Intrepid Witness to History

Essays in Honor of Boris Blick

EDITED BY SARAH BLICK AND JOHN PEPPLE

AuthorHouse™
1663 Liberty Drive, Suite 200
Bloomington, IN 47403
www.authorhouse.com
Phone: 1-800-839-8640

First published by AuthorHouse 6/2/2008

ISBN: 978-1-4343-5976-6 (sc)

Library of Congress Control Number: 2008900401

Printed in the United States of America
Bloomington, Indiana

This book is printed on acid-free paper.

On the cover: The Corner of Politics by Honoré Daumier, Boris Blick Collection

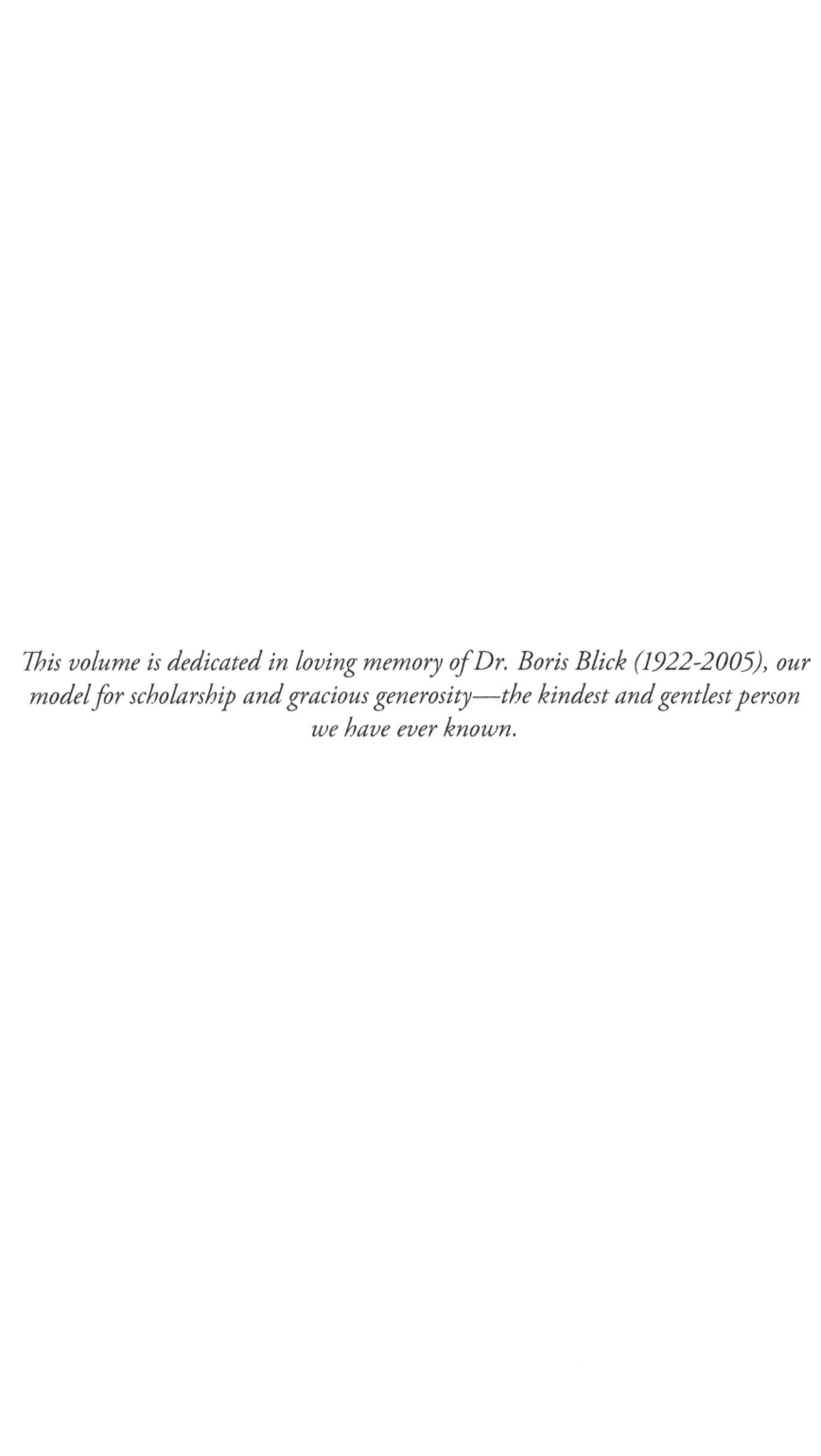

This volume is dedicated in loving memory of Dr. Boris Blick (1922-2005), our model for scholarship and gracious generosity—the kindest and gentlest person we have ever known.

Contents

Acknowledgments

It is with enormous gratitude that we thank the following people for their wonderful support and encouragement: Louis Patsouras, June Burton, and Katherine Harper.

Preface

Boris Blick. Scholar, soldier, teacher, husband, father, brother, friend, and collector. Philanthropist, too, as no charity's request ever passed his desk or came to his door without a contribution. He made friends with everyone he encountered — mailman, exterminator, and lawyer—and these people showed their appreciation for him by attending his funeral. Boris was also fiercely interested in politics and its effect on people's lives. He was particularly devoted to Israel after having experienced anti-Semitic treatment in WWII, becoming a life-long supporter. Yet he was not dour, and when he wished to be, he was a very entertaining storyteller.

Born in 1922 to a working-class, immigrant family, Boris worked hard throughout his childhood. Money earned at delivery jobs was given over entirely to his mother. Reaching young adulthood at the end of the Depression, he worked as a Western Union messenger and as a factory worker operating a small drill press and wiring lamps. These jobs were few and far between, so in April of 1942 (when he was 19 years old) he joined the army and was shipped to Europe. While there he served as an airline mechanic, chauffeur, and rifleman, fighting in some of the war's worst battles, including the first wave on Omaha Beach on D-Day (where, as far as he knew, he was the only one in his battalion not wounded or killed) and the Battle of the Bulge (where he remembered the fierce cold). His bravery was recognized by a series of medals including the silver star. Once V-E Day was declared, he was shipped to the Philippines to fight against the Japanese, but V-J Day ended the war, and after a wait of six months, he was sent home to Brooklyn, almost four years after entering the army.

Although Boris remained a private (and private first class) during the war, he had a few brushes with the rich and famous. On one occasion, he attended a show featuring Glen Miller, and the revered bandleader wanted a soldier to join him on the stage. It was decided by his fellow soldiers that since Boris was such a fine singer, he should be the one. He must have acquitted himself well, because at another performance (in London) Mr. Miller recognized him and asked him to again join him on the stage.

On another occasion, he was at a café in Paris shortly after it had been liberated. A waitress asked him and his buddies if they wanted to see an artist's studio, and although no one else wanted to, Boris persuaded them that it would be worth while. The artist turned out to be a chain-smoking old man whose paintings Boris had little regard for, but when the artist asked if any of the soldiers had any cigarettes he could have, Boris (who didn't smoke) gave him not just a cigarette or even a pack, but an entire carton (worth, at the time, $500 in gold). The artist was so overcome with gratitude he offered Boris two paintings, which Boris refused. He later learned the artist was Picasso. Years later when he and his wife Judy were in Paris, she suggested that he call on the artist and claim a couple of paintings, but the ever-humble Boris refused.

In England on leave, visiting a luxurious country home and scanning the books in its magnificent library, he was approached by the man who owned the house who introduced himself as G.M. Trevelyan, to which he replied he was Boris Blick. Later this short interaction became humorous as he came to realize that it was the distinguished historian, who at that time meant nothing to the young Boris.

After the war, he first sought training as a radio repairman at the Melville Radio Institute, but the teacher in the course told him (rightly so) that he had no talent for repairing radios and suggested that he take a vocational aptitude test at a local college. The results of this test made it clear that Boris was destined to be a teacher, and using the GI Bill, he became the first in his family to complete a college degree. He attended Brooklyn College, majoring in history, becoming a member of Phi Beta Kappa, and getting his degree in 1950. Because he enjoyed studying history so much, he decided to pursue a graduate degree, and he was accepted into the acclaimed program at the University of Wisconsin in Madison, where in 1958 he earned his Ph.D. with a dissertation on a French politician from a century ago named Rene Waldeck-Rousseau.

While earning his degree, he met Judith Rosenbloom, an undergraduate in history at Wisconsin, and they married in December of 1953. A telegram sent by a prankster friend to the couple read, "Heartfelt felicitations upon the occasion of your nuptials. P. Picasso and G.M. Trevelyan." Boris was awarded a Fulbright Scholarship in 1954, and he and Judith sailed across the Atlantic to France to live in Paris for a year. In recognition of his excellent scholarship, this award was extended for another year. In order to win this award, Boris told a forgivable falsehood, saying he was proficient in French. Since he thought he had no chance to win the award, he never dreamed this lie would come back to haunt him, but when he actually did win, he was forced to acknowledge to the language qualifier that he wasn't as fluent as he had claimed. He promised to learn French as fast as possible. He not only lived up to this promise by beginning a crash course in French, but kept up his knowledge by reading French magazines, newspapers, and scholarly books, and by listening to French broadcasts on short wave radio every day till the day he died.

The years followed, and he taught at the University of Wisconsin Extension in Sheboygan and Manitowoc from 1956-1959, then at Rockford College from 1959-1964 (where he served as chairman of the History Department and Chairman of the Division of Social Sciences), and finally at the University of Akron in 1964, where he would teach courses in 19th and 20th century European and military history until his retirement in 1989. As a scholar, he suffered the disappointment of being scooped, for while finishing his dissertation on Waldeck-Rousseau, whom scholars had previously ignored, a prominent historian published a study on this same politician shortly after Boris finished. Boris's confidence was sapped, and he was reluctant to submit his dissertation for publication. In spite of this, his thesis quoted widely by later scholars interested in the politician's career. After this, Boris became interested in French Liberal Anti-Socialism from 1880-1914, placing it in a wider political, social, and intellectual context. Looking beyond the typical documentation, he sought to gauge public opinion by reading contemporary novels and examining political caricatures. He even used the sensitive response of the Paris Bourse to explicate the broad social and political changes, and his later scholarship reflects this.

Meanwhile, he had an obvious interest in the military, which continued throughout his life. One highlight was his participation in the ROTC seminar in Military History at West Point in 1984, choosing that over the D-Day 40th-year re-union. He regularly gave talks about WWII and did such varied things as serve as a commentator for the Center for Peace Studies at the University of Akron on the film *To Die in Madrid* (covering the Spanish Civil War 1931-1939). He published articles as varied as "French Icarians in St. Louis" in *The Bulletin of the Missouri Historical Society* (1973), "Life in New Icaria, Iowa: A 19th Century Utopian Community" (with H. Roger Grant) in *Annals of Iowa* (1974), and "Influence of the French" in the *Encyclopedia of Southern History*, "What is Socialism? French Liberal Views in the 1890's" in Louis Patsouras, *The Crucible of Socialism* (1987), and he co-edited *Rebels Against the Old Order: Essays in Honor of Morris Slavin* (1994) with Louis Patsouras, contributing the essay "On Morris Slavin." He also regularly gave public talks on a wide variety of topics from "De-Christianization in 19th century France" to "D-Day," and was featured on radio and TV programs.

Beyond his exemplary scholarship, what set Boris Blick apart was his generosity and enthusiasm for all kinds of historical and political topics. He would happily discuss these topics with friends and students, sharing his insights and thoughtful opinions and listening with great interest to those with whom he spoke. He believed in a meritocracy open to all and was disdainful of social climbers. He believed in the essential goodness of others.

Sadly, his life was marred by tragedy as his wife died young from cancer at the age of 39 in 1971 and two of his three children were mentally ill, his eldest Lee dying at the young age of 25. He worked diligently to support them and to rebuild his shattered life. His pain made him compassionate and he became a beloved and proclaimed teacher, teaching thousands of students who regularly wrote of his dedication and concern. He inspired many of his students to continue their studies of history in graduate school. He served on numerous graduate committees, generously sharing his time and insight. He was the Director of the Seminar in Russian and East European Area Studies for the Regional Council for International Education (1967-1968), Director of the Masters Graduate Program for the Department of History at the University of Akron (1971-1975) and Organizer and Director of the University of Akron Paris Semester in the fall of 1974. Others, particularly those he taught in the ROTC, cited his influence on the development of their character—honorable, clear-eyed, and brave. An excellent writer, he was generous with his editing skills, reading over the works of colleagues, students, friends, and relatives.

Finally, Boris was also a collector. He collected prints, pocket watches, fountain pens, and a variety of antiques. He admired the exquisite craftsmanship found in watches, and he loved the historical weight and beauty of prints, pens, and antiques. He was also a passionate bibliophile who amassed a stunning scholarly library. Its 15,000 tomes covered such topics History (French, European, American, and Military), classical antiquity (especially Rome), the Middle Ages (particularly the Carolingian Period), Forestry, Art History, and Political Science. He read voraciously and was interested in and knowledgeable on all sorts of topics. However, he regularly donated enormous numbers of books to the University of Akron library, and he gave books to almost everyone he met, carefully choosing volumes that would interest and enlighten their recipients. Upon his death, various individuals and libraries were rewarded (the University of Akron, Akron Public Library, Kenyon College Library, and the Bibliotheque Nationale) with some of the many books he owned. His antique and print collection, too, was donated to the Art History Department at Kenyon College, forming the core of the Boris Blick Teaching Collection.

This volume, a collection of unpublished essays written by Boris combined with essays from those with whom he worked and admired, is a *liber amicorum*. The first part of the volume features two unpublished articles by Boris. The first article, "French Liberal Response to the Political Consequences of Industrialization, 1880-1914," explores the "social panic" of the 1890s, revealing that the literature of liberal anti-socialism did not generally or characteristically show acute anguish, anxiety, panic. Instead, when discussing the seriousness of the socialist threat, liberal publicists, economists, and politicians had an infinity of opinions that exposed the inanity of that crude Marxist notion of the bourgeoisie reacting and thinking in unison which many historians almost imply.

The second article examines "The Failure of Political Organization in Late Nineteenth- Century France: The Case of the Moderate Party" which explores how a number of influential Moderate republicans, who had long condemned the weakness of their party, attempted to transform it into a strong, centralized, coherent organization, taking the English Conservative party as their model. Why they failed, and why the opportunity to renovate the party came to nothing, is the subject of this paper. It is essentially the story of the inability of the French, excepting the Socialists and later the Communists, to create national, coherent, and disciplined parties.

The second part is composed of essays that reflect Boris's broad interests and the warm gratitude his kindness engendered. These include Morris Slavin's investigation of Trotsky's fight against fascism in Germany and his urging of the communist party to counter fascism and how Stalin thwarted this movement against the rise of the Nazi party. Slavin answers the question of why the Soviet Union, the Comintern, and the KPD followed the suicidal course that guaranteed Hitler's accession to power.

Then James Friguglietti examines how the French Communist Party viewed the French Revolution during the period from its creation until its dissolution in 1939 and how its historians interpreted the French Revolution, concentrating on a single historian, Jean Bruhat (1905-1983), whose career exemplifies Communist historiography during the later 1930s. This is followed by Roy Wortman's classic article which researches the outcomes and reasons for the failure of the I.W.W. Rubber strike in Akron in 1913. Continuing with the theme of exploring the approaches to creating a better society through political movements, Robert Zangrado writes of the life of Walter F. White and his pivotal role in the NAACP and the organization's establishment of the Legal Defense and Educational Fund, Inc. Howard Reinmuth Jr., carries the thread further in his "Planning Parks in the Seventies: Federal and Provincial Parks in the Gaspé," examining how a well-meaning attempt at central planning to try to bring people to where the jobs were did not work and how ultimately the people who were expropriated resulted in major electoral changes. The final essay in this section, by Louis Patsouras, brings forth a discussion of the Communist Manifesto, of its content and its continuing relevance to the plight of the workers today.

The third section of this volume is composed of essays on philosophical and art historical topics, which intrigued Boris. John F. Pepple writes of how Plato tried to create a system of moral experts and how and why it failed and what he proposed in the end as a possible solution to the lack of moral experts in our world. William McMahon writes against a school of thought that has developed within the philosophy of science over the last forty years which is noted for its skepticism with respect to objectivity in science. Against these epistemological relativists, McMahon advocates instead a common-sense approach similar to that of G.E. Moore and argues that Moore's approach is more sophisticated that it might seem on first acquaintance. Rounding out the volume, Sarah Blick's essay explore the symbolic impact of using saints and their lives to communicate royal power in the reign of Richard II.

Boris Blick, while experiencing tragedies and hardship, made a contribution to the world in many different way. Wise, kind, and compassionate, like Chaucer's Knight in the *Canterbury Tales*:

He was of sovereign value in all eyes
And though much distinguished, he was wise.
And in his bearing modest as a maid
And never yet a boorish thing had said
In all his life to any, come what might
He was a true, a perfect gentle knight.

He will be very much missed.

Chapter 1

French Liberal Response to the Political Consequences of Industrialization, 1880–1914

Boris Blick

Most historical works that cast even a cursory glance at French society of the late nineteenth century remark on the phenomenon of the *peur sociale*, the social disquiet that gripped the bourgeoisie on the apparition of socialism. Panic, obsession, hysteria, convulsive fear, we are often told, characterized the unheroic and mean reflex of the bourgeoisie.[1]

It is difficult in the present state of our knowledge of French "public opinion" of the later nineteenth century, in the as-yet inadequate instruments of measuring political sentiment in the age before opinion polls, to assess these portentous pronouncements. Attempts, often ingenious, to determine the popularity of imperialism[2] in this period have not yet succeeded, no more than testing the dogmatic assertion that the Dreyfus Affair divided France into "two camps,"[3] or that most Frenchmen were indifferent to both.[4] But an exploration of the large contemporary anti-socialist literature which doubtless influenced and reflected the opinions of the propertied classes offers insight into the social disquiet.

The literature of liberal anti-socialism did not generally or characteristically show acute anguish, anxiety, panic. The reader emerges from it seeing—however confusedly—the complexity, not the stark simplicity of the matter of socialism. On the seriousness of the socialist threat, liberal publicists, economists, and politicians had an infinity of opinions that exposes the

1

inanity of that crude Marxist notion of the bourgeoisie reacting and thinking in unison which our historians almost imply.

To avoid listing and drowning in the polemical ocean of anti-socialism, the traveler must discriminate between different currents of anti-socialist opinion. He needs to chart the long-range pull of opinion against the sudden threatening, subsiding squalls, to discern the broad waves of national from the narrow eddies of local opinion. Nor can the wary mariner relax his watch for the treacherous shoals separating genuine feeling and tactical advantage. Particular discrete episodes—the socialist political advance of the early nineties, the anarchist "outrages," the rash of major violent strikes—sometimes released fear tremors that abated as the crises faded.[5]

The Commune illustrates this phenomenon. It set off acute fear, a genuine social disquiet, to judge from the vehement condemnation and dread foreboding of many celebrated writers.[6] But this most notorious uprising of the Third Republic did not prove a dress rehearsal for social revolution and its fear-inspiring power fell off sharply in the 1880s.[7] As scarecrow or argument, the Commune is inconspicuous in the anti-socialist literature of the nineties.[8] It is, perhaps, instructive that the onset of socialism in the 1890s produced no comparable explosion of fear and outrage by the literati.

Harsh local conflicts (as in the coal mining region of Carmaux) producing prolonged social unrest, violence, the appearance of demagogues and meneurs, the Socialist capture of municipalities, and the election of socialist deputies set off anti-socialist alarms, apocalyptic cries, and the creation of anti-socialist leagues.[9] But, it must be stressed, the intensity of regional anti-socialist reaction, often advanced as proof of anti-socialist panic, cannot be equated with "national" opinion.

Nor ought the anti-socialist alarms of politicians such as Jules Méline, often invoked as evidence of the political elite sharing the bourgeois panic, be taken at face value.[10] A careful reading of their pronouncements sometimes shows bewildering inconsistency.[11] The problem of measuring the intensity of anti-socialist anxiety is magnified by the difficulty of separating genuine sentiment and the ritual denunciation of collectivism. The tactical exploitation of the red scare[12] resembled the tireless trumpeting of the clerical threat.[13] The social disquiet, though real and possessing a momentum of its own, emerged from the Third Republic's plot and polemical tradition and fits nicely as the obverse of the perceived threats of clericalism,[14] caesarism, and reaction. And their unmasking required a heightening of danger through rhetorical exaggeration.

Fear of socialism blended with fear of all sorts of contemporary changes. The political languages of the nineties must then be read with care. To speak of the fear of socialism, to cite anti-socialist philippics, can be misleading, for socialism represented a protean entity on whose nature and significance there was no agreement.

Anti-socialist assessment of the *péril social* can be roughly subsumed under three broad reactions: those who feared its reality, those who doubted that socialism could ever succeed but knew that it would generate disorder, and those who dismissed the uproar as largely empty noise. None of these perceptions can be correlated with such anti-socialist elements as the patronat, liberal economists, or moderate liberal parliamentarians, since none of them had a single, coherent view of socialism.

The troubled anti-socialists brooded about a general socialist advance over weak institutions and ineffective resistance made possible by a general weakening of governmental authority.[15] Catholic anti-socialists stressed equally erosion of moral authority in the anti-clerical onslaught that had weakened one of the great barriers to revolutionary subversion.[16] These anti-socialists apprehensively watched an aggressive Socialist parliamentary phalanx battering the state from within,[17] while anarchist bombs exploded from without. If government appeared bending before the Socialist cyclone, others flinched before the apparition of state power advancing over the battlefield of social conflict.

State socialism, as vague and multiform a concept as socialism and sometimes loosely equated with almost any state initiative in the social sphere, appeared to anti-socialists in many guises, such as the sudden flood of ameliorative legislation; the unprecedented concern with the social question reflected in the proliferation of groups, parties, and factions attacking the laissez- faire state; and egotistical capitalism.[18]

In their malaise, heightened by the thunderclaps and lightning flashes of strikes and industrial disorder, anxious anti-socialists observed the formation of armies of subversion—demagogues, agitators, ring-leaders, doctors of socialism—a new, dangerous class, a kind of political priestcraft leading the "laborious classes" astray.[19]

Many anti-socialists, while discounting an explicit socialist danger, argued that socialism, in its flight through the social atmosphere on the way to oblivion, left a trail of fire and destruction. The real socialist threat they found in the fevers generated by its passage through the healthy organism of liberal democracy. Socialism might not seize the machinery of state power but its spirit and measures discouraged ambition, initiative, invention, discipline, work. Already some claimed the socialist blight touched the French economy, lowering productivity and scaring off capital.[20] Ironically socialism thereby doomed its own proclaimed ideal: the "amelioration of the moral and material condition of the poor and disinherited."[21]

Of the fevers induced by socialism, none troubled liberals more than "state socialism." Paul Leroy-Beaulieu, the renowned liberal economist, in the preface to the French translation of a celebrated German anti-socialist tract, described state socialism as a kind of creeping socialism, socialism on the installment plan. Socialism, he wrote, would not come by way of revolution but through insidious small doses of socialist poisons such as income tax and nationalization.[22]

Socialism, often described by liberals as retrograde and counter-revolutionary, could also destroy liberal democracy by frightening the country into the protective arms of reaction. France faced a reprise of 1848 and the triumph of caesarism.[23] Socialism, which many liberal anti-socialists declared German in origin, and the class war divided and weakened France, opening the prospect of another military catastrophe[24] and the triumph of German autocracy.

Other than state socialism, it is difficult to say which of these many offshoots of careening socialism were thought most dangerous and which reflected conspiracy-mongering. Since anti-socialists thought socialism utterly chimerical and few seemed convinced it could take power, the dark vision of socialism unable to conceive a new world and able only to trouble the old, more than technical and philosophical demonstrations, constituted the ultimate anti-socialist argument.[25]

Immersion in French anti-socialist literature of the late nineteenth century leads a reader instinctively to the conviction that tranquil liberals outnumbered the fearful—or at least those who supposed socialism an imminent possibility. Certainly confident anti-socialists eclipsed their anxious fellows with an imposing panoply of arguments.

Against the background of bourgeois panic limned by historians, some eminent representatives of French capitalism displayed an astonishing serenity. Baron Alphonse de Rothschild, serenely denying the socialist peril, wouldn't even agree that there was a crisis. Albert Cristophle, Gourverneur du Crédit foncier, contemptuously dismissed the socialist peril as nothing more than "des rêves d'Allemands qui ne peuvent pas se concilier avec les besoins de clarté de l'esprit français. C'est un brouillard."[26] Many contemporaries, sharing Rothschild's tranquility, saw no advancing red armies on the political landscape,[27] but rather several heights of the French national character that they confidently believed socialism could never scale.

Liberal anti-socialism derived deep satisfaction from the conviction of the essential conservatism of the French people, which they often observed in the profound tranquility of a country tired of "sterile agitation" and impervious to demagogic blandishments.[28] It was difficult to imagine socialism progressing in a country of seven million security holders and eight million landowners or overcoming the "solid good sense of our rustics" and their "resistance to subversive doctrines."[29]

From that confidence moderate liberal republicans in the nineties insisted that Radical and Socialist electoral progress did not reflect the true balance of political forces. They found the country more conservative than its representation, that the large number of voters who normally stayed away from the polls were neither Radicals nor Socialists but rather citizens disgusted by chronic government instability and the prevailing political mores. Their abstention enabled the better-organized Left to enjoy a greater representation than its actual following. René Waldeck-Rousseau predicted in 1895 that the "day when men of property will make to defend themselves, a tenth of the agitation that others make to threaten them, they will be the masters. They are the many and they are the force."[30] The unprecedented barrage of Socialist, Radical, and Anarchist propaganda and the absence of an effective counter-response, it was also argued, gave a misleading impression of collectivist strength.[31]

Socialist gains in the 1893 general election were minimized on the grounds that many socialist candidates and deputies were arrivistes parading under false colors. A good number of Socialists emerged as trimmers exploiting the then-current infatuation with socialism and the social question or ambiguous protest figures fathered by the incestuous union of the French electoral system and the French political temperament.[32] J. E. C. Bodley, who observed French political life closely and who reflected the opinions of the *centre gauche* liberals, remarked in 1898 that "the Socialist vote in France is rather an expression of discontent or of disorder than a serious evolution towards collectivist doctrine."[33]

A quest for the "real socialism," identified by a moderate republican publicist as "the collectivist and anti-French socialism of M. Jules Guesde," suggested a minority dwarfed by pseudo- or quasi-socialists, parlor anarchists, anti-Semites, Christian democrats, and opportunistic Radicals.[34] Socialism's irregular armies, liberal anti-socialists noted, had been further swelled by the votes of ex-Boulangists and Reactionaries practicing la politique du pire, spreading disorder through socialism[35]

Earlier fears of socialist advances subsided as dreaded developments did not materialize. The first of May 1890 did not generate paralyzing general strikes, nor did the Radicals massively enter Socialist ranks. In Parliament the anti-socialist majority in the Chamber had blunted the Socialist offensive while the Senate, an anti-socialistic bastion, kept vigilant watch.[36]

Underpinning these developments and reinforcing them was a generational change of climate of opinion that appeared to be taking the country away from the instability and crises that bred all sorts of dangerous protests, from Boulangism to socialism. Moderate liberal leaders detected a deep shift of opinion in the country, which they saw as a profound reaction to the abuses of the parliamentary system and sterile agitation, as well as a yearning for government stability and a "policy of results."[37]

Determined anti-socialists thought that a tough government and a show of resistance would have the better of socialism. And there were encouraging signs of a forthcoming restoration of authority—repeated calls for energetic leadership, strong governments, disciplined and coherent parliamentary majorities, and political parties "worthy of the name."[38]

Observed closely, socialism inspired hope rather than alarm. To many liberal observers, the socialist phenomenon represented an amalgam of political opportunism, quackery, and disunited elements of social protest. Not too formidable a machine and one that appeared neither monolithic nor the oracle of an unanswerable dialectic.[39] Already its momentum had been slowed by the inertia of reformist socialism. Renouncing its mission as "a party of struggle and attack" in its sobering exposure to reality, had, these critics argued, divested socialism of its revolutionary essence. Emergence of reformist factions such as the possibilistes was seen not as a sign of flexibility or creative adaptation but as loss of momentum, sinking into respectability and domestication.[40]

An ideological disarray mirroring the internal anarchy of socialism confirmed the permanent and insoluble crisis of socialism. Riddled with contradictions and avoiding a fatal synthesis, socialism seemed to have slipped into ideological bankruptcy. Socialist leaders, their theories refuted, fell back on noise, abuse, and mechanical representation of their hackneyed conceits.[41]

The hopelessly chimerical, the utterly utopian character of socialism offered perhaps the ultimate assurance that it did not imperil the existing order. Socialism, flying in the face of human nature and the laws of economics, stood condemned to remain forever outside the sphere of objectivity, reality, practical ability, and power. Socialism that had never existed was denied a future existence by the judgment of history. Socialism's abortive and limited historical experience—the utopian communities, the abstractly naive communist thinkers, the National Workshops, the Communes—all had ended in total failure.[42]

A glance at the political scene, largely missing in this paper, may help in sorting out the contradictory perceptions of the reality of the *péril social*. Historians dwelling on the "social disquiet" find confirmation in, for instance, the extreme anti-labor reaction of the patronat buttressed by governmental force, the panic generated by the May 1, 1890 procession, the truly panicky reaction to socialism of major personages of the haute banque and grande industrie, and the anguished, almost terrified warning of approaching storms by the venerable politician and embattled anti-socialist, Bernard Lavergne.[43]

Undeniably this evidence bears witness to anti-socialist anxieties. But in this one-sided demonstration our historians have uncritically processed their raw facts and have ignored or overlooked events and opinions that make it difficult to accept the idea of a badly frightened bourgeoisie.

Anti–trade union action was not always and everywhere synonymous with the anti-socialist crusade, though it is undoubtedly true that strike leaders and strikes were, like so much else, indiscriminately equated with "socialism." The May 1, 1890 argument ignores major liberal and anti-socialist organs deriving satisfaction from contemplating a volcano that fizzled. The invocation of troubled bankers can be matched by an equal and possibly greater number of tranquil capitalists. Bernard Lavergne, the personification of the anti-socialist fright, should be seen as an aged politician who lost his bearings, and possibly the only major moderate republican politician to passionately announce the coming eruption of social revolution.[44]

Instructively the bourgeois writers of the eighties and nineties did not, like the literary observers of the Commune, produce a large, fearful, hate-filled anti-socialist literature. Nor did a petrified bourgeoisie follow the example of 1848 and embrace caesarism. Boulangism had been neutralized essentially by the resistance of moderate republicanism and the exalted Nationalists of the later nineties had flopped even more dismally.

Why had not French politics split into two camps, the Socialist and the anti-Socialist, as some observers had confidently predicted?[45] Why had not the numerous anti-socialist ligues—politically oriented businessman groups, moderate liberal anti-socialist extra-parliamentary associations—achieved prominence and force rather than all having been weak and transitory? The very brief and almost unnoticed existence in 1892 of the Ligue anti-socialiste, headed by Yves Guyot, anti-socialism's most militant spokesman, showed the vanity of the vaunted alliance of the Catholic and republican anti-socialist bourgeoisie.[46] Vastly more pertinent, the much-publicized but abortive republican-ralliés coalition demonstrated that to many bourgeois, clericalism remained more of a danger than socialism.[47]

A final, revealing note. In June 1899, Waldeck-Rousseau's government of Republican Defense (including the then-notorious Socialist Millerand, the first Socialist minister of the Third Republic) received the votes and vocal support of a number of unyielding liberals such as Edouard Aynard and Charles Jonnart, who not very long before had stood out among the major personalities of anti-socialism. Did not their vote signify their conviction that the observed anti-republican danger superseded, for the time being, at least, the *péril social*?

Where did the notion of "social panic" of the 1890s arise? No doubt it was, in part, the perpetuation of a mistaken view, a myth, a generalization that went long unchallenged. Certainly it corresponds to a "Marxist" image of the ignoble bourgeois. Perhaps the idea of a panic-stricken bourgeoisie came from a reading of the Socialist press of the nineties where the bourgeoisie stood naked, trembling in all its ugliness.

Endnotes

[1] Michelle Perrot, *Les ouvriers en grève France 1871–1890* (Paris, 1974), 11, p. 717; Pierre Sorlin, *Waldeck-Rousseau* (Paris, 1966), pp. 358–60; Roland Trempé, *Les mineurs de Carmaux 1848–1914* (Paris, 1971), 11, pp. 886–87.

[2] For the authorities who deny the popularity of imperialism in the late nineteenth-century France and stress indifference see, for example, Henri Brunschwig, "L'impérialisme en Afrique noire," *Revue historique*, no. 505 (1973), p. 1932; J. Valette, "Note sur l'idée coloniale vers 1871," *Revue d'histoire moderne et contemporaine* XIV (1967), p. 158; Charles-Robert Ageron, *L'Anticolonialisme en France de 1871 à 1914* (Paris, 1973), pp. 42–44; Roger B. Brown, *Fashoda Reconsidered: The Impact of Domestic Politics on French Policy in Africa 1893–1898* (Baltimore, 1970), p. 7; Henri Brunschwig, *Le Patrage de l'Afrique noir* (Paris, 1971), pp. 1965–68; Pierre Renouvin, *Histoire des relations internationales*, (6 vols., Paris, 1955–1958), VI, p. 41.

[3] On the difficulty of determining the "emotion collective" during the Dreyfus Affair see, for example, J.-P. Peter, "L'Affaire Dreyfus," *Annales Économies Sociétés Civilisations*, XVI (Nov.–Dec. 1961), 1141–1152.

[4] It is probably not possible to determine how much and what kind of influence newspapers have on public opinion. I have tried very roughly to "measure" anti-socialist reaction by carefully reading major liberal organs across periods when anti-socialist fears were, a priori, likely to be strong. Thus I have read *La République Française* for 1893, the year of the great Socialist advance, and found little trace of anxiety and much confidence in the tranquility and "good sense" of the country.

[5] Scheurer-Kestner Papers, *Journal, Nouvelles Acquisitions Françaises*, tome VII, 12710 (Bibliothèque Nationale).

[6] Paul Lidsky, in a study of the hostility of French writers to the Commune, remarked how quickly the "ruling class" recovered from its fear, invokes the testimony of Ludovic Halévy writing in June 1871. *Les écrivans contre la commune* (Paris, 1970), p. 159.

[7] See, for example, Jean T. Joughin, *The Paris Commune in French Politics, 1871–1880* (Baltimore, 1955), 11, pp. 441, 447, 455, 478–86, 488.

[8] This statement is based on a wide reading of anti-socialist literature of the nineties in which references to the Commune are relatively infrequent and those that saw it as an omen are rare.

[9] Jean-Michel Gaillard, "Le 1er mai 1890 dans le bassin houiller du Gard," *Le mouvement social* (94) (Jan.–Mar., 1976), 70; Trempé, *Les minuers*, 11, 874–87.

[10] Méline, sometimes cited as an instance of a major politician petrified by socialism, often took a different tack. *La République Française* (Nov. 21, 1893); *Discours de M. Méline au groupe des republicains progressistes le 24 février 1899* (Paris, 1899), pp. 12–13.

[11] A careful reading of politicians' opinions on the socialist danger shows much inconsistency. If the opinions of politicians must be treated with some caution, the rumblings of a press that some observers contend created the Dreyfus Affair (Patrice Boussel, L'Affaire Dreyfus et la presse [Paris, 1960], pp. 5–6.) requires even more circumspection. Bernard Lavergne wrote in his *Mémoires* in May 1893: "Du reste, Carnot est convàincu comme moi, que la source de tout notre mal est dans la loi de 1881 sur la Presse." *Mémoires de Bernard Lavergne, Nouvelles Acquisitions Françaises*, t. VI, 14639, p. 1060 (20), Bibliothèque Nationale.

[12] *La Petite République* (Oct. 10, 1894); Georges Dupeux, *Aspects de l'histoire sociale et politique du Loir-et-cher 1848–1914* (Paris, 1962), pp. 582–84; J. Kayser, *Les grandes batailles du radicalisme, 1820–1901* (Paris, 1962), p. 257; Pierre Miqel, *L'Affaire Dreyfus* (Paris, 1959), p. 13.

[13] The terminological confusion reached its climax in the anti-socialist attacks on the Radicals, sometimes denounced as dangerous as the Socialists, and often indiscriminately equated with them. Lavergne, *Mémoires*, VI, p. 1081; *La République Française* (Jul. 30, Sept. 5, 1893); *Mémorial de la Loire et la Haute Loire* (Aug. 12, 1904); Georges Picot, *La lutte contre le socialisme révolutionnaire* (Paris, 1896), p. 8. The documentation on this and most other points of this paper is indicative or representative and in no way exhaustive.

[14] It would be difficult to dispute the assertion that "enemy number 1" of the Third Republic's "political ruling class" was clericalism. See, for example, *Centenaire de la Troisième Republique: Actes du colloque de Rennes 15–17 mai 1975* (Paris, 1975), p. 42.

[15] Lavergne, *Mémoires*, VI, p. 1075.

[16] L'Abbé Elie Méric, *Les erreurs sociales du temps present* (Paris, 1884), pp. 238–240; Louis Joubert, "Chronique politique," *Le Correspondant*, 184 (July 10, 1896), 177–80.

[17] Lavergne, *Mémoires*, VI, p. 1067; Scheurer-Kestner, *Journal*, VII, pp. 318–19.

[18] See, for example, A. Daniel, *L'Année politique 1891* (Paris, 1892), pp. 166–167.

[19] *La République Française* (Oct. 18., Nov. 1, Nov. 7 1893); Paul Deschanel, *La question sociale* (Paris, 1892), pp. 11–13, 26–28, 34. Yves Guyot put the matter this

way: ". . .par notre apathie la France risque-t-elle donc de devenir la proie d'une bande de farceurs, de fous, de rheteurs. . ." *La comédie socialiste* (Paris, 1897), p. 468.

[20] *La République Française* (Nov. 7, 1893); *Le Temps* (June 11, 1893); *La Petite Gironde* (Sept. 9, 1904); E. Levasseur, *Salariat et salaires* (Paris, 1909), pp. 417, 456–57.

[21] *La République Française* (Sept. 29, 1893).

[22] Eugène Richter. *Où mene le socialisme: Journal d'un ouvrier* (Paris, 1892).

[23] *La Loire Républicaine* (Aug. 15, 1894); *La République Française* (July 30, 1893); Paul Deschanel, *La question*, 15–16.

[24] *La République Française* (Sept. 29, 1893).

[25] Archives de la Préfecture de Police, Ba/1077 4e partie, report July 18, 1889; Agence Havas (Nov. 23, 1895); *La République Française* (Oct. 11, Oct. 18, Dec. 6, 1893).

[26] Jules Huret, *Enquête sur la question sociale en Europe* (Paris, 1897), pp. 35, 59, 63–64, 121, 126.

[27] *La République Française* (July 1, 1893); *Le Matin* (Aug. 20, 1896).

[28] *Le Matin* (Aug. 30, 1896); *La République Française* (July 23, Aug. 23, Sept. 14, 1893); *Discours de M. Méline. . .le 24 fevrier 1899*, pp. 12–13.

[29] *Le Matin* (Aug. 20, 1896); *La République Française* (Dec. 20, 1893); Maurice Block, *Le socialisme moderne* (Paris, 1891), p. 28; Picot, *La lutte*, pp. 10–13; Guyot, *La comédie*, 468; Huret, *Enquête*, 111.

[30] *Agence Havas* (Nov. 23, 1895); *Le Matin* (July 9, 1896); *Le Temps* (Oct. 24, 1897); Louis Joubert, "Chronique politique," *Le correspondant*, CLXXVIII (Mar. 10, 1895), 978–79 and CLXXXVII (May 10, 1897), 579–80; René Waldeck-Rousseau, *Pour la République* (Paris, 1904), pp. 200–02, 336–39; Guyot, *La comedie*, 468.

[31] Picot, *La lutte*, 8.

[32] *La République Française* (Aug. 22, 23, 25, 1893); Lavergne, *Mémoires*, VI, pp. 1099.

[33] J. E. C. Bodley, *France* (London, 1898), 11, p. 445.

[34] *La République Française* (Aug. 24, 1893).

[35] *La République Française* (Sept. 6, 1893).

[36] *Le Matin* (Nov. 6, 1896); Scheurer-Kestner, *Journal*, VIII; Lavergne, *Mémoires*, VI, p. 1060 (18); Daniel, *L'Année. . .1891*, 164–67.

[37] *Paris* (Nov. 19, 1893); *Le Temps* (June 11, 1893); *Journal de Montbrison* (Loire) (Mar. 17, 1895); *Le Journal de Roanne* (Loire) (Sept. 30, 1894); Daniel, *L'Année. . . 1891*, 100; *L'Année politique 1893* (Paris, 1894), p. 189.

[38] See, for example, *Le Rappel* (Nov. 15, 1895); *Le Temps* (June 11, 1893).

[39] *La République Française* (Aug. 25, Sept. 5, 1893); P.-E. Laviron, *Le socialisme français et le collectivisme allemande* (Paris, 1895), p. 1.

[40] *La République Française* (Sept. 16, 1893); Huret, *Enquête*, IV; Maurice Vanlaer, *Démocratie et socialisme* (Arras, 1900), pp. 9–10.

[41] E. Spuller, "Quatorze mois de législature," *Revue politique et parlementaire*, III (Jan. 1895), 8.

[42] *La République Française* (Sept. 17, 1893); Yves Guyot, *La tyrannie socialiste* (Paris, 1893), p. VII; Léon Say, *Contre le socialisme* (Paris, 1896), pp. 90, 107.

[43] See, for example, Pierre Sorlin, *Waldeck-Rousseau* (Paris, 1966), pp. 356–61.

[44] Lavergne, *Mémoires*, VI, pp. 1063, 1086, 1091.

[45] *Le Rappel* (Nov. 15, 1896); *Le Temps* (June 11, 1893); Deschanel, *La question*, 39.

[46] *Le Temps* (May 12, 1892).

[47] See, for example, *La Croix* (Dec. 28, 1897); *La Vérité* (Dec. 23, 1897); *L'Oeuvre Electorale* (Feb. 9, Apr. 20, 1898); *La Dépêche* (Toulouse) (Mar. 17, 19, 1898).

Chapter 2

The Failure of Political Organization in Late Nineteenth-Century France: The Case of the Moderate Party

Boris Blick

The political parties that emerged slowly in the first two decades of the Third Republic had neither central organization nor coherence. They were torn by dissension and weakened by fragmentation. Constituency groups, where they existed, were generally small, short-lived, and inert between elections. Party cadre and supporters had little sense of party loyalty and parliamentarians were not amenable to party discipline.

In the early eighteen-nineties, however, a change in the political climate foreshadowed the possibility of the fusion and consolidation of many existing parties and movements. A sharp reaction against the defects and abuses of the parliamentary system—ministerial instability, weak and shifting coalition governments, the party system, and demagoguery—swept the country. With the wave of criticism came demands for strong government and parties. A national vogue for effective organization stirred numerous groups such as trade unions, cooperatives, and employer associations. In that atmosphere the contribution of effective organization to the dramatic emergence of the Socialists as a political force made a deep impression on the other parties. The Socialist example, the "contagion from the Left," inspired imitation.

At the same time many changes in the political world such as the irreversible decline of royalism, an apparent weakening of anticlerical sentiment, a rapprochement between numbers of Moderate republicans and moderate Catholics, and the widening gulf between Moderate and Radical republicans were seen by contemporaries as encouraging signs of political renovation. Leading politicians from every point of the political spectrum agreed that a new era in French politics had begun.

Against this background a number of influential Moderate republicans who had long condemned the weakness of their party attempted to transform it into a strong, centralized, coherent organization, taking the English Conservative party as their model. Why they failed, and why the opportunity to renovate the party came to nothing, is the subject of this paper. It is essentially the story of the inability of the French, excepting the Socialists and later the Communists, to create national, coherent, and disciplined parties.

The Moderate republicans were the dominant political group in France from the late 1870s to the end of the nineteenth century. During much of this time the Moderates had a majority in Parliament, formed most of the ministries, and controlled the greater part of the departmental political and administrative machinery. Their influence was sufficiently pervasive to mark the era as the Opportunist Republic. Yet in their years of power the Moderates, who insisted that they alone could give France strong and stable government, never created the political machinery that would have enabled them to govern effectively.

The Moderate party lacked many of the elements of a modern western parliamentary party, such as central organization and open membership. As late as 1897 the Moderates did not have a central office. There was no formal medium to coordinate party policy or to run a national election campaign. The Moderate parliamentary groups, the extra-parliamentary associations centered in Paris, and the local and departmental organizations operated independently of each other. And in Parliament no Moderate prime minister had secure control over his majority.

Who were the Moderate republicans? As there were moderates in all the parties, and the political press of the early decades of the Third

Republic commonly spoke of Catholic, conservative, republican, and Radical moderates, defining the term modéré and fixing the identity of the Moderate republicans is not easy. Like so many terms of the French political lexicon, modéré cannot be defined precisely. Jules Simon noted in 1868 that there were "so many parties in France, and so many divisions within the parties" that there did not "remain a single word of the language of politics which is perfectly clear."[1]

In the eighties the term modéré took on, in addition to its broad connotation, a narrower focus, a more precise association. It was used almost interchangeably with the term Opportunist, then in vogue, to describe those members of the "political class" who were associated with the Moderate republican groups led by Gambetta and Ferry as opposed to the "extremist" Radicals and Socialists. By the early nineties the term Opportunist had become somewhat discredited[2] and many Moderate politicians preferred calling themselves Moderate republicans, Republicans of Government, or Progressists,[3] the three terms being used quite interchangeably. Certainly by the mid nineties the term modéré had become linked in the public mind with the Moderate republicans.

Political labels provide only surface identification. The Moderate republicans can be distinguished by their political outlook and more certainly by their "political temperament" and the language in which they expressed it. In the last quarter of the nineteenth century the Moderate republicans embodied the moderate political temperament of the Left spiritual family. A conscious opposition to the "extremist" Radicals profoundly influenced their temperament in those years.

Moderates habitually compared their moderation and calmness with the overexcited Radical temper. Moderate politicians contrasted Moderate realism, practicality, sense of proportion, appreciation of the complexity of things, subordination of theories to facts to Radical recklessness, muddled thinking, and utopian fantasies. They opposed their clear, sober, frank appeal to the electorate to Radical verbal ambiguity and chronic outbidding. Tirelessly they juxtaposed their "sense of government," attachment to order, and stability with Radical demagoguery, systematic opposition, and sterile agitation.[4]

The cautious conservatism of the Moderate republicans appeared unmistakably in the predilection of Moderate orators for such words as judicious, prudent, practical, useful, reasonable, serious, and reflective, and in the favored Moderate slogans of the nineties, "order and progress" and "neither revolution nor reaction."[5] Their social conservatism manifested itself in the frequent use of such key phrases as "defense of the interests" and "avoiding irritating questions." The Moderates also absorbed some characteristic conservative terminology as the honnêtes gens, the decent people threatened by troublemakers and agitators.

Although the flattering composite portrait sketched above was the one Moderates generally drew and accepted as accurate, some Moderates admitted its flaws. These critics of the party's weakness saw the portrait as an ideal that they hoped organization and discipline could realize.

Another question remains. Was the Moderate party, for all its influence, really a political party, or was it merely the moderate tendency of the "Republican party," which, together with the "Conservative party," formed the two spiritual families of France that bound people sharing the same community of views?

It is generally accepted that what "defines a political party—and makes it different from other interest and pressure groups—is its willingness or constitutional ability to take power; to achieve its desired ends through the given structure of political power in society."[6] The Moderate party fits this description; and rather than being a "community of opinion" was in fact an example of the classic type of later nineteenth-century middle-class parliamentary cadre party with its weak system of articulation, decentralized structure, and closed caucuses.[7]

If the Moderate party had no central organization, it had an informal power group, a network of personal relations at the ministerial, parliamentary, and departmental levels which, despite personal and factional rivalry, provided some leadership and direction. There was enough sense of common interest among Moderate parliamentarians,[8] much of the time, to ensure the Moderate orientation of governments, to keep the Radicals from power, to beat down Radical legislation, to keep control of key committees, and to assure election of Moderates to key positions such as the presidency of the Republic and of the Chamber of Deputies. Prefects appointed by Moderate governments were not remiss in promoting the interests of the Moderates. During elections there was interaction between Moderate governments and provincial party groups through the medium of the prefectorial administration.[9] Though it is difficult to assess the scope and importance of government support, it was, at times, important.[10] As the quest for material advantages for constituents was an overriding purpose of politics, the judicious distribution of government favors such as public works projects and employment, counted. Besides, the voters knew that the "government's candidate" was in a better position to get what they wanted.[11]

In some departments and constituencies the Moderates possessed a cohesion far superior to the parliamentary party.[12] In Isère, for instance, the "Opportunist coterie" dominated the department from about 1880 to 1895. Organization and power centered in the community of interest of like-minded Moderate deputies. These deputies, strongly rooted in their constituencies, controlled the local caucuses, had a working majority in the departmental general council, and usually succeeded in getting compliant prefects.[13]

The Moderate party really existed, but its loose, informal, incomplete machinery functioned erratically and unpredictably. As early as 1871 Léon Gambetta proposed the formation of a "true republican party" with a cadre, discipline, a program, and clear "boundaries."[14] Gambetta's goal of a strong party did not get very far in the 1880s. Many Moderates were suspicious of or hostile to Gambetta, who regarded himself as the natural leader of a united Republican party. Moreover, the Moderate party itself was divided by factional and personal rivalry. Those Moderates who wanted to strengthen the party's organization were clearly a minority in that age of extreme individualism. And they themselves disagreed how the party might be strengthened. Jules Ferry, like Gambetta a champion of strong government, homogeneous majorities, and disciplined parties, but more realistic and skeptical, doubted that these objectives could be easily reached in a country without "political mores."[15]

Gambetta's idea of a coherent party of like-minded people was incompatible with his ardent championing of the union of all republicans. The ambiguous relationship of the Moderates and Radicals stood in the way of a cohesive Moderate party. In the eighties the Moderates were marked off from the Radicals by temperament, competition for power, and sharp differences over important issues. Antagonism between them was often extreme.[16] The strong party Moderates,[17] though publicly regretting the splintering of the Republican party, wanted clearer separation from the Radicals. A clean separation was the precondition for a coherent Moderate party; but in the eighties the final break did not come.

The habit of mind that some Moderates still shared with the Radicals of seeing political conflict mainly in terms of the eternal struggle between republicans and "reactionaries," the memory of common struggles, the determination to defend the Republic against its enemies, the continuing strength of the conservatives in many departments, and the resurgence of conservative power in 1885 and Boulangism all contributed to maintaining or renewing ties with the Radicals. The vagueness of some professions *de foi*, the equivocal use of party labels,[18] the lack of clarity so much decried by strong party Moderates, at times obscured the lines separating the parties. The coherence of the Moderate party suffered from the practice of republican concentration and the quest for Radical votes when a majority was lacking or uncertain. Moreover, some Moderate politicians sought closer ties with the Radicals, while others, fewer in number at the time, leaned toward the more moderate conservatives out of necessity, expediency, or from a sense of affinity. These contradictory pressures reflected the centrist character of the Moderate party.

The cohesion of the Moderate party in the provinces, the sense of being clearly separated from the Radicals, varied greatly from department to department so that a unified, coherent national Moderate party was not possible in the eighties. Party cohesion was affected by many factors, such as how quickly republicans won power, the presence or absence of a strong Radical current, and the political temperament of the population. Like other parliamentarians, Moderate deputies absorbed the dominant coloration of their constituency. Putting the constituency over the party was far more common than disregarding local opinion in the interest of the party.

In the Loire, for instance, the republicans won power quickly and by the early seventies a sharp cleavage separated Moderates and Radicals. The conservative temper of the population and the dominant power of the Moderates made any accommodation with the Radicals unnecessary. In the Côte-d'Or, where the republicans were solidly entrenched by the mid seventies, hostility between Moderates and Radicals produced competing congresses and rival electoral lists. In the Loir-et-Cher, where the Moderates were the dominant party, Radical candidates in

1885 dubbed themselves the "anti-opportunist candidates."[19] But in many departments, as in the West where the Right remained strong, the fundamental divide lay between republicans and conservatives. Differences between Moderates and Radicals were blurred, and a single electoral list prevailed.[20] Between areas of clear-cut Moderate-Radical opposition and the battlegrounds of the Republican and Conservative parties, where the Moderate party had no autonomous identity, there were intermediary zones where, lacking a majority, the coherence of the Moderate party was jeopardized by the necessity of accommodation and compromise.[21]

The disheartening organizational history of the Moderate party in the 1880s did not discourage those Moderates intent on strengthening their party. In the closing years of the decade a bitter quarrel over republican reverses in 1885 and Boulangism intensified hostility between Moderates and Radicals. Moderates blamed the Radicals for the resurgence of the Right, the rise of Boulanger, and, in general, for the broad discontent in the country. A break with the Radicals was pressed by the strong party Moderates. The full-scale attack on Radicalism was accompanied by a declaration of ideological independence, a condemnation of ambiguous and outdated catchwords and combinations, a call for clarity, and a demand that the Moderates go to the electorate under their own flag. Cautious overtures to the moderate conservatives considered possible allies against the Radicals were a startling departure from republican tradition and underscored the seriousness of these developments.[22]

Moderate spokesmen insisted that the country was tired of weak, unstable government, of "organized anarchy." A strong government, backed by a "truly compact government majority, judicious and disciplined," responding to the conservative, tolerant, practical mood of the country, would regain the confidence of the disaffected and win over the conservative masses more interested in defending their interests than in restoring a monarchy. The Moderate party alone could bring about "le bon ordre dans la République" that the country wanted. But to do this the Moderates had first to end the organized anarchy in their own ranks.[23]

During the critical period of Boulangism the strong party Moderates pleaded the benefits of party organization. Jules Ferry's organ L'Estafette observed that the Moderate republicans "ont eu le grand tort de laisser le champ libre, out peu s'en faut, à des adversaires qui, eux, n'ont point désarmé un seul instant."[24] Eager to take advantage of a new mood in the country that seemed favorable to the Moderate cause, to resist Boulangism and Radicalism, and to organize the Moderates for the "decisive battle" of the 1889 election, they formed the first of the Moderate extra- parliamentary associations, the Association nationale républicaine. A second Moderate association, the Union libérale républicaine, also emerged during the election period. Though the associations had been formed primarily to fight Boulangism, they also intended to provide the party structure and leadership. As the new decade got underway more associations appeared. The proliferation of Moderate groups was seen by the strong party men as evidence that Moderates really wanted organization.[25]

Whatever the original intent, the main activity of the Moderate associations in the 1890s became "political education," not political organization. Radicalism and Socialism were fought with tracts and lecture series, not with a network of branches centrally directed. "La bonne parole opportuniste" was widely disseminated among the smaller provincial newspapers by press services of the Association nationale and the Union libérale. Some Moderate candidates received financial assistance from the associations and, at times, there was interaction between the associations and the administrative agents of Moderate governments. But essentially the associations were "propaganda mills" centered in Paris with committees in a few of the larger cities. They were, as contemporary observers noted, general-staffs without troops.[26]

Although the associations shared the same general orientation they did not merge, and new associations continued to be formed. The proliferation of associations resulted in part from the ambition of their leaders. Associations could be launched with little effort and then used to advance the parliamentary influence of the organizers. But beyond the play of ambition, the diversity of the associations reflected the different tendencies of the Moderate party, each with its following, sphere of influence, and organs of opinion.

The Union libérale represented the survival of the old centre gauche, the most conservative republican faction. Among Moderates the Union libérale was the most enthusiastic in welcoming the Ralliement, some of its members even favoring modifying the lois scolaires. Later it vehemently attacked the Waldeck-Rousseau ministry.[27]

The Association nationale républicaine was more representative of the mainstream of the Moderate party in its cautious drift to the Right, and in its ambiguous attitude to the Ralliement. Closely identified with the Méline ministry, the Association nationale also later attacked the Waldeck-Rousseau ministry.[28]

Founded in 1894 by the Gambettistes, surviving friends and associates of Gambetta, the Association gambettistes remained more faithful to the old republican tradition, and later supported the "government of republican defense." Committed to "perpetuating the memory and realizing the program" of Gambetta, the Association gambettistes more emphatically than other associations championed a strongly organized party. At the time of its inception the Association gambettistes intended setting up committees all over France that would have close and continuous ties with the central committee in Paris.[29]

Although the expectations that the associations had generated had not materialized, an optimistic mood prevailed in the early nineties among the Moderates, who noted fundamental changes in the world of politics that seemed highly favorable for the prospects of the Moderate party and for the possibility of strengthening it.

Moderate leaders such as Jules Ferry, Eugene Spuller, Léon Say, and René Waldeck-Rousseau detected a deep shift of opinion in the country, which they saw as a profound reaction to the abuses of the parliamentary system and sterile agitation, as well as a yearning for government stability and a "policy of results." In that "turning point" of French history, as Ernest Constans described in 1893, the changes that were altering the structure of Third Republic politics, the optimism of the moderates, seemed warranted.[30]

The Moderates had in mind not only the virtual disappearance of the royalist parliamentary groups, the flowering of the Ralliement, and the 1893 general election, which gave them a majority in the Chamber. Even Radicals agreed that the great issues of the eighties—constitutional revision, separation of Church and State—left the public indifferent. Many of the obstacles to a coherent, centralized Moderate party seemed to be crumbling. Concentration ministries that had favored the minority Radicals and for so long contributed to the ambiguous atmosphere that enveloped parliamentary politics, were condemned by leaders of all the major groups, from the Monarchists to the Socialists. The old Republican party, judging from mutual anathemas and categorical pronouncements, appeared finally to have come apart. For many Moderates the enemy was now on the Left, and "republican discipline" was widely ignored in the 1893 election. With a majority of constituencies having two (or more) republican lists, the separate identity of the Moderates on a national scale came closer to reality.[31]

Once the basic issue of the political system had been settled, many politicians assumed that a realignment and simplification of the party system would follow. The air was filled with talk and plans for launching new parties or investing old ones with backbone. There was clearly a widespread desire for renewal, for efficacy through organization.[32]

In the 1880s all the French political groups, excepting the Socialists, were weak in organization. But in the early nineties a revolution in the state of the parties seemed in the making. The Socialists, though splintered into many factions, were well along in the process of creating the first of the mass parties with annual congresses, a system of branches, control over membership, effective propaganda methods, and parliamentary discipline. The Radicals, influenced by the Socialists, were entering the path of organization. A surge of Radical grass-roots militancy and persistent demand for stronger organization and leadership led to the multiplication of departmental federations and cantonal comités and to the creation of a rudimentary national organization.[33]

The example of the Socialists, the "contagion from the Left," touched the Catholics too. Enthusiasm for the institution of the Congress swept over the Catholic community in the 1890s. Congresses of Catholic journalists, teachers, and political partisans met for pious purposes, study, or political action. Even the clergy, traditionally confined to their diocese, were caught up in the vogue for organization. Many proposals were advanced and some steps taken toward the creation of Catholic electoral organizations and political parties or a non-sectarian party in which Catholics could freely participate.[34]

Enthusiasm for organization[35] spread to the trade unions, employer associations, and agricultural cooperatives. The 1890s witnessed a significant increase in trade union effectives and a multiplication of employer federations. And, as in the case of the political parties, the momentum of organization led to attempts to unify on a national scale.[36]

Against this background of ferment and expectation, strong party Moderates believed that the transformation of the Moderate party into a party "worthy of the name" was now possible. Some of them even regarded the coming of an English-type two-party system as a realistic possibility, with the Moderate party as the French Tory party. Many politicians agreed that national parties were emerging from the breakup and regrouping of the old parties.[37] There was widespread agreement that there were now only two tendencies in French politics—what Léon Say described as liberal and radical, J.-L. de Lanessan as conservative and democratic, and Marcel Sembat as socialist and anti- socialist. The incipient polarity of French politics was emphasized in the frequent use of the labels Whig and Tory. Confirmation of these trends was seen in the formation of the first homogeneous government of the Third Republic (Casimir-Perier) supported by a homogeneous Moderate majority followed by an alternation of the first all-Radical ministry (Bourgeois) supported by the Socialists and the Moderate Méline government supported by the conservatives.[38] Further proof of the emergence of a two-party system was seen in the rapprochement of the Ralliés and the Moderates and in the "splitting" of the Radical party. Moderates such as Méline, Waldeck-Rousseau, and Deschanel insisted that the Radicals were ideologically bankrupt, increasingly falling under Socialist influence, and being abandoned by their moderate followers.[39] The moderate Radicals, the radicaux de gouvernement, were, Moderates claimed, coming over to their side.

The rapprochement of the Moderates and Ralliés was stimulated by a common fear of Radical and Socialist strength as well as broadly similar views on the need for a strong executive and defense of the "interests."[40] Only the religious question separated them. But even this obstacle seemed no longer formidable. Many observers in the early 1890s noted that anticlericalism had greatly subsided.[41] Practical political cooperation between them began discreetly in those years. Moderate candidates in the 1893 election benefited from Ralliés votes. In some departments, as in the Loire, Nord, and Tarn, Ralliés and Moderates worked together openly against the "collectivists."[42] In the Chamber of

Deputies Moderate ministries became increasingly dependent on the Ralliés.

Optimistic Moderates saw a prospect of uniting the "middle classes," or what Moderate spokesmen often called the "propertied classes" or the "interests," behind their party. The progress of "Radical-Socialism," the specter of the income tax, the militancy of the trade unions, had convinced many businessmen that the political neutrality they had observed was no longer compatible with the defense of their interests. The Bourgeois ministry and its income tax bill, which had given the business community a bad scare, led to the formation of politically oriented businessmen's associations. Prominent industrialists and many of the major syndicats patronaux joined the Société d'économie industrielle et commerciale and the Comité national républicain du commerce et de l'industrie. The fact that Moderate politicians had been instrumental in the formation of these associations foreshadowed collaboration between powerful groups of the business community and the Moderate party.[43] Moderate leaders such as Gambetta, Waldeck-Rousseau, and Méline had long favored a greater and more active participation of businessmen in politics.

The stirring of the business community led some Moderate politicians to hope that they might also win the support of many of the large number of Frenchmen who normally stayed away from the polls. They assumed that most of them were neither Radicals nor Socialists, but rather citizens disgusted by chronic government instability and the prevailing political mores. Their abstention, Moderates argued, enabled the better-organized Left to have a greater representation than its actual following.[44] Waldeck-Rousseau predicted in 1895 that the "day when men of property will make to defend themselves, a tenth of the agitation that others make to threaten them, they will be the masters. They are the many and they are the force." If only the pays réel could be organized—and that was what the strong party Moderates proposed to do.[45]

In June 1897 René Waldeck-Rousseau proposed a new, dynamic association to realize the old gambettiste dream of a coherent, centralized national party. The older Moderate associations had provided neither leadership nor organization. Unprecedented opportunities, it seemed, had not been exploited. At the same time a sizeable Moderate majority proved unable to assure the life of Moderate governments. The opportune moment for revitalizing the party had come, Waldeck-Rousseau argued, because all Moderates were keenly aware of the party's weaknesses and of the imperative need to overcome them.[46]

The projected Grand cercle républicain, in the mind of its organizers, was to be radically different from the other associations. They intended bringing together in one centralized organization all Moderate parliamentarians, party cadre, and extra-parliamentary organizations. They meant to profit from the painful experience of the past as well as from the experience of those parties, regardless of doctrine or nationality, which had achieved discipline and efficacy. They were interested in more than winning votes: they wanted a party capable of setting national policy through effective parliamentary and governmental action. They hoped to end the "abuses" of the parliamentary system, to strengthen the executive, and, by attracting all moderates, to advance the coming of a two-party system.[47]

The Grand cercle differed from the other associations not only in its wider ambition, but also in the greater and acknowledged influence of English political practices. Though the Moderates generally admired England's political system, they disagreed over its relevance to France. Moderate opinion on this question in the nineties ranged, as it had among Frenchmen generally since the Second Empire, from those who thought it feasible to introduce features of the English party system into France[48] to those who merely believed that an understanding of what made the English system work so well might yield helpful insights, to the more widespread conviction that what worked in England would not work in France. At the same time Moderate opinion divided between those who believed that a two-party system was a realistic expectation and those who thought it an illusion and hoped more modestly that the Moderates might form a stronger center party between the extremes.[49]

The organizers of the Grand Cercle believed in the imminence of a two-party system and in the feasibility of forming English-type parties in France. Indeed, the English Conservative party served as their model.

They visualized the cercle as a combined directorate, central office, and political club. Parliamentary and electoral strategy would be decided there. Elaborate party machinery—councils, assemblies, and an annual congress—would round out the national party organization. Determined that the Grand cercle would not become just another Parisian association, the organizing committee planned a network of branches throughout the country, buttressed by a permanent cadre and sustained by militants of the kind that the Moderate party sorely lacked. Party activity would go on, even in the dead season between elections. A continuing program of "political education," more aggressive than the mild-mannered diffusion of "sound ideas" by the other associations, would counteract Radical and Socialist propaganda and instill a "new faith" in a party having little partisan feeling. It was hoped that the dining facilities, the regular dinners, the meeting of party leaders and interest groups, and the creation of a library of political and parliamentary information, would create the kind of atmosphere that prevailed in the London political clubs. New elements would be attracted such as businessmen and youth.[50]

As the organizers of the Grand cercle intended appealing to a broad range of groups, they proposed, following the English example, grades of membership and degrees of participation. Annual dues were set at two hundred francs for the party elite down to five or ten francs for members of associated popular leagues to be organized later.[51]

The experience of the Grand cercle clearly revealed the difficulties and the ultimate frustration facing the strong party Moderates. Although the Grand cercle was welcomed by the Gambettistes and some of the younger leaders such as Poincaré and Jonnart, it ran into resistance with other Moderates. Not all of them shared Waldeck-Rousseau's sense of urgency or felt that traditional methods were obsolete. Some Moderates thought that there were already too many organizations and that another would only further divide the party. In some departments Grand cercle organizers ran up against the incurable suspicion of anything organized and directed from Paris. Certain people invited to join refused on the ground that Waldeck-Rousseau was a "reactionary," reflecting the opposing tendencies of the Moderate party. But the most determined resistance came from the older associations fearful of absorption by the centralizing Grand cercle.[52]

Some Moderates, though favorable to the concept of the Grand cercle, thought that the necessary conditions for its success were as yet lacking. Le Temps contended that the "arrondissement spirit" must first be overcome and that regional decentralization was the answer. Only when local issues were settled locally, and when the deputy was no longer the agent of local interests, could parliament's attention be centered on national questions. Then, perhaps, a coherent majority and opposition could function as in England.[53] Other Moderates felt that there wasn't much point providing the party with a centralized structure without first changing the political behavior that undermined all discipline. Was such a change possible, and if so, how was it to be done?

Still other Moderates, contemplating the "national character," doubted that it could ever be done. More hopefully a number of Moderate politicians launched a campaign to restrict the "excessive" powers of the deputies by revising the procedural rules of the Chamber,[54] a strategy earlier favored by Gambetta. They expected that a stronger executive and a less omnipotent Chamber would promote parliamentary discipline. During the 1898 election campaign Waldeck-Rousseau, Poincaré, Deschanel, and other Moderates made the reform of parliamentary procedure a major issue. As one Moderate noted, it was easy enough to say that political mores needed changing. But could it be done? "Manners," he observed, "are stronger than the laws."[55]

In the face of opposition and skepticism, the organizing committee made a forceful effort to convince the Moderates of the necessity of central organization. In the meantime violent attacks in the Radical and Socialist press publicized the cercle, membership increased steadily, and in February 1898 the Grand cercle was formally constituted.[56]

The Grand cercle was born in the midst of the 1898 general election. Having been organized barely six weeks before the first ballot, it could not play the directing role to which it aspired. There had been no time to set up elaborate machinery or to form branches in the provinces. Nevertheless, the Grand cercle entered briskly into the campaign with the purpose of demonstrating to the Moderates, if only on a small scale, the manner in which a well-organized party should run a campaign. Agents were sent to the departments to gather detailed information on candidates, issues, and drift of opinion. In Paris a semblance of a political machine, with committees operating in the arrondissements, was set up. The cercle seconded efforts to coordinate the national campaign by presenting a common party program. It sought to persuade more businessmen to run as Moderate candidates to help the party financially.

The cercle sponsored Moderate candidates, contested seats hitherto abandoned to the Left, and tried to unseat Socialist deputies.[57] The "invasion" of Radical and Socialist strongholds was an unheard-of audacity on the part of moderates.[58]

But these exertions were clouded by untoward developments that jeopardized the aspirations of the strong party Moderates of the Grand cercle. In early 1898 they, along with all the other Moderates, found themselves fighting on difficult, sometimes treacherous terrain. Some of the trends of the early nineties that Moderate observers assumed would benefit them had in the long run had the opposite effect. The surge of Socialist strength and the emergence of the Ralliement did not lead to a simplification of the party system; these, in fact, greatly confused the political scene. The Socialist "threat" did not unite the "anti-Collectivists" and the "interests" behind the Moderate party. Nor did the Ralliement bring over the mass of conservatives to the Moderate camp.

Though Moderates shared a common hostility to the Socialists, they disagreed how they should be resisted. They did not all turn to the conservatives for allies. In some departments counterweight to the Socialists was found in entente with the Radicals, thereby reviving or continuing "republican concentration" to the detriment of party coherence.[59]

The Ralliement had profited the Moderate party, but it had also deeply divided and weakened it. Moderate response to the Ralliement ran a wide gamut from enthusiastic approval to unconcealed hostility. The Ralliement was not a single, unified movement with which the Moderates could have easily come to terms. It was a movement of bewildering complexity, composed of many elements whose attitude toward the Moderates ranged from eagerness for meaningful collaboration to militant hostility. The Ralliés closest in outlook to the Moderates made overtures to them for closer ties. But excepting the ultra-Moderates of the Union libérale (some of whom favored modifications of the Laic Laws) and a small number of parliamentarians from departments of particular Catholic strength, Moderates rarely went beyond endorsing the abstract principle of the Ralliement. Even the leaders of the Grand cercle, who thought in terms of a two-party system in which the conservatives would enter their "Tory" party, were vague on the subject.

Moderate hesitation on the Ralliement exposed the rifts and the divided purpose of the Moderate party. The Ralliement forced insistently on the Moderates the choice of alignment with the conservatives or the Radicals, a question that profoundly divided them. The opposing pressures that beset the Moderate party and undermined its coherence were more acute in the later nineties than they had been in the eighties, when an alignment with the conservatives was inconceivable for most Moderates.

The ambivalence of the Moderates, their treatment of theRalliés as untouchables, their refusal to change the Laic Laws, made any broad agreement with the conservatives, any hope of creating a new republican conservative party, impossible. Ill feeling between the groups had deepened during the by-elections of 1896 and the senatorial election of 1897. Incensed Ralliés accused some Moderate candidates who had had no chance of winning of retiring on the second ballot in favor of Radicals. Indignant Moderates charged Catholics in some departments of spitefully voting for Radicals.[60]

The uneasy relationship of Moderates and Ralliés provided the Radicals with an issue that they brilliantly exploited. In the mid nineties the Radicals began a violent anticlerical campaign aimed in part at working up republican opinion against the rapprochement of the Ralliés and the Moderates. They stirred up the anticlericalism, which had lost some of its old virulence, to such an extent that the religious question became the sharpest issue in the long 1898 election campaign. They succeeded in shifting some of the concern over the danger of socialism to an anxiety over the "clerical threat."[61]

In that charged atmosphere the Radicals touched the Moderates in their most sensitive spot, their fear of being called false republicans and of being excluded from the republican spiritual family. The courting of Ralliés support, the relaxation of government pressure on the congregations, the very idea of the esprit nouveau provoked impassioned Radical charges of clericalism and apostasy. For all their social conservatism, dislike of the Radicals, and fear of socialism, few Moderates wanted to leave the Republican party or to be identified with Reaction.

The strength of tradition only partly explains the defensive reaction of the Moderates, who vehemently denied Radical accusations. They were gripped by a truly profound apprehension of being irremediably compromised in the eyes of republican voters. Fear that too open an alignment with the "clericals" would cost them heavily at the polls was widespread in 1897 and 1898.[62] Many Moderate politicians intimidated by the Radicals asserted their republican orthodoxy, castigated clericalism, and tried to outdo the Radicals in the ardor of their professed attachment to the Republic. Not all Moderates, however, reacted so defensively. Some of them, decreasing in number as the election approached, agreed with Méline that the Ralliement had been "a great victory for the Republic" and a blow to the Radical party, whose plans and calculations it had frustrated.[63]

Moderate sensitivity to Radical criticism, Moderate fears during elections that their support of moderate measures and men might antagonize the electorate, the "cowardice of the Moderates," had long weakened the party. In the eighties strong party Moderates such as Gambetta, Ferry, Waldeck-Rousseau, and Joseph Reinach had bitterly observed how easily Moderates gave way to the rage accusatrice of the Radicals, and of the lack of courage so often shown by them. In the nineties the same lament was heard from the strong party Moderates and those Ralliés who really wanted accommodation with the Moderates.[64]

The hesitation and confusion of the Moderates were greatly aggravated by the politicization of the Dreyfus Affair. The agitation of the Nationalists, the dynamic militancy of the Assumptionists, the aggressively antiparliamentary tone of conservative electioneering, the biting attacks against the Moderates in the Assumptionist press, the links between many Ralliés and the new extreme Right had far-reaching repercussions on the Moderate party. Many Moderates turned from looking to the conservatives (now seen as reactionary rather than conservative) to a rapprochement with the Radicals, reviving, once again, the ambiguous Moderate-Radical relationship. But as other Moderates refused a turn to the Left, the rift in the Moderate party widened. The climate of opinion was no longer that of the early nineties. The recrudescence of anti-parliamentarianism and of militant anticlericalism produced an atmosphere in which the Moderates were peculiarly vulnerable to Radical attack.[65]

The Grand cercle républicain did not escape the dilemmas of the Moderate party. Its response to them was conventional: it was vague on the Ralliement, avoided taking sides on the Dreyfus Affair, and reacted defensively to the Radical offensive. These reactions reflected the cautious Moderate temperament rather than the bold approach of a dynamic party.

During the last two years of the sixth legislature (1893–1898), a number of conservative deputies had regularly supported the Méline ministry and so assured its longevity. Although Méline refused to conclude an overall election agreement with the conservatives, he and some Moderate politicians wished to acquit their debt by not running Moderate candidates against prominent supporters of the government, such as Denys Cochin. When the Radicals and Socialists learned that pressure had been put on a number of Moderate arrondissement committees, including those of the Grand cercle, to withdraw candidates running against the "friends" of the government, they saw in this action substantiation of their un-wearying accusation of the Republic betrayed by the Moderates. They denounced the choice of certain Moderate candidates as offensive to all good republicans.[66]

In the furor of charges and countercharges the Grand cercle and other Moderate groups expediently withdrew their support from suspect candidates and affirmed their opposition to any modification of the lois scolaires. More than ever the Moderates were on the defensive. Everywhere, the Radical Lockroy observed, Moderate candidates felt obliged to "show themselves more Radical than the Radicals and almost more revolutionary than the revolutionaries." Many a Moderate ostentatiously rejected the support of the Ralliés. By the intransigent proclamation of their laïcité these Moderates accelerated the revival of anticlericalism to the profit of the Radicals.[67]

The post-election period was gloomy for the Moderates, who came out of the election divided, on the defensive, and their majority lost. They could command a majority only by greater dependence on the Right, which most Moderates refused. At the same time the tacit support of the Right was no longer certain. With neither the Moderates nor the Radicals able to govern alone, sentiment developed in both groups in favor of a government of "republican concentration." The possibility of a concentration ministry, of a reconciliation between Radicals and Moderates, threatened the coherence and distinctiveness of the Moderate party so strongly favored by the strong party Moderates. Not surprisingly the leadership of the Grand cercle opposed any "equivocal combination" and reaffirmed the necessity of homogeneity and clarity.[68]

The election also showed the tenaciousness of those bad political habits the strong party Moderates had imagined to be on the decline. In some departments Moderate discipline was almost totally absent. There were instances of Moderate candidates withdrawing in favor of Socialist candidates. But it wasn't only the Moderates who were affected by the breakdown of party discipline. Party programs were often submerged in a flood of issues and vague formulas behind which candidates concealed the most contradictory opinions. Besides a "confusion of ideas," there were in many localities so many candidates that at times party labels lost their meaning. The two clear-cut "currents of opinion," the precursor of a two-party system predicted by many observers in the early nineties, did not materialize.[69]

The portent of the election and the growing dissension within the Moderate party did not outwardly discourage the leaders of the Grand cercle. In January 1899, the Grand cercle opened a center of "contact, political action, and propaganda." Meetings of political and business groups were sponsored. An effort was made to get Moderate deputies and senators to meet at the cercle. The atmosphere at the cercle's headquarters consciously resembled the London political clubs where members worked out parliamentary strategy, dined, and relaxed.[70]

Waldeck-Rousseau and his colleagues planned to increase the scope of the cercle's activities. But the times were less favorable than ever. In the post-election period the Dreyfus Affair splintered the Moderates more profoundly than any other party. The goal of a coherent, unified party became increasingly remote. The Grand cercle faced the prospect of becoming no more than just another extra-parliamentary association. The other associations showed no signs of subordinating themselves to it. Nor was the Grand cercle immune from the effects of the many counter-currents eddying through the Moderate party. The moment that Waldeck-Rousseau intervened publicly in the Dreyfus debate, and from a Dreyfusard position, the cohesion of the cercle dissolved. And when in June 1899 Waldeck-Rousseau formed his government of Republican Defense, which included not only Radicals, but a Socialist, the Moderate party split—a break that extended to all its parts. Acrimonious debate and resounding public resignations shook the Moderate extra-parliamentary associations. There was much feeling against Waldeck-Rousseau in the Grand cercle: some members demanded his removal as president. In April 1900, the Grand cercle closed its doors almost unnoticed.[71]

Had the signs observed by many Moderate leaders foreshadowing the emergence of a two-party system and the renovation of the Moderate party been an illusion? Not entirely. There had been in the early nineties a reaction against "pure politics," ministerial instability, concentration ministries, and corruption.[72] The vogue for organization, the desire for efficacy, had been both widespread and real. At times fear of socialism and income tax seemed to be bringing the "propertied classes" into a de facto alliance with the majority Moderate party. Undeniably the conjuncture of the early nineties had been favorable to the Moderates. But years slipped by before the Grand cercle was organized, and the favorable climate of politics passed. Temperamentally the Moderates moved cautiously, preparing opinion and waiting for the opportune moment. Characteristically they disagreed on how to exploit opportunities.

There were not only opportunities lost, but also illusions harbored. "The decade of the 1890s, seen in retrospect," Gordon Wright has observed, "stands out as an era of political transition, a time of general shifting of political forces."[73] At such times expectation and illusion run high. The illusion that decisive political changes were imminent was a fairly common phenomenon during the Third Republic. The Moderates were not alone in the early nineties in viewing the future with excessive optimism; so did many other groups such as the Socialists and the Ralliés.

Some of the developments encouraging to the Moderates turned out very differently than anticipated; others proved to be superficial rather than profound changes. The castigation of political mores so marked in the early nineties, which had been one of the hopeful signs observed by the strong party Moderates, did not produce a moral reorientation. Condemnation of political mores, however sincere, was part of the ritual of French politics. Talk about change, reform, and organization that had become part of political ritual more often than not, led nowhere. Writing in 1896 about the aspirations of the conservatives for organization, Louis Joubert remarked: "Nous savons que dans tous les banquets, de quelque opinion que soient, les convives, républicains de l'union libérale, monarchistes, conservateurs, on nous promet qu 'on va s'organiser. Il y a vingt ans qu 'on l'announce; il vaudrait mieux le répéter moins souvent, et le faire une fois." Writing in 1958, Hubert Beuve-Méry noted that the "refonte des institutions politiques de la France est à l'ordre du jour depuis une trentaine d'années. Malheuresement aucune des réformes tentées n'a reussi à modifier profondément les moeurs politiques du pays, moeurs déplorables que chacun condamne tout en leur restant plus ou moins attaché."[74]

Strong party Moderates had been a convergence of all who, regardless of party labels, wanted "order, stability, economy, practical reforms, and liberty for all." They assumed that the Moderate party would be the beneficiary of this convergence, since they believed that it reflected the "middle opinion" of the country.[75]

The unity of view of "middle" or moderate opinion upon which rested the hope of a two-party system proved unreal. A temporary and limited rapprochement inspired by a sense of common danger was mistaken for a permanent and broad change. Thus the attempt of the Moderate-sponsored businessmen associations to mobilize the business community encountered resistance from those businessmen who wanted the syndicats patronales to maintain their traditional neutrality and Catholic entrepreneurs who formed their own groups.[76] The Moderates who favored alignment with the conservatives thought the main political dividing line would henceforth be between the collectivists and the anti-collectivists. "Collectivism" was a dividing line, but not the only one, nor in 1898–1899 the most important one. Fear of socialism had subsided while passion over the religious question had mounted. Republican tradition had certainly weakened among the Moderates in the 1890s, but what remained was sufficient to compromise the rapprochement with the conservatives and to keep alive ties with the Radicals.

Le Temps noted after the 1898 election that there were no majorities in France, only majorities on certain questions.[77] However wide the agreement between the moderate Ralliés and the Moderates on social conservation and government stability, they remained divided on what proved, in spite of appearances, to be the immense gulf of the religious question.

Of the hopes of the strong party Moderates none was less real than introducing English political ways into France. The English political system was a different world, and the French Moderates did not much resemble the English Conservatives. The conditions that assured the discipline and coherence of the English parties were absent in France.

By the 1890s the English parties had known a continuous existence of more than two centuries.[78] For at least a century they had elements of central organization and, at times, even well before the first Reform Act, they possessed a strong sense of group identity and party loyalty.[79] Many MP's, owing nothing to their party for their seats, willingly accepted party discipline. In the second half of the nineteenth century defection of disappointed politicians and the breaking away of dissident groups were rare in comparison to the French parties. Men in sharp disagreement with party policy commonly did not press their differences too far or else kept their discontents from public view and settled quarrels privately.

A sense of identification with the parties extended beyond Parliament to the nation. Public opinion had been won over massively by the parliamentary parties at least a generation before the full development of national party organizations. This phenomenon radically differentiated English from French politics at the constituency level.

In the Victorian age the English parties realized a cohesion unimaginable in France by their capacity to embrace a wide span of interests and viewpoints as well as men of moderate and extremist tendencies. In France it was impossible to assemble in one party all republicans, or royalists, or socialists, to say nothing of a party that could accommodate proletarians and their employers. Even men of similar outlook found it hard to work together. Party cohesion was reinforced in England and further fractured in France by different electoral systems. The system of simple-majority-single-ballot promoted English party coherence as well as the two-party system, while the French scrutin d' arrondissement had the opposite effect.

There were fewer lines of division in the English political world. England experienced no trauma such as the French Revolution leaving deep scars constantly reopening. Landlords, tenants, yeomen farmers, large and small spoke with one voice on most issues and they spoke through the Tory party, the party of the "agricultural interest." Moreover, the Socialist movement in the later nineteenth century was insignificant and few English workers subscribed to the doctrine of class war. Most workers voted Liberal but a surprising number backed the Tories. The world of English labor contrasted sharply with the turbulent and important French Socialist movement, itself torn by factionalism, and the acute class consciousness of the French workers. Differences over religious and educational policy in the late Victorian years did not touch off political lightning and passionate storms as in France. Religious controversy was dying down and was no longer at the center of political concern. And neither the Anglicans nor the Dissenters were homogeneous in their politics.

The social homogeneity of the local and national leadership of both parties and, above all, of the parliamentary parties was crucially important in attaining coherence and in overcoming differences of attitude and opinion. The deeply rooted habit of deference to the upper classes constituted a major element of stability and continuity. Until fairly late in the century, deference communities such as far tenants and workers of large enterprises in smaller towns voted for the party of their landlords and employers.

In the nineteenth century English public opinion expressed itself powerfully through the proliferation of extra-parliamentary movements, which, unlike the small number of their weak French counterparts, significantly affected the course of politics. The power of opinion was heightened by the clarity of the great issues that dominated politics, such as the Reform bills, the Corn Laws, and the Irish question. Most national elections were fought around a single, clear-cut issue. By the 1870s the attention of the electorate shifted increasingly from local to national issues, among them questions of foreign policy, which were sometimes decisively important in general elections. Clear and, at times, acute differences on foreign and defense policy separated the parties. In France foreign affairs hardly ever counted as an election issue.

The emergence of powerful leaders who came to symbolize their parties and had mass appeal sharpened the national character of the parties. In France, most political leaders and heads of government were scarcely known in the country. There, fame and exceptional qualities were, except in times of extraordinary crisis, disabling handicaps exciting envy, fear, and hostility.[80]

As the suffrage was extended Liberals and Conservatives were forced to appeal to a wider and more heterogeneous electorate. They had the insight and flexibility to transform themselves from cadre into mass parties. The intense rivalry of the closely matched parties made effective organization essential. Electoral defeat spurred the parties to searching inquests, overhaul of party machinery, and greater effort.

The impressive discipline of the English parties in the later decades of the century came not only from party loyalty and pressure from the whips and the extra-parliamentary organizations. An increasing number of constituency candidates became dependent on the support of the national party. A candidate needing financial and moral support looked to the party and not to the government, for, unlike France, the influence of the government on elections was negligible. Politicians could not, as in France, further their ambition by striking out on their own. Recognition, honors, and advancement were possible only within the framework of the parties. There was no future or place for the independent or the creator of splinter groups.

The goal of a coherent, disciplined party was beyond the reach of the strong party Moderates. They had always been a minority in the party, and they were of different minds how the goal could be reached. The strong men of the departments, secure in their fiefs, did not clamor for a strong, centralized party.[81] No pressing appeal for stronger organization came from the provincial cadre. The organizers of the Grand cercle had to persuade Moderate politicians, none too successfully, of the necessity of central organization.

There was no secure nucleus from which to build a coherent party. The Moderate party never synthesized the conflicting tendencies of its followers. The divisions in the Moderate party were a permanent condition. So deep-rooted were the cleavages of the nineties between those Moderates who wished to work with the Radicals, those who wanted accommodation with the conservatives, and those who clung to an unstable position in the middle of the center party, that all of these divisions reappeared in 1900 inside the anti–Waldeck-Rousseau Progressivist group which then constituted the right wing of the old Moderate party.[82]

The dynamic party visualized by the Grand cercle was really incompatible with the Moderate temperament. The defensive character of Moderate electioneering reflected their cautious temperament. As Jules Ferry remarked in 1887, "Qu' est-ce qu' une armée qui dit à ses chefs: Surtout pas de bruit, qu' on ne vous voie ni vous entende?"[83]

The strong party Moderates did not see that the social groups who supported them or whose support they sought—the "propertied classes," the comfortable bourgeoisie, the liberal professions, and businessmen[84]— were uncomfortable in the world of mass democratic politics. They had little taste for political action and felt sufficiently informed to be indifferent to, and even irritated by, political indoctrination.[85]

A divided party that had no doctrine, whose electoral appeal was negative, that exploited fears and lacked imagination, could not generate enthusiasm or attract an army of dedicated party members. In the 1890s many Moderate leaders agreed that the party needed to go beyond the posture of a "party of resistance." But those Moderates who, like Waldeck-Rousseau, Paul Laffitte, Barthou, and Méline, tried to formulate a positive party program were conspicuously timid or vague.[86]

To succeed, the strong party Moderates had not only to overcome the multiple weaknesses of their own party, but also traditional French political behavior. All the French parties, even the centralized and structure Guesdiste P. O. F., suffered from factionalism and "Latin individualism." Like the other parties, the Moderates could not escape the deeply rooted "arrondissement spirit" and the putting of the constituency over the party. As a center party the Moderates were more subject than other parties to the contradiction between local and national alliances and orientation. In the nineties the strong party Moderates had no answers, or rather, many uncertain answers to this fundamental obstacle to coherent parties.

In the eighties many strong party Moderates believed the answer to the "arrondissement spirit" lay in a change of electoral system, in the elimination of the scrutin d'arrondissement, which they regarded as the fundamental vice of the parliamentary system.[87] Experience had shown that the scrutin d'arrondissement tended to produce a multiplicity of loosely organized, undisciplined parties and groups, favored the primacy of constituency politics, and increased the influence of the extremists. The Gambettistes pushed a change to the scrutin de liste[88] that theoretically favored coherence, discipline, and the authority of the party over the deputy. But when the scrutin de liste was introduced it did not at all produce what its partisans had confidently expected. The test of the scrutin de liste in the 1885 election had been a most unhappy experience. It is not surprising that the Moderates in the nineties were divided and confused over the issue of electoral systems.[89]

All the efforts of the strong party Moderates in the eighties and nineties ended in failure. Other Moderate reformers during the Third and Fourth Republics promoted the formulation of an English-type conservative party, the reformation of political mores, and the limiting of the powers of the deputies. None succeeded, all broke against the same obstacles as had the Grand cercle. Periodically a sense of danger—from Boulangism, socialism, income tax, and later communism—revived the old dream of the fusion of the moderates. But when the danger passed, so did the superficial unity, while the old divisions and profound individualism remained.[90]

Endnotes

[1] Jean Dubois, *Le vocabulaire politique et social en France de 1869 à 1872* (Paris, 1962), p. 367.

[2] J. E. C. Bodley, *France* (London, 1898), II, p. 417; Pierre Miquel, *Poincaré* (Paris, 1961), p. 119.

[3] The more discriminating observers in the later nineties employed the term *Progressiste* to identify the Moderates hostile to the Radicals and favorable to the *esprit nouveau*. Sometimes *Mélinistes* was used interchangeably with *Progressistes*. Earlier in the decade, however, the designation *Progressiste* was adopted by Moderates wishing to remain close to the Radicals. André Siegfried, *Tableau politique de la France de l'Ouest sous la Troisième République* (Paris, 1964), p. XVI.

[4] See, for example, *La République Française* (June 12, 1893); *Journal des Débats* quoted in *La Loire Républicaine* (Jan. 5, 1897); *Le Temps* quoted in *La Loire Républicaine* (Oct. 6, 1894); A. Daniel, *L'Année politique 1888* (Paris, 1889), pp. 354–59; *L'Année politique 1895* (Paris, 1896), pp. 95–96; Joseph Reinach, *La Politique opportuniste* (Paris, 1890), pp. 295–96.

[5] Variations of the slogan "neither revolution nor reaction" were numerous: as, for instance, "it is necessary to hold back those who want to go forward too quickly and to push those who are trying to impede the forward march" and "a policy without timidity, without rashness." Raymond Long, *Les élections législatives en Côte-d'Or depuis 1870* (Paris, 1958), p. 83; *L'Estafette* (June 29, 1896).

[6] Peter Nettl, "The German Social Democratic Party, 1890–1914 as a Political Model," *Past and Present*, XXX (Apr. 1965), p. 65.

[7] Maurice Duverger, *Political Parties* (London, 1964), pp. 20–21, 59, 152, 185.

[8] Consultation between Moderate leaders was frequent during crises, the fall of ministries, and before and during elections to key parliamentary posts.

[9] See, for example, Archives de la Préfecture de Police, Ba/1076 2e partie, report 26, Jan. 14, 1886; Félix Faure, "Mon élection à la Présidence," *Hommes et Mondes* (Jan. 1954), 158; Pierre Barral, *Le département de l'Isère sous la Troisième République, 1870–1914* (Paris, 1962), p. 358; Siegfried, *Tableau politique*, p. 288; A. Daniel, *L'Année politique 1893* (Paris, 1894), p. 299.

[10] Control of the Ministry of the Interior, particularly during general elections, was always a major objective of the Moderate party. Moderate candidates frequently

sought government help. At times the Moderates even had government agents find suitable candidates.

[11] Jean-Paul Charnay, *Les scrutins politiques en France de 1815 à 1962* (Paris, 1964), pp. 90–91; François Goguel, ed., *Nouvelles études de sociologie électorale* (Paris, 1954), p. 99.

[12] The state of the Moderate party varied greatly from area to area. In some localities party organizations simply didn't exist, or existed with little life. Sometimes Moderate groups were infiltrated by Radicals. Elsewhere, as in the Loire, Loir-et-Cher, the Marne, and Isère, they were cohesive and effective.

[13] Barral, *Le département de l'Isère*, pp. 329–30, 349, 358, 381.

[14] Pierre Sorlin, "Gambetta et les républicains Nantais en 1871," *Revue d'histoire moderne et contemporaine*, X (Apr.–June 1963), 126; Daniel Halévy and Emile Pillias, eds., *Lettres de Gambetta 1868–1882* (Paris, 1938), Letter 115.

[15] *Lettres de Jules Ferry, 1846–1893* (Paris, 1914), pp. 489–90, 511, 513; D. W. Brogan, *The Development of Modern France (1870–1939)* (London, 1949), p. 131.

[16] The conviction that the split between Radicals and Moderates was close to a final rupture was often expressed in the eighties. Jacques Kayser, *Les grandes batailles du radicalisme, 1820–1901* (Paris, 1962), pp. 148–49; Paul Robiquet, ed., *Discours et opinions de Jules Ferry* (Paris, 1898), VII, pp. 10–11.

[17] The term "strong party Moderate" is used to designate those Moderates who wanted a centralized, coherent, national Moderate party. In general the strong party Moderates stood for a strong executive, ministerial stability, reduction of the "excessive" powers of the deputies, and the primacy of national over local interests.

[18] For examples of the ambiguous use of the Radical label in the eighties, see Kayser, *Les grandes batailles*, pp. 160, 180–81.

[19] See, for instance, Laurent Boyer, *Les élections politiques dans le Département de la Loire au temps de l'Assemblée Nationale et du Maréchal Mac-Mahon* (Paris, 1963), pp. 60–61, 89, 92, 95–96, 123, 162–63, 209–11; Long, *Côte-d'Or*, pp. 62–66, 68–71; Georges Dupeux, *Aspects de l'histoire sociale et politique du Loir-et-Cher 1848–1914* (Paris, 1962), p. 507.

[20] Jacques Ameye, *La vie politique à Tourcoing sous la Troisième République* (Lille, 1963), p. 18; André Siegfried, *Géographie électorale de l'Ardèche sous la IIIe République* (Paris, 1949), pp. 82–85; Siegfried, *Tableau politique*, pp. 463–65.

[21] See, for instance, Jean Micheu-Puyou, *Histoire électorale du Département du Basses-Pyrénées sous la IIIe et la IVe République* (Paris, 1965), pp. 310–12, 320–22.

[22] *Lettres de Jules Ferry*, p. 487; Reinach, *La politique opportuniste*, pp. 199–200;

Daniel, *L'Année politique 1888*, pp. 274–75, 354–59, 368–70, 375.

[23] *L'Avenir de Rennes* (Sept. 27, 1887); René Waldeck-Rousseau, *Pour la République (1883–1903)* (Paris, 1904), pp. 92–96; A. Daniel, *L'Année politique 1889* (Paris, 1890), pp. 116–17; Robiquet, *Discours et opinions de Jules Ferry*, VII, p. 139.

[24] Archives de la Préfecture de Police, Ba/1077 4e partie, report July 18, 1889, brochures distributed by *L'Estefette*.

[25] *Le Figaro* (Dec. 12, 1888); *La République Française* (Apr. 12, 1889); *Le Temps* (June 11, 1893); Marcel Fournier, "L'Organisation du parti progressiste," *Revue politique et parlementaire* XIV (Nov. 10, 1897), pp. 237–39; Robiquet, *Discours et opinions de Jules Ferry*, VII, pp. 137–42; *Lettres de Jules Ferry*, pp. 523–24; Daniel, *L'Année politique 1889*, p. 114.

[26] Archives de la Préfecture de Police, Ba/654, report Mar. 26, 1898; *Le Figaro* (Mar. 22, 1891); *L'Avenir du Tarn* (Mar. 6, 1898); Waldeck-Rousseau, *Pour la République*, pp. 332–33.

[27] *Discours prononcés par MM. Barthelémy Saint-Hilaire, Henri Barboux, Léon Say, Ed. Aynard au banquet de l'Union Libérale Républicaine du 30 mars 1892* (n.p., n.d. [1892]); *L'Estafette* (Feb. 3, 1897); *La France* (Mar. 16, 1897); *Le Siècle* (Feb. 8, 1901).

[28] *Le Figaro* (Mar. 22, 1891); *Le Forézien* (Loire) (June 30, 1899); *La Dépêche* (Apr. 23, 1898).

[29] *L'Estafette* (June 29, 1896); *La Loire Républicaine* (Aug. 15, 1894); *Le Temps* (Jan. 6, Mar. 25, 1902).

[30] *Paris* (Nov. 19, 1893); *Le Temps* (June 11, 1893); *Journal de Montbrison* (Loire) (Mar. 17, 1895); *Le Journal de Roanne* (Loire) (Sept. 30, 1894); Félix Roussel, "Chronique politique et parlementaire," *Revue politique et parlementaire*, I (July 1, 1894), 99; Louis Joubert, "Chronique politique," *Le Correspondant*, CLXXIX (June 10, 1895), 994; A. Daniel, *L'Année politique 1891* (Paris, 1892), p. 100; *L'Année politique 1893*, p. 189.

[31] *L'Estafette* (Oct. 13, 1894); *Le Matin* (Mar. 15, 1895); Jacques Kayser, ed., *Le Presse de province sous la Troisième République* (Paris, 1958), pp. 59, 169; Kayser, *Les grandes batailles*, pp. 200, 204; Daniel, *L'Année politique 1893*, pp. 2–5, 144, 189.

[32] See, for example, *Le Rappel* (Nov. 19, 1895); *Le Matin* (Dec. 14, 1892); Paul Laffitte, *Lettres d'un parlementaire* (Paris, 1894), p. 32; Jacques Chastenet, *La République triomphante 1893–1906* (Paris, 1955), p. 53; Aaron Noland, *The Founding of the French Socialist Party 1893–1905* (Cambridge, 1956), pp. 30–31; Barral, *Le département de l'Isère*, pp. 331, 412–13.

[33] Léon Blum, "Les congrès ouvriers et socialistes français," in *L'Oeuvre de Léon*

Blum (Paris, 1954), pp. 391–489; François Goguel, *Histoire des institutions politiques de la France de 1870 à 1940* (Les Cours de Droit, Université de Paris, 1951–1952), pp. 361, 367–71; Kayser, *Les grandes batailles*, pp. 214–19, 241, 254–57, 261–63.

[34] Jean-Marie Mayeur, "Les congrès nationaux de la 'Démocratie Chrétienne' à Lyon (1896–1897–1898)," *Revue d'histoire moderne et contemporaine*, IX (July–Sept., 1962), 172; René Rémond, *Les deux congrès ecclésiastique de Reims et de Bourges 1896–1900* (Paris, 1964), pp. 1–3.

[35] The vogue for organization in the nineties was, indeed, widespread. See, for instance, the case of the free-thinkers, Pierre Lévêque, "Libre pensée et socialisme (1889–1939): Quelques points de repère," *Le mouvement social*, 57 (Oct.–Dec. 1966), p. 104.

[36] Edouard Dolléans and Gérard Dehove, *Histoire du travail en France* (2 vols: Paris, 1953), I. p. 389; Paul Louis, *Histoire du mouvement syndical en France* (Paris, 1947), I. pp. 148–49, 157; Edouard Dolléans, *Histoire du mouvement ouvrier 1871–1920* (Paris, 1953), pp. 31, 33–35; Dupeux, *Aspects de l'histoire sociale*, pp. 519–24; Barral, *Le département de l'Isère*, p. 537.

[37] Albert de Mun, Raoul Duval, Jacques Piou, Léon Say, Paul Deschanel, Charles Jonnart, René Waldeck-Rousseau, Raymond Poincaré, Léon Bourgeois, J.-L. de Lanessan, and Marcel Sembat were among the politicians who between 1891 and 1897 expressed the belief that a two-party system was in the making.

[38] For example, see *Le Rappel* (Nov. 15, 1895); *Le Temps* (June 11, 1893); Leo A. Loubère, "Left-Wing Radicals, Strikes, and the Military, 1880–1907," *French Historical Studies*, III (No. 1, 1963), 96; René Bloch, *Le régime en France sous la Troisième République* (Paris, 1905), pp. 107, 151, 153–54; Laffitte, *Lettres*, p. 216.

[39] This description of the state of the Radical party was emphatically denied by Radical spokesmen, who insisted that the diagnosis of ideological sterility and internal disintegration could be applied with greater accuracy to the Moderates, prisoners of the "financial oligarchy, the Right, and of clericalism," *La Dépêche* (Apr. 24, 1898); A. Daniel, *L'Année politique 1894* (Paris, 1895), p. 80. The approaching demise of the Radical party was often predicted by Moderates during the Third Republic. See, for instance, L. Bodin and J. Touchard, *Front populaire 1936* (Paris, 1961), p. 64. Socialists were not lacking in the 1890s who also believed that the end of Radicalism was in sight.

[40] *Le Journal de Roanne* (Sept. 16, 30, Oct. 7, 11, 1894); Louis Joubert, "Chronique politique," *Le Correspondant*, CLXXIX (Apr. 25, 1895), 385, (May 10, 1895), 598, CLXXX (July 10, 1895), 188–89, CLXXXI (Nov. 25, 1895), 770, CLXXXII (Feb. 10, 1896), 594, CLXXXIII (May 10, 1896), 578, 580; G. d'Avenal, "Chronique de la quinzaine," *Revue des deux mondes*, CXXI (Jan.–Feb. 1894), 947–48.

[41] "Who today," asked the Radical journalist Emanuel Arène, "still speaks of the

separation of the Church and State?" *Le Matin* (Mar. 11, 1895); "Il est incontestable," *Le Temps* remarked in September of 1893, "que, dans la politique républicaines, comme dans le pays, une grande pacification s'est opérée. Là même où la paix n'est pas faite, l'animosité a disparu. Sans doute, on n'a rien sacrifié des lois scolaires et militaire; mais il est bien certain que personne ne demande qu'on en fasse des armes de combat, et que chez les plus fanatiques de part et d'autre, la raison et l'équité ont gagné ce qu' ont perdu le fanatisme et la passion." Quoted in R. P. Lecanuet, *L'Eglise de France sous la Troisième République* (Paris, 1910), II, p. 591. Even so astute an observer as Bodley asserted that anticlericalism had gone "out of fashion" before the Dreyfus Affair changed the political climate. J. E. C. Bodley, *The Church in France* (London, 1906), p. 56.

[42] See, for example, Archives départmentales de la Loire, 10 M 102, Rapports sur la situation du département, situation économique, situation politique, esprit publique (Jan.–June 1894) and Situation politique dans l'arrondissement de St. Etienne (Mar. 10, 1894); *Journal de Roubaix* (Nord) (Apr. 4, 5, 12, 19, 25, 30, 1898); *Le Mémorial de la Loire* (Mar. 23, 1896); R. Trempé, "Du royalisme à la République ou le 'ralliement' du Marquis de Solages député de la 2e circonscription d'Albi (Tarn)," *Annales du Midi* LXXI (1959), pp. 64–67.

[43] *Le Figaro* (July 9, 1896); *L'Eclair* (May 2, 1897); *L'Avenir du Tarn* (Mar. 6, 1898); *Le Temps* (Oct. 24, 1897); Louis Joubert, "Chronique politique," *Le Correspondant*, CLXXXII (Mar. 25, 1896), 1219; *Compte rendu des travaux de l'Année 1896* [Société d'économie industrielle et commerciale] (Paris, 1897), pp. 27–32; *Comité national républicain du commerce et de l'industrie* (n.p., Mar. 31, 1897) (brochure); François Goguel, *La politique des partis sous la 111e République* (Paris, 1946), p. 83.

[44] These assumptions and contentions were disputed by Radical and Socialist spokesmen, who argued that many citizens were indeed disillusioned, but by a succession of Moderate governments that had not given the people the reforms it wanted. The country, Jaurès asserted, was "certainly more radical than its representation." And Alexandre Millerand told the Socialists in 1893 that they could and should attract the "great mass of disillusioned voters." *La Dépêche* (May 28, 1898); A. Daniel, *L'Année politique 1893*, p. 156.

[45] *Agence Havas* (Nov. 23, 1895); *Le Matin* (July 9, 1896); *Le Temps* (Oct. 24, 1897); Louis Joubert, "Chronique politique," *Le Correspondant*, CLXXVIII (Mar. 10, 1895), 978–79, CLXXXVII (May 10, 1897), 579–80; A. L. Lowell, *Governments and Parties in Continental Europe* (Boston, 1896), I, pp. 84–85; Waldeck-Rousseau, *Pour la République*, pp. 200–02, 336–39.

[46] Circular of the *Grand cercle républicain*, insert in *Le Temps* (Jan. 8, 1899); E. Spuller, "Quatorze mois de législature," *Revue politique et parlementaire*, III (Jan. 1895), 10–15; Waldeck-Rousseau, *ibid*, p. 364.

[47] Draft of a circular by René Waldeck-Rousseau for the *Grand cercle républicain*,

undated. Préparations aux élections de 1898, Papers of Waldeck-Rousseau (Bibliothèque de l'Institut de France); circular of the *Grand cercle républicain, ibid.*

[48] See Edmond Demolins, *A quoi tient la supériorité des Anglo-Saxons* (Paris, n.d.]1897]), pp. 411–61, on the stir occasioned by the publication of Demolin's book with its high praise of English mores and institutions.

[49] Félix Roussel, "La vie politique et parlementaire en France," *Revue politique et parlementaire*, I (July–Sept. 1894), 495; Raymond Poincaré, "Vues politiques," *La revue de Paris* (Apr. 1, 1898), 648–49; *Discours prononcés dans la Loire* [Waldeck-Rousseau] (Paris, 1896), pp. 11–12; Pierre Guiral, *Prévost-Paradol 1829–1870* (Paris, 1955), pp. 494–97; Theodore Zeldin, *The Political System of Napoleon III* (London, 1958), p. 152; Laffitte, *Lettres*, pp. 12, 216.

[50] Drafts of the circulars of the *Grand cercle républicain*, Papers of Waldeck-Rousseau; Marcel Fournier, "La Fondation, l'inauguration et l'avenir du 'Grand cercle républicain'," *Revue politique et parlementaire*, XVI (Apr. 10, 1898), 11, 15–17, 28, 31–32; *Conférence sur les syndicats professionels faite à Roubaix, le 30 avril 1898* (Paris, n.d.) (brochure of the *Grand cercle*); Waldeck-Rousseau, *Pour la République*, pp. 365–68.

[51] Marcel Fournier to Waldeck-Rousseau, Aug. 18 [1897]. Papers of Waldeck-Rousseau.

[52] A. Labrouse to Waldeck-Rousseau, Aug. 26, 1897; Charles Ladet to Waldeck-Rousseau, Aug. 23 [1897]; P. Deschanel to Waldeck-Rousseau, July 20, 1897; H. Audiffred to Waldeck-Rousseau, Oct. 28, 1897, Papers of Waldeck-Rousseau.

[53] *Le Temps* (June 20, 1897).

[54] Among the procedural reforms proposed by Moderate leaders were restraining the deputy's right of interpellation, restricting the number of amendments that could be introduced during the course of a debate on a bill under consideration, disallowing motions proposed during budgetary debate increasing expenditure that did not have prior government approval, making extra-parliamentary sessions the exception rather than the rule, and shortening the regular parliamentary sessions. In addition, some Moderates favored the executive using its power of dissolution when a divergence existed between "national opinion" and legislative opinion.

[55] Félix Roussel, "Chronique politique intérieure," *Revue politique et parlementaire*, XIX (Feb. 10, 1899), p. 433; Alcide Ebray, "Les clubs politiques Anglais: Leur but, leur action, leur organisation," *Revue politique et parlementaire*, XV (Jan. 10, 1898), p. 17.

[56] Waldeck-Rousseau, elected president by acclamation, announced that the *cercle* had more than nineteen hundred members and predicted that before long the membership would greatly exceed that number. *La Cloche* (Jan. 2–3, 1898); *Le*

Matin (Mar. 23, 1898); Fournier, "La fondation," 16–18; Waldeck-Rousseau, *Pour la République*, pp. 411–12.

[57] In districts considered safe for the Socialists, the *Grand cercle* discreetly ran "pseudo-anarchist" candidates and "dissident Socialists" against regular Socialist candidates. One of the Socialist deputies the leaders of the *Grand cercle* tried to retire was Alexandre Millerand, who a year later was to join the Waldeck-Rousseau ministry!

[58] See Préparations aux élections de 1898, Papers of Waldeck-Rousseau.

[59] See, for example, Long, *Côte-D'Or*, pp. 86–88.

[60] *La Croix* (Dec. 28, 1897); *La Vérité* (Dec. 23, 1897); *L'Oeuvre Electorale* (Feb. 9, Apr. 20, 1898); *La Dépêche* (Mar. 17, 19, 1898); Zedyx, "Chronique politique," *Revue du droit public et de la science politique* IX (Jan.–July 1898), 289; Louis Joubert, "Chronique politique," *Le Correspondant*, CLXXXVII (Apr. 25, May 25, 1897), 389–90, 775–76; Abel Bonnard, *Les modérés* (Paris, 1936), pp. 54–57.

[61] Archives de la Préfecture de Police, Ba/654, Élections législatives à Paris (1898), election posters; *La Lanterne* (Nov. 29, 1897); *Le Radical* (Feb. 7, 1895); *La Dépêche* (Mar. 8, 11, 17, 1898); Kayser, *Les grandes batailles*, pp. 252–53.

[62] Some Moderates suspected that public opinion was more "advanced" than themselves. A number of Radical by-election victories and the increase of Radical representation in the Senate appeared to confirm their suspicions. This view obviously contradicted the assumption of other Moderates that a majority of the electorate shared their views. The dread of being branded false republicans by the Left haunted the Moderates throughout the Third Republic. Many Moderates categorically denied that they were conservatives. It took courage for a Jules Ferry and a Waldeck-Rousseau to frankly admit that they were conservatives.

[63] Archives de la Préfecture de Police, Ba/654, Élections législatives à Paris (1898), election posters; *La Croix* (Dec. 28, 1897); *L'Oeuvre Electorale* (Apr. 20, 1898); J.-M. Mayeur, "Droites et Ralliés à la Chambre des Députés au debut de 1894," *Revue d'histoire moderne et contemporaine*, XIII (Apr.–June 1966), p. 120, 127, 130; Miquel, *Poincaré*, pp. 151–52; Kayser, *Les grandes batailles*, p. 252.

[64] *Le Journal de Roanne* (Oct. 25, 1896); *Journal des Débats* (July 25, 1893), quoted in Bodley, *France*, II, p. 403; Jules Delafosse, "Au Palais-Bourbon," *Le Correspondant*, CLXXXXII (July 10, 1898), 18–19; Joseph Reinach, *Le ministère Gambetta* (Paris, 1884), pp. 7–8; *Lettres de Jules Ferry*, pp. 374–75, 389, 434.

[65] See, for example, *L'Oeuvre Electorale* (Feb. 16, Mar. 9, Apr. 6, 1898); Mgr. Eugene Jarry, "L'orientation politique de 'la Croix' entre les années 1895 et 1900," *Documentation Catholique* (Aug. 23, 1953), 1045–58; Chastenet, *La République triomphante*, p. 121; Long, *Côte-D'Or*, pp. 88–89.

[66] Archives de la Préfecture de Police, Ba/654, Ba/657, Élections législatives à Paris (1898), election posters; *La Dépêche* (Mar. 11, Apr. 23, May 12, 21, 1898); Jacques Piou, *Le Comte Albert de Mun: Sa vie publique* (Paris, 1924), pp. 175–77; David Shapiro, "The Ralliement in the Politics of the 1890s," in *The Right in France 1890–1919* (London, 1962), p. 44.

[67] Archives de la Préfecture de Police, Ba/654, Ba/657, *ibid*; *Le Radical* (May 9, 1898); *La Dépêche* (Apr. 24, May 12, 21, 1898).

[68] *Le Temps* (June 17, 18, 19, 1898); Kayser, *Les grandes batailles*, pp. 268, 271.

[69] *L'Aurore* (Apr. 30, 1898); *Le Radical* (May 9, 1898); *La Dépêche* (Apr. 21, May 12, 1898); Félix Roussel, "Chronique politique intérieure," *Revue politique et parlementaire*, XVI (June 1898), 701–03.

[70] *Le Temps* (June 17, 1898); Circular (insert) in *Le Temps* (Jan. 8, 1899); Fournier, "Le fondation," 31–32; Joseph Caillaux, *Mes mémoires* (3 vols.; Paris, 1942–47), I, p. 119.

[71] *Le Forézien* (Loire) (June 30, July 7, 8, 1899); *La Petite République* (Apr. 23, 1900); Circular (insert) in *Le Temps*, *ibid*; *Journal des Débats* (Jan. 21, 1900); *L'Eclair* (Jan. 21, 1900).

[72] The shift of opinion discerned by Moderate leaders in the early 1890s was a good deal more complex than they allowed. If the change in public sentiment could be represented as a call from many for a more vigorous defense of the social order, a case could also be made for interpreting the criticism of the times as expressing the demand of other citizens for the fulfillment of the "social promises of the Republic."

[73] Gordon Wright, *France in Modern Times* (Chicago, 1960), p. 316.

[74] *Le Monde* (sélection hebdomadaire) (Sept. 25–Oct. 1, 1958); Louis Joubert, "Chronique politique," *Le Correspondant* CLXXXII (Feb. 10, 1896), 598.

[75] See, for example, Archives de la Préfecture de Police, Ba/656, Élections législatives de 1898, poster of the Union du commerce et de l'industrie pour la défense nationale; *L'Intransigeant* (May 2, 1897); Laffitte, *Lettres*, pp. 32–34, 59–60, 128, 145–46, 216.

[76] *L'Eclair* (May 2, 1897); *L'Avenir du Tarn* (Mar. 6, 1898); *L'Intransigeant* (May 2, 1897); See, also, Roger Priouret, *Origines du patronat Français* (Paris, 1963), pp. 235–36.

[77] *Le Temps* (May 24, 1898).

[78] This section on English parties is based largely on: Samuel H. Beer, *British Politics in the Collectivist Age* (New York, 1965); E. J. Feuchtwanger, *Disraeli,*

Democracy and the Tory Party (Oxford, 1968); Norman Gash, *Politics in the Age of Peel* (London, 1953); H. J. Hanham, *Elections and Party Management: Politics in the Time of Disraeli and Gladstone* (London, 1959); Henry Pelling, *The Origins of the Labour Party 1880–1900* (Oxford, 1966); Robert Robson, ed., *Ideas and Institutions of Victorian Britain* (London, 1967); John Vincent, *The Formation of the British Liberal Party* (New York, 1966).

[79] See the illuminating observations of Donald E. Ginter, "Problems of Party," *The Times Literary Supplement* (Feb. 29, 1968), p. 205.

[80] Bodley observed in 1898 that the "constituencies, excepting at election of quasi-plebiscitary character, such as those conducted by Gambetta before or after Seize Mai, or such as that of 1889 might have been but for General Boulanger's flight, never take into consideration the name of any man nor the merits of any policy. During the elections of 1893 no one ever heard of the Prime Minister [Dupuy] or of his successor, M. Casimir-Perier, any more than of his predecessors, MM. Ribon and Loubet. So when M. Dupuy was dismissed from office on the assembling of the new Chamber, it did not mean that he had lost the confidence of the country, for he had never had it in the sense in which the word is understood in England. The country was neither pleased nor displeased either when he resigned office in November 1893, or when he became Prime Minister again in May 1894." Bodley, *France*, I, p. 287.

[81] See, for instance, Charles Ladet to Waldeck-Rousseau, Sept. 8, 1897. Papers of Waldeck-Rousseau.

[82] Archives nationales, F7 12553, Situation politique 1899–1905, report Apr. 1900.

[83] *Lettres de Jules Ferry*, pp. 434–35; Un Député, "Le parti progressiste: Ce qu'il peut et doit être," *Revue politique et parlementaire*, XII (June 10, 1897), 489–91.

[84] The history of French employer groups up to 1914 (and beyond) is a story of painfully slow growth and perennial weakness. Their members had little enthusiasm and less discipline and showed concern, above all, for promoting their particular interests. The *patrons* were poor militants. Dolléans and Dehove, *Histoire du travail*, I, p. 392; Prioret, *Origines du patronat*, pp. 235–36.

[85] Goguel, *Histoire des institutions*, pp. 362–63.

[86] Félix Roussel, "Chronique politique intérieure," *Revue politique et parlementaire*, XV (Mar. 10, 1898), 682; Un Député, "Le parti progressiste," 496–97; Daniel, *L'Année politique 1895*, pp. 95–96; *L'Année politique 1897* (Paris, 1898), pp. 122, 222–23; Laffitte, *Lettres*, pp. 46–48, 128–30, 145–46.

[87] These Moderates supposed that adoption of the *scrutin de liste* would remove all the evils of the parliamentary system. Joseph Reinach, *Du rétablissement du scrutin*

de liste (Paris, 1880), pp. 15–30; Reinach, *Le ministère Gambetta*, pp. 39–40, 347, 491–92.

[88] Essentially the *scrutin de liste* provided for the election of all the deputies of a department on one ticket, while the *scrutin d'arrondissement* was the system of single election districts.

[89] *La Dépêche* (June 23, 1897); René Waldeck-Rousseau, *L'état et la liberté* (second série) 1883–1885 (Paris, 1906), pp. 320–25; Joseph Reinach, *La réforme électorale* (Paris, 1912), p. 184; Philip Williams, *Politics in Post-War France* (London, 1954), pp. 310–13; Daniel, *L'Année politique 1897*, pp. 241–42.

[90] See, for example, Nicholas Wahl, "Aux origines de la nouvelle constitution," *Revue française de science politique*, IX (Mar. 1959), 59–66; Marcel Merle, "Les Modérés," in *Partis politiques et classes sociales en France*, ed. Maurice Duverger (Paris, 1955), pp. 245–48, 274–76; René Rémond, *Les Catholiques le communisme et les crises 1929–1939* (Paris, 1960), pp. 148–49.

Chapter 3

Trotsky's Fight against Fascism[1]

Morris Slavin

Mit der Dumheit Kämpfen Götter selbst vergebens.
(Against stupidity the very gods contend in vain.)
—Friedrich Schiller

Our world is largely the product of two major events: the Russian Revolution and the Holocaust. The first promised a new stage in humanity's progress to freedom but turned into its opposite. The Stalinist counterrevolution destroyed the Bolshevik party and corrupted the very ideal of socialism. The second turned back the clock of civilization to its primitive beginnings. The Nazis exterminated all dissenters and brought into question the very nature of humanity. Yet there was nothing inevitable in the triumph of Stalinism or Nazism. Just as there was a choice for the Bolshevik leaders in what direction to lead the Soviet Union after the death of Lenin, so there was a choice for the leaders of the Social Democrats and the Communist party of Germany on how to stop the rise of Hitlerism. "Man makes his own history," wrote Karl Marx, even if "he does not make it out of whole cloth."

Anyone acquainted with the history of Germany following World War I must realize what a blow to revolutionary politics was suffered when Karl Liebknecht and Rosa Luxemburg were murdered by the proto-fascists of 1919. The removal of these two leaders from the scene paved the way for the future subservience of the KPD (Kommunistische Partei Deutschlands) to the Soviet Union's CP headed by the Troika, that is, Zinoviev, Kamenev, and Stalin. Not one of the men who headed the German party—neither Heinrich Brandler, nor August Thalheimer, and, later, Ernst Thälmann, Hermann Remmele, or Heinz Neumann— possessed the independence of mind or the personal courage of his predecessors. It is inconceivable that Liebknecht or Luxemburg would have embraced the suicidal policy of the KPD after it had become a creature of Stalin's personal ambition, Russian chauvinism, and xenophobia.[2]

Experts on the crisis of Germany in 1923, when the French occupied the Ruhr and the swelling inflation was destroying the German economy, disagree whether a successful proletarian revolution was possible.[3] Trotsky, who knew something of revolutionary situations, was convinced that Germany was ripe for revolution. Ruth Fischer, leader of the KPD's left wing and author of *Stalin and German Communism*, wrote: "Foreign observers agreed that the threat of a social revolution in Germany was imminent."[4]

Trotsky contrasted the failure of the German party with the success of the Bolsheviks in a brilliant brochure entitled *Lessons of October*.[5] Among other things, he pointed out that unlike in Russia "The proletariat composes the overwhelming majority of the population in Germany. . . [where] the insurrection would have immediately blazed in scores of mighty proletarian centers." He rejected what he called "the tendentious calculations" made by the faint-hearted "in order to justify the policy that led to the debacle," and he condemned "the passive fatalism" of the KPD leaders, Brandler and Thälheimer, as "only a cover for irresolution and even incapacity for action." Trotsky warned that "The hopes of the masses change into disillusionment as a result of the party's passivity. . ."[6] A warning that went unheeded almost a decade later. He recalled that the KPD had the majority of the working class behind it, and that even in May 1924, when the ebb tide had already set in, it still received a greater percentage of the proletarian votes than in 1930.[7]

In contrast to Trotsky's exhortations urging the German party to prepare the insurrection, Stalin was advising a different course. While Zinoviev, as head of the Comintern, was hesitating, Stalin wrote a letter to him and Bukharin urging that they discourage the German militants from acting. "Should not the Communists. . . strive to seize power without the Social Democrats?" he asked, and replied that "In my opinion, the Germans must be curbed, and not spurred on."[8] Why did he take this position? We know today that Stalin was willing to subordinate the fate of the German revolution to his own factional interests. A successful revolution in Germany would have strengthened the Zinoviev faction and would certainly have raised Trotsky to new heights. In either case Stalin's ambition, disloyalty, and animal-like craftiness would have suffered immeasurable blows, if not total defeat. This does not preclude, of course, his own conservative evaluation of the crisis in Germany.

Thus, the German party had suffered two body blows even before the appearance of the Nazis on the scene—the failed uprising of the Spartacus Bund in 1919 that led to the murders of Liebknecht and Luxemburg and, now, the abortion of a revolution that might have succeeded in 1923. One year later the KPD was fatally disoriented by a resolution of the Fifth Congress of the Comintern held in July 1924. This stated that "The more bourgeois society decays, the more all the bourgeois parties, particularly Social Democracy, take on a more or less fascist character. . . Fascism and Social Democracy are the two sides of a single instrument of capitalist dictatorship."[9] Who had inspired such a fatal "theory"? It seems that some months later in the same year of 1924 Stalin wrote an article entitled "The Period of Bourgeois-Democratic Pacifism." This is what he said: "Fascism is the bourgeoisie's fighting organization that relies on the active support of Social Democracy. Social Democracy is objectively the moderate wing of fascism. . . . These organizations [i.e. the fascist and the social democratic] do not negate, but supplement each other. They are not antipodes, they are twins."[10]

It is not difficult to imagine how Lenin would have replied to this idiocy had he been alive to update his *Left-Wing Communism: An Infantile Disorder.* He had written in 1920: "To carry on war for the overthrow of the international bourgeoisie, a war which is a hundred times more difficult, prolonged and complicated than the most stubborn of ordinary wars between states, and to refuse beforehand to maneuver, to utilize the conflict of interests (even though temporary) among one's enemies, to refuse to temporize and compromise with possible (even though transient, unstable, vacillating and conditional) allies—is not this ridiculous in the extreme?"[11] But, of course, had he been alive and in good health, such a fatal resolution would never have been adopted by the Comintern in the first place, and Stalin would not have dared utter such nonsense.

To supplement this "theory" the Sixth Congress of the Comintern, held in September 1928, adopted a resolution to the effect that "In countries where there are strong Social Democratic parties, fascism assumes the particular form of social-fascism. . . . The leading cadres of Social Democracy. . . are now threatening the German working class with open fascist dictatorship." The Social Democracy, the resolution concluded, "organizes the crushing of the working class by fascist methods."[12] Thus, the KPD was instructed by the Comintern that it could not fight fascism by making a united front with "social-fascists." The two parties were not antipodes but twins, Stalin assured its members.

Still, it was obvious to all except Stalinists that Nazis were not just bourgeois democrats; they made no distinction in their hatred of socialists, or communists, or democrats, or bourgeois liberals, for that matter. Moreover, the Italian example should have given the Stalinists pause. The KPD leadership insisted, however, that there was no such thing as a "lesser evil." The Social Democrats were no better than Nazis, they repeated. If the socialists were a lesser evil to the Hitlerites it was only because they could not suppress the workers for the moment. What was the way out, then? Thälmann replied, in "a united front from below": that is, making a united front with the rank and file socialists against their leaders. This meant, Thälmann assured the Central Committee of the KPD, a "relentless struggle against social fascists of every hue," mobilizing the masses from below. "The united front cannot come about through negotiations in parliament, nor via arrangements with other parties or groups." Thus, there were to be no joint demonstrations, no parallel committees, no common action to defend themselves against the Nazis.[13]

It takes little imagination to see the bankruptcy of this policy. If one was a Social Democrat and was slandered as a "social fascist" by the KPD he would hardly accept its invitation to join the Communists "from below." But aside from this, what is decisive is that if he were a socialist it meant that he retained enough confidence in his party and its leaders to follow their direction. Why would he "unite from below" with a party that was not his? If the KPD was serious about fighting fascism then there was only one way to do so; it had to negotiate with the Social Democratic party for specific joint action against the Nazis. This could be everything from mutual defense of meeting halls to joint strike action, from common demonstrations to aggressive attacks on Nazis when they marched provokingly in working-class neighborhoods. Each party would maintain its independence, with its own slogans, its own candidates; but although they marched separately, they would strike together. Against the devil one should not hesitate to unite with his grandmother.

The elections of September 1930 were ominous in their results. The KPD vote rose from roughly 3,300,000 to 4,600,000, an increase of 1,300,000 votes. The Socialists lost only a few of their supporters: from 9,150,000 to a little less than 8,600,000. But the Nazis increased their vote from 800,000 to 6,400,000. Despite this warning and despite the fact that the Social Democrats had considerably more workers behind them than did the Communists, the latter boasted of their "prodigious victory."[14]

Immediately after the election Trotsky warned that "Fascism in Germany has become a real danger." "The bourgeois regime was helpless to arrest the crisis," he wrote; the SPD (Sozialistische Partei Deutschlands) was still playing its traditional, conservative role, and the KPD was too weak to take power. There was danger that as the crisis deepened the only potentially revolutionary party, the KPD, was impotent to resolve it. Thus, the tragedy of 1923 could be repeated, he warned. The parliamentary gains of the Communists were of little consequence in light of the far greater victory of the Nazis. "Whoever denies this," wrote Trotsky, "is either blind or a braggart."[15]

Trotsky then proposed that the KPD repudiate the Stalinist policy of "social fascism," work out a genuine united front program between the Soviet and German trade unionists in order to solve the problem of unemployment, and, instead of repeating the slogan of the Nazis on repudiating the treaty of Versailles, raise the revolutionary slogan of the "Soviet United States of Europe."[16]

Finally, the KPD should adopt a policy of defense against the fascists. This would close the ranks with the workers of the SPD against the fascist threat. The KPD must defend the historic gains of all workers, that is, their political organizations, trade unions, newspapers, printing plants, clubs, libraries, and meeting halls. This kind of action would cement the ranks of the workers. Thus, the more the fascists appeared as aggressors to the Social Democrats and the unaffiliated masses, the more would the KPD appear as their defender. But this defense had to be vigilant, active, and bold. It had to take all changes into account and stand ready to launch a general assault on the Nazis.[17]

The leadership of the KPD refused to open their eyes, however. In July 1931, Thälmann and Company did an incredible thing—they made a united front with the Nazis against the socialist government of Prussia. Taking a page out of Orwell's future *1984*, they called it a "red referendum," as if giving this infamous act a radical term hid the shameful reality behind it. Both the KPD and the Nazis campaigned against the Social Democratic government of Otto Braun and Carl Severing, mustering together 9.8 million votes to their opponents' 13 million. It is not difficult to imagine how such a united front demoralized the workers and gave the Nazis a new legitimacy.

Trotsky analyzed the results of this action shortly thereafter. The KPD leaders had addressed the upper strata of the SPD and when the latter rejected their advances the KPD made a united front with the Nazis. In the process they obviously threw overboard their "united front from below." If the Social Democracy is a variety of fascism how can one make a united front with "social fascists" to defend democracy? asked Trotsky. The KPD argued that Heinrich Brüning (prime minister and leader of the Center Party) and Otto Braun were paving the way for fascism. This is correct, but helping the Nazis to replace this government was only shortening the road to fascism, he warned.[18]

The KPD argued that the referendum was "a united front from below." It saw no difference between a party that betrays and deceives the workers (that is, the Social Democracy) and a party that wants to kill them off. "To come out into the streets with the slogan 'Down with the Brüning-Braun government!' at a time when, according to the relationship of forces, it can only be replaced by a government of Hitler-Hugenberg, is the sheerest adventurism," Trotsky warned. He then contrasted the Bolshevik experience of patiently winning over the proletariat against the "conciliators" rather than refusing to unite with them against Kornilov.[19]

In November 1931 Trotsky analyzed the situation further. The weakness of the German proletariat stems from the fact that the reformist Social Democracy continues to enjoy the support of the majority of the workers, while the inability of the KPD to unite the proletariat under it sharpens the crisis, he wrote. This inability of the KPD is due to its continued adherence to the theory of "social fascism" and the experience of its "red referendum" in Prussia. "The decisive hour is very close," he continued, while the CPSU says nothing, thus risking defeat during the whole of the next historical epoch. Inside Russia the Stalinists are faced with a sharp crisis and want to be left alone, hence their silence on Germany. Meanwhile, the KPD is beginning to think that fascism's victory is inevitable. It is preparing its retreat without having fired a shot. If this becomes its policy it will equal the betrayal of the working class on a scale comparable to that of the Social Democracy in 1914, "with more frightful consequences," he added. The KPD is preparing an enormous catastrophe.[20]

If the Nazis seize power, Trotsky went on, they will exterminate the flower of the German proletariat. They will eradicate its belief in the future. Italian fascism will appear as an almost humane experiment in contrast to the Nazis. If the KPD evades the struggle it means that it will deliver the proletariat to its mortal enemy, since the workers have no place to retreat and no place to hide. "Ten proletarian insurrections, ten defeats, one on top of the other, could not debilitate and enfeeble the German working class as much as a retreat before fascism would weaken it at the very moment when the decision is still impending on the question of who is to become master in the German household," warned Trotsky.[21]

The mood of capitulation in the leadership of the KPD will push the vacillating bourgeoisie and petty bourgeoisie into the hands of the Nazis. The fascists are still hesitating and they realize that they can break their necks, but the policy of the KPD will facilitate their coming to power. If this should happen, the victory of fascism would mean a break in the continuity of revolutionary development, the collapse of the Comintern, and the triumph of world imperialism in its most bloody form. "A victory of fascism in Germany would signify an inevitable war against the USSR," he predicted correctly. Once the German proletariat is crushed nothing will stand in Hitler's way to make war on the USSR. He will act in the Far East with Japan, and will become the super-Wrangel of the world bourgeoisie. The USSR will be isolated. The war that will come will be fought to the death. Crushing the German proletariat would comprise "half of the collapse of the Soviet republic," he emphasized.[22]

The key to the international situation is in Germany, Trotsky repeated, and that key is still held by the KPD. But anyone who preaches a "strategic retreat" now is a traitor. The elementary duty of the KPD is to say that "fascism can only come into power after a merciless, annihilating civil war to the bitter end. "The world proletariat must know it. The Red Army must know it." The historic capitulation of the German CP in 1923 encouraged the rise of fascism. It is true that the Nazis have received many votes, "but in a social struggle votes are not decisive. The main army of fascism still consists of the petty bourgeoisie and the new middle class, petty officials, employees, the technical personnel, the intelligentsia, and the impoverished peasantry. In an election, a thousand fascist votes equal a thousand Communist votes. But in revolutionary action a thousand workers in one big factory represent a force a hundred times greater than a thousand petty officials, clerks, their wives, and their mothers-in-law. The great bulk of the fascists consists of human rubbish," he declared.[23]

It is true that the fascists have serious fighting cadres, but soldiers, not officers, decide, and in this case the proletarian army is immeasurably superior, he continued. After the conquest of power the fascists will easily find their soldiers with the help of the state apparatus. But fascism is still not in power. "And can we assume, even if only for a moment, that the German workers, who have the powerful means of production and transportation in their hands, who have been bound together by the conditions of their work into an army of iron, of coal, of railroads, of electrical wires, will not prove to be immeasurably superior in the decision struggle to Hitler's human rubbish?" he asked.[24]

Trotsky then called for a "realistic inventory" to learn just what forces the Nazis possessed. Their strength lies in the present schism within the proletariat, he explained. This fascist threat must push the workers to unity in the name of self-defense. Here again, the key is in the hands of KPD. Furthermore, since a fascist triumph would mean an inevitable war on the USSR Trotsky repeated, "It should be axiomatic for every revolutionary worker that the attempt of the fascists to seize power in Germany must lead to the mobilization of the Red Army." This will be a revolutionary self-defense for Russia. Germany is not only Germany but the very heart of Europe, and Hitler is its super-Wrangel, Trotsky warned again. "But the Red Army is also not only the Red Army. It is the arm of the proletarian revolution," something that it had been under Trotsky's leadership but was to become quite a different instrument under Stalin.[25]

One year before the Nazis came to power Trotsky published a comprehensive analysis of the German situation entitled *What Next?*[26] The Social Democrats were trying to stabilize capitalism at a time when it was decaying and undermining the gains that workers had made over several generations. Yet fascism would destroy all organizations of the proletariat, including the SPD and the trade unions. Just as the Lassalleans were wrong to dump the liberal bourgeoisie and feudal reactionaries into one mass, as Marx and Engels taught, so it is equally wrong to equate Social Democrats with fascists by regarding them as "social fascists."[27] The Social Democratic leadership relies on Prussian police to help them ("Staat, greif zu!") and thinks that Brüning will fight fascism. This is nonsense. First of all, former workers who become policemen are no longer workers, they are policemen. Secondly, a functionary who is neutral will reason that if millions of Social Democrats with enormous resources are relying on him to help them, he will save his own skin and join the Nazis. Hilferding[28] writes that since the Social Democrats and the Communists have only 40% of the votes they cannot come to power. But Brüning enjoys only 20% of the votes yet he rules. Thus the other 40% are Nazi votes, and only one of the three parties can hold power.[29]

Besides, parliamentary figures do not give the proper correlation of forces. Hilferding insists that the Social Democrats must support Brüning in order to prevent Hitler from coming to power, but if they broke with him and opted for revolution, victory would be theirs. Whole strata would leave the Nazis and come over to the side of the workers. Struggle would be inevitable, but a firm decision to fight until victory could change the balance of forces. The leadership of the SPD cannot change, but its ranks can and would if they were helped. The KPD, however, encourages the workers to stay with the SPD by its suicidal policy.[30]

Stalinists insist that fascism and capitalist democracy are one and the same. This is untrue; contradictions exist between the two. Social Democracy is the chief representative of the bourgeois-parliamentary regime that derives its support from the workers. Fascism, however, rests on the petty bourgeoisie. Without the organized workers the SPD can have no influence. But fascism cannot enrich itself without annihilating these same workers' organizations. Parliament is the main arena of the SPD. But fascism is based on the destruction of parliament. It is true that for the monopolistic bourgeoisie parliamentary or fascist regimes represent only different vehicles of rule. But for the SPD and for the Nazis the choice of one over the other has an independent significance. It becomes a question of political life or death.[31]

The Stalinists, who do not recognize any difference between Hitler and Brüning, are saying, in reality, that it makes no difference if proletarian organizations exist or not. They write that there is no difference whether one starves under Brüning or under Hitler. But to revolutionaries it is not a question under which regime it is better to die, but rather how to fight and to win. Before destroying the workers' organizations the fascists must launch a major offensive. Stalinists lie when they accept Hitler's victory as inevitable. The working class is split and disoriented but it is not crushed; it is not exhausted. It is still powerful. If one identifies Brüning with Hitler, as the Stalinists do, one identifies the conditions before the battle with those after the defeat. It means that one appeals for surrender before the battle.[32]

Trotsky then excoriated the KPD for its "ultimatism," which insists that the workers accept its leadership or be treated as counter-revolutionaries. It refuses to be patient and to educate the workers.[33] In 1917, it will be recalled that Lenin insisted on "patiently explaining" the program of the Bolshevik Party. Trotsky then pointed to the lessons of Italy. There the reformists (that is, the Social Democrats) shouted "Victor Emmanuel, Help! Intervene!" One of their leaders, Turati, let loose the following dazzling motto: "One must have the manhood to be a coward." The German Social Democrats say the same thing: "Courage under unpopularity. (Mut zur unpopularität)." The young

Communist Party of Italy also opposed united fronts and saw fascism as only "capitalist reaction." It failed to understand the *particular* traits of fascism, wrote Trotsky, which springs from the mobilization of the petty bourgeoisie against the proletariat. Only Gramsci understood this.[34]

The workers, he continued, still have potent political, economic, and sports organizations. This is true under the present regime of Brüning; it will no longer be true under Hitler. If these organizations are weak it is only because of their poor leadership. The Bruchsal and Kliengenthal defense organization is essentially a soviet of workers' deputies, even though it does not call itself such, he wrote.[35] Were this form of organization transferred to Berlin it would be a soviet of workers' deputies.[36]

"Is the situation hopeless?" asked Trotsky. Not at all, he replied. Despite the defeats of 1919, 1921, and 1923, and the conservative nature of workers' organizations in Germany, the solidarity of the workers has not permitted fascism to penetrate them. A united front is a defensive strategy, but its success opens up great offensive possibilities. Once an offensive is launched against the Nazis it will attract all strata of the proletariat to fight. Even the Stalinist apparatus, he thought, was beginning to turn. Furthermore, he believed that the tiny Left Opposition could still influence the KPD to prepare for the struggle. He was opposed to building a third party under the present circumstances and saw the crisis weakening the bureaucracy's hold on the party ranks. Present leaders of the KPD who refused to prepare for the fight would be swept aside, he wrote, in the process of democratizing the party.[37]

Members of the KPD must be convinced of the correctness of a united front policy. He was optimistic that "On the very next day after the victory of the German proletariat, even before, the hoops that bind the Comintern will burst. The bareness of the ideas of bureaucratic centrism [i.e. Stalinism], the national limitations of its outlook, the anti-proletarian character of its regime—all these will at once be revealed in the light of the German Revolution, which will be immeasurably more brilliant than the light of the October Revolution. The ideas of Marx and Lenin will gain their inevitable hegemony within the German proletariat.[38]

Less than five months before Hitler took power Trotsky launched another appeal for the KPD to change course.[39] He began by briefly tracing the position of Germany in world affairs. The Bonapartist regime of Brüning could not solve the crisis and gave way to the Papen-Schleicher regime. The barons and magnates of capital would prefer the latter government to that of Hitler's for no other reason than to save expenses and stop the greedy petty bourgeoisie from taking their share of the spoils. Nevertheless, they have confidence that, should Hitler be necessary, they can tame him. Meanwhile, the Social Democrats are hoping for a miracle and still lead millions of workers. At the same time the KPD confuses the workers by referring to the Brüning regime as "fascist," yet warning against Hitler. It is still pursuing the suicidal policy of "social fascism."[40]

The Reichswehr is independent of the Papen regime, but no 100,000 soldiers can keep a nation of sixty-five million in crisis continually under siege. Moreover, the army is still to be tested should the civil war come. Schleicher cannot last even 100 days, he predicted. The only way out is either Hitler or the proletarian revolution.[41]

Any political analysis must examine the relations between the petty bourgeoisie (which includes the peasantry), the bourgeoisie, and the proletariat, he wrote. The bourgeoisie cannot rule alone; it must use the petty bourgeoisie to uphold its rule. It did so when it was revolutionary as a Jacobin regime. Later it replaced Jacobinism with Social Democracy. Today it must use the fascists not because it wants to (there is always a danger in this), but because it has no choice if it wants to defeat the proletariat.[42]

The Social Democracy is principally responsible for the growth of fascism. Since World War I it has uprooted from the consciousness of the proletariat the idea of an independent policy and, instead, has implanted the belief that capitalism is eternal. The petty bourgeoisie will follow the workers only if they see their party as a new chief, not a lackey. Not having done so, the SPD converts the petty bourgeoisie into cannon fodder of fascism.[43] The Stalinists, despite the great crisis of capitalism, and because of their opportunistic policy and adventurism, cannot win over the proletariat and, thus, push the petty bourgeoisie into the hands of the Nazis. Stalinism, too, is responsible for the growth of the Nazis.[44]

Thälmann tells the Social Democratic worker that the KPD is sincere in its desire for a united front because it favors the overthrow of capitalism. Trotsky replies that "A skilled propagandist would have answered in the following manner: 'You put your stakes on democracy; we believe that the only way out lies in the revolution. Yet we cannot and we do not want to make the revolution without you. Hitler is now the common foe. After the victory over him we shall draw the balance together with you and see where the road ahead leads.'"[45] What is decisive is that the bourgeoisie wants to abandon its compact with the SPD, even if the latter does not. "The reign of the fascist terror will and can only mean the abolition of the Social Democracy," Trotsky emphasized yet again. "In any event, the 'social fascist' cherishes his skin. The Communist united-front policy at the present time must proceed from concern of the Social Democracy for its own hide. That will be the most realistic policy and at the same time the most revolutionary in its consequences," concluded Trotsky.[46]

Why did the Soviet Union, the Comintern, and the KPD follow the suicidal course that guaranteed Hitler's accession to power? No one should minimize the role of stupidity and the irrational in the Stalinist apparatus during the 1930s. There is little question that in contrast to the policy followed by Lenin and Trotsky in the Russian Revolution, the approach of the KPD alienated the vast majority of the Social Democratic workers. The "united front from below," the so-called "Red Referendum," the slanderous term "social fascism," the capitulation implied in the boast "After Hitler, We!"—these and a dozen other such fantasies destroyed the KPD as a revolutionary instrument. But in addition to the role of the party and its apparatus, the Soviet Union's diplomatic game also added to the German debacle.

Almost from the foundation of the Soviet government the difficulty of reconciling state policy with party politics plagued the Soviet leaders. The Polish War (1920) had brought Russia and Germany closer together. Had the Soviet Union succeeded in conquering Poland the Versailles Treaty would have become a scrap of paper. Winston Churchill acknowledged that "Poland was the linchpin of the Treaty of Versailles."[47] Long before Churchill, Lenin had written: "If Poland had become Soviet the Versailles peace would have been crushed and the whole international system forced by the victors on Germany would have collapsed."[48] This was why all Germans were hoping that the Red Army would prove successful as it approached Warsaw. "Everyone in

Germany, even the blackest revolutionaries and monarchists, said that the Bolsheviks would save us. . . ." Lenin recalled.[49]

After the retreat of the Red Army and, despite the hatred of Bolshevism, Germany had to turn to Russia for trade or be strangled by the Entente. To bring this about the Soviet government made important economic concessions to German capitalists, but, in return, began to acquire factories, capital, and industrial products. Russia was willing to make the same concessions to England and France, of course, but since only Germany was willing "to knock on the Eastern gate," the two powers drew closer together. At first a distinction was made between the bankers and industrialists of Germany and "the oppressed masses." Soon, however, this contradictory appeal to the German bourgeoisie and to Germany's proletariat, lost all distinction.[50]

The Trade Treaty of 1921 between the two powers was soon followed by the important Treaty of Rapallo, concluded in April 1922. Full diplomatic relations were established, and the right of reparations was surrendered by the Soviet Union in return for Germany's renunciation of compensation for property nationalized by the Bolsheviks. In addition, the treaty included the "most favored nation" clause. Its most important article, however, was Article 5, which held that "the two Governments shall cooperate in a spirit of mutual goodwill in meeting the economic needs of both countries."[51]

While Britain and France became alarmed over the inherent threat of Rapallo, the Bolsheviks were divided as to its real meaning. Trotsky denied that it was a counterweight to the Entente and insisted that the Soviet Government was ready to sign similar treaties with all capitalist states. Radek, on the other hand, stated that "the policy of throttling Germany implied as a matter of fact the destruction of Russia as a great power, for no matter how Russia is governed it is always her interest to see that Germany exists." Others, like G. Chicherin, saw new international forces emerging. Steklov, the editor of *Izvestya*, the official government newspaper, vacillated, while still others were confused.[52]

In Germany the same division of opinion occurred. While Walter Rathenau was unhappy with the treaty, General von Seeckt favored it. The Social Democrat Friedrich Ebert was "surprised and embittered," while Hermann Müller, the last Social Democratic Chancellor before Heinrich Brüning of the Center Party, wanted to couple it with a "policy of fulfillment towards the West." Arthur Crispien of the Independent Socialists saw it as a "betrayal of socialism," while Paul Frölich, the KPD's spokesman, was embarrassed and denied its importance.[53] The main thing was that for Germany the treaty was a weapon against the Allies and Versailles. For Russia it was a defensive measure in that it prevented a united front of the capitalist powers against her. Germany was neutralized, it was true, but in return the Russians had to support the German bourgeoisie against Versailles. In doing so, they gave aid to German nationalism.[54]

The threat implied by the Rapallo Treaty induced Britain to detach Germany, if possible, from Russia, and to turn it toward the West. With this end in view Germany signed the Locarno Treaty in 1925, thus reestablishing the balance of power on the Continent between Germany and France.[55] Shortly thereafter Germany entered the League of Nations.

Needless to say, the Soviets saw the menace of Locarno to themselves. It threatened to isolate Russia again, and it made Britain the dominant power on the Continent. *Izvestya* wrote: "Germany is subordinating itself to English policy. . . a *place d'armes* for future attacks against the Soviet Union."[56] Thus, both Britain and Russia saw the importance of Germany to maintain the balance of power in Europe. If the threat to Russia did not materialize it was because Gustav Stresemann, the German Chancellor, was too astute to line up with either.[57]

The limits of this essay do not permit a detailed examination of the vicissitudes undergone by the Rapallo and Locarno treaties, nor of the continuous diplomatic maneuvers by the European powers. Suffice it to say that, although the Soviet Union never closed the door on the Western Powers, throughout the 1920s and into the early 1930s it supported Rapallo and feared Locarno. Thus, any political party in Germany that repudiated the former and favored the latter was seen by the Soviets as a threat to themselves. The Social Democrats of Germany were "the greatest enemies of Rapallo and the foremost supporters of Locarno." They had drawn attention to the Reichswehr–Red Army contacts and had been attacked by *Izvestya* (23 May 1928) for their pro-Western orientation. "Although it cannot be proved, it is likely that the all-out attack on the German Social-Democrats was a response to the demands of Russian foreign policy," writes Kochan, the historian of this subject.[58] Here, surely, is one explanation for the uncompromising war launched by the Comintern and its KPD on the "social fascists."

Furthermore, Stalin's policy of making the Social Democrats the main enemy by 1928 was closely linked to his fight against his own so-called "right wing" of the CPSU, that is, against Bukharin, Rykov, and Tomsky. In the course of this struggle Stalin was forced to assume a "left tactic" by the Comintern.[59] Russia feared a rapprochement between France and Germany, which the Social Democrats of the latter country supported.[60]

By 1930 Germany was in a much stronger position than it had been in 1923 and began to turn away from Russia. Communist gains of 23 seats in the Reichstag for a total of 77 and a 4,500,000 vote for the party encouraged an attack on "communism" by the German press. "From now on, in relation to Germany, Stalin was less the master of a situation than mastered by a situation. *It is doubtful whether the KPD was expected to achieve its aim of a German revolution. It is even more doubtful whether its policy was formed with this end in view.*"[61] If, therefore, Germany did not repudiate Rapallo it was because it still had not gained the Polish Corridor and Upper Silesia (in Polish hands) and wanted an Anschluss with Austria.[62]

One week before Hitler came to power Molotov stated that "we have had and now have the strongest economic connections with Germany. That is no accident. It arises from the interests of the two countries."[63] Moreover, he was convinced of "a substantial strengthening of the international position of the Soviet Union."[64] In November 1932, as seen above, the Nazis lost two million votes and the KPD picked up 700,000, giving it 100 deputies in the Reichstag. This development could have been the reason for Molotov's complacency. After Hitler came to power Russia still hoped to revive the Rapallo Treaty. Gustav Hilger, Germany's economic expert in Moscow, was assured by the manager of TASS that the Soviet press had been ordered to avoid any criticism of German policy. Russia feared that the transition period under Hitler would be disturbing "before normal relations could again be achieved."[65] At the same time Hitler seemed ready to continue friendly relations with Russia because he lacked an army as yet. On 23 March 1933 he declared that his fight against Communism was an internal affair and would not affect relations with the Powers.[66] This was the smoke screen behind which he was to destroy the Versailles Treaty.

Meanwhile, the Russians and the Comintern were convinced that Hitler's reign would be ephemeral. The Social Democratic workers, under the pressure of National Socialism and the arguments of the KPD, would quickly lose their reformist illusions. They would flock to the KPD and, thus, the temporary Nazi counter-revolution would pave the way for a communist victory. When Hitler's purge of the S.A. (storm troops) occurred on 30 June 1934, the Stalinists were more convinced than ever that Germany was ripe for Hitler's overthrow. "This attitude towards the Nazis," writes Kochan, "is equivalent to saying that a defeat is a victory, or that it at least contains within itself the seeds of victory."[66] For the time being, however, Stalin was still holding out "a fraternal hand to Hitler," a hand that Hitler was to grasp in 1939 before turning against the Soviet Union in June 1941.

More than seventy years has gone by since the Nazis took over the government in Germany. It is clear today that Stalin and his Comintern misunderstood the nature of the Nazi party and the reciprocal influence that the petty bourgeois masses had on it, as Trotsky understood so well. Some think that the Russians hoped for a Communist conquest of power, or an acute conflict between a Nazi Germany and France. Others believed that Stalin put his trust in the dependence of the NSDAP on the Reichswehr, with which Russia had mutual military agreements. In either case, the policy of "social fascism" played into Hitler's hands. The Comintern saw fascism as a mere instrument of the bourgeoisie or the Reichswehr and not its intrinsic racist ideology. The Stalinists thought that the Nazis were dependent on the bourgeoisie, that is, that they were not an independent entity. They could not believe that the desperate petty bourgeoisie could have separated themselves from the capitalists, since the latter possessed the economic and military power and were, therefore, in control. The Nazis, they were convinced, had a desire for plunder, not a real ideological conviction.[67] It is hardly necessary to add that no knowledgeable Marxist believes there is a direct one-to-one relationship between a social class and a political party.

Finally, it is essential to stress the theoretical roots of Stalin's "national Bolshevism." The Bolshevik leaders were convinced, from the very beginning, that their revolution was only a prelude to proletarian revolutions in the West. It was an axiom accepted by all that, without the assistance of at least one industrialized country, their regime was doomed. Writing of the eve of the insurrection, Lenin declared that should the Bolsheviks take power "the proletariat will have *every* chance of retaining it and of leading Russia until a victorious revolution in the West." At the second Congress of the Soviets Trotsky stated: "If the people of Europe do not rise and crush imperialism, we will be crushed. . ."

On 7 March 1918, Lenin repeated his warning: "The absolute truth is that without a revolution in Germany, we shall perish." Writing in the party textbook, *The ABC of Communism*, Nikolai Bukharin and E. Preobrazhensky began the chapter on "The Second and Third International" with the following statement: "[T]he communist revolution can be victorious only as a world revolution." As late as April 1924, Stalin asked if the proletariat of one country, after overthrowing the bourgeoisie, "can finally consolidate socialism and fully guarantee that country against intervention and, consequently, also against restoration?" He replied: "No, it does not. For this the victory of the revolution in at least several countries is needed." The premise accepted by everyone was if the Soviet Union was not rescued by the working class of the West, it would be crushed. The prospect of building socialism in a backward, largely peasant nation never entered the head of any Bolshevik.[68]

The revolution in the West failed to occur but the Bolshevik regime remained in power. To justify the new state of things Stalin, with the help of Bukharin, reversed himself by December 1924 and began to preach the possibility of building "socialism in one country." Shortly thereafter, it had become a major doctrine. This theory was an unconscious expression of the disappointment with the failure of the expected revolution in the West and, at the same time, a manifestation of Russian nationalism, a feeling that Stalin knew how to exploit and to encourage. The inevitable conclusion that followed from the theory was that if socialism could be built by Russia alone, it had no need for revolutions in the West. The Communist parties must, therefore, change their role. Henceforth, they must become mere agents of the Russian Foreign Office and help promote the Soviet Union's foreign interests. When the Hitler-Stalin Pact unleashed the Second World War, the CP of USA raised the slogan, "The Yanks Are Not Coming." After Hitler attacked his erstwhile partner, the slogan was "Open the Second Front." The German CP paid the inevitable price, and its capitulation to Hitler only encouraged Molotov to declare that "fascism was a matter of taste."

The history of Trotsky's struggle to reorient the KPD more than three years before the Nazis came to power leaves little doubt that had he still enjoyed his former influence on Soviet policy a Nazi victory would have been unlikely. A Trotskyist policy would never have permitted the split between the two working-class parties to continue. Whatever profound differences still existed between the KPD and the SPD, the dire necessity to defeat fascism would have forced a united front on the SPD. Led by a Marxist party uncorrupted by Russian and German chauvinism, the German workers, supported by the Third International and the military resources of the Soviet Union, might have triumphed over the Nazis. Let us put it another way. Suppose for a moment that Lenin had been in good health and still had a decade or so of life. Can anyone imagine his allowing the adoption of such a suicidal policy as "social fascism," or "the united front from below," or the obscene "red referendum," or the continued misdirection of the German party by deceitful puppets of Stalinism? Together, Lenin and Trotsky would have stopped the rise of fascism in the heart of Europe. And this defeat of fascism would have prevented Stalin's destruction of the Bolshevik party, the creation of the gulags, and, possibly, the outbreak of World War II. Our world would have been quite different.

But, as the poet wrote, "For of all sad words of tongue and pen, the saddest are these: 'It might have been.'"

Endnotes

[1] *This article originally appeared in *Essays on Socialism*, eds. Louis Patsouras and Jack Ray Thomas (San Francisco: EMText, 1992). Reprinted by permission.

[2] The KPD gradually abandoned democracy and expelled all dissenters. This resulted in a subservient leadership ready to do the bidding of Stalin in promoting his foreign policy. Moreover, it was torn by various factions. See Ossip K. Flechtheim, "The Role of the Communist Party," in *The Path to Dictatorship 1918–1933: Ten Essays by German Scholars* (Garden City, N.Y., 1966), pp. 99–108, *passim*.

[3] E. H. Carr, *A History of Soviet Russia: The Interregnum, 1923–1924* (New York, 1924); Werner T. Angress, *Stillborn Revolution: The Communist Bid for Power in Germany, 1921–1923* (Princeton, 1963); C. L. R. James, *World Revolution 1917– 1936: The Rise and Fall of the Communist International* (New York, 1937); Ruth Fischer, *Stalin and German Communism: A Study in the Origins of the State Party* (New Brunswick and London, 1982), first published in 1948. See her discussion in Part 3, "The Communist Uprising in 1923," pp. 291–383. Pierre Broué, *Révolution en Allemagne, 1917–1923* (Paris, 1971), the best study of all.

[4] Fischer, p. 301. In June the mark stood at .5 million to the British pound; in July its value declined to 1 million, and in August it took 1.5 million marks to buy one English pound. Fischer writes: "paradoxically, the only group convinced that Germany could not proceed to revolution was the Central Committee of the (German) Communist Party." *Ibid.*

[5] Translated by John G. Wright (New York, 1937).

[6] *Ibid.*, pp. 69, 72.

[7] 3,693,000 or 12.6% as against 4,592,100 or 10.6% in 1930. The latter figure was for September 1930.

[8] Cited by Fischer, p. 306.

[9] David Beetham, ed., *Marxists in Face of Fascism: Writings on Fascism from the Inter-War Period* (Totowa, New Jersey, 1984), pp. 152–153.

[10] *Ibid.*, pp. 153–154.

[11] V. I. Lenin, *The Communist International, Selected Works*, vol. 10 (N.Y., 1938), p. 111.

[12] Beetham, pp. 156–157.

[13] *Ibid.*, pp. 164–167.

[14] Leon Trotsky, *The Turn in the Communist International and the Situation in Germany* (New York, 1930), p. 6. The two working-class parties accounted for 40.4% of the votes.

[15] *Ibid.*, p. 11.

[16] *Ibid.*, pp. 28–29.

[17] Not in the brochure; see Leon Trotsky, *The Struggle against Fascism in Germany* (New York, 1971), pp. 72–73.

[18] Against National Communism! (Lessons of the "Red Referendum"), (August 25, 1931), in *The Struggle Against Fascism in Germany*, pp. 93–114, *passim*.

[19] *Ibid.*, pp. 96, 97–98.

[20] *Germany: The Key to the International Situation*, translated by Sam Gordon and Morris Lewis (New York, January 1932), pp. 13–17, a remarkably perceptive analysis of the catastrophe in the making.

[21] *Ibid.*, pp. 17–18.

[22] *Ibid*, pp. 18–20.

[23] *Ibid.*, pp. 20–21.

[24] *Ibid.*, pp. 22–23.

[25] *Ibid.*, p. 24.

[26] The subtitle is *Vital Questions for the German Proletariat*, translated from the Russian by Joseph Vanzler (New York, January 27, 1932).

[27] *Ibid.*, pp. 11, 13. The authoritarian and hierarchical structure of the SPD is discussed by Flechtheim, pp. 95–96. The party's watchwords were not "Revolt, Rebellion, or Anarchy," writes the author, but "Reform, Compromise, Order, Authority." The result was that the SPD underrated the danger of reaction and deluded itself that if it behaved with caution and modesty its enemy would become reasonable and conclude an honorable compromise with it. *Ibid.*, pp. 97–98.

[28] Rudolf Hilferding (1877–1941) was one of the Social Democratic leaders in Germany and author of a pioneering work in political economy, *Finance Capital*. He fled to France in 1933. The Petain government turned him over to the Gestapo in 1940 and he died shortly thereafter in a German prison.

[29] *What Next?* pp. 20, 23.

[30] *Ibid.*, pp. 24-25, 25-26.

[31] *Ibid.*, pp. 38–40.

[32] *Ibid.* See Chapter Three, "Bureaucratic Ultimatism," pp. 41–52.

[33] *Ibid.*, pp. 84–85, 86–87.

[34] *Ibid.*, pp. 163–164. Trotsky cited the workers of Bruchsal and Kliengenthal where the local Communist party, together with the SAP (the centrist Sozialistische Arbeiter Partei) and the trade unions, organized an effective defense against fascists despite an attempted sabotage of the reformist leadership. See Theodore Abel, *The Nazi Movement: Why Hitler Came to Power* (New York, 1966), pp. 93–112, wherein the author gives examples of clashes between the Nazis and the Reichsbanner and Red Front workers.

[35] *What Next?* p. 165.

[36] *Ibid.*, pp. 177–178, 184–185.

[37] *Ibid.*, pp. 186–187.

[38] *The Only Road for Germany*, translated from the German by Max Shachtman and B. J. Field (New York, April 1933).

[39] *Ibid.*, pp. 7–16.

[40] *Ibid.*, pp. 18–19.

[41] *Ibid.*, pp. 21–23.

[42] *Ibid.*, pp. 27–28.

[43] *Ibid.*, p. 28.

[44] *Ibid.*, p. 39. Perhaps an equally telling argument would have been that it was impossible to maintain a democratic regime (Trotsky speaks of "democracy" without qualifying it), since the Bonapartist regimes of Brüning, Papen, and Schleicher had abandoned the democracy of the Weimar Republic some time ago and there was no prospect of returning to it in 1932.

[45] *Ibid.*, pp. 40–41.

[46] *The World Crisis—the Aftermath* (London, 1929), p. 262, cited by Lionel Kochan, *Russia and the Weimar Republic* (Cambridge, England, 1954), p. 35, n. 1.

[47] *Sochineniya*, vol. 25, p. 402, cited by Kochan, above.

[48] *Sochineniya*, vol. 25, p. 418, cited by Kochan, p. 37.

[49] The German Foreign Minister, Dr. Simons, stated: "Communism as such is no reason why a German republican bourgeois Government should not trade with the Soviet Government." Kochan, p. 40.

[50] *Ibid.*, pp. 52–53.

[51] *Ibid.*, pp. 55, 56–57.

[52] *Ibid.*, p. 58.

[53] *Ibid.*, p. 59. The bargain was that "Russia promised Germany her aid against Versailles and Germany promised Russia her neutrality," writes Kochan. Rapallo also provided military cooperation between the two powers. Tank and aviation training schools were established with German cooperation on Russian soil. German industry produced poison gases, artillery shells, etc. *Ibid*, p. 60.

[54] The treaty or Pact guaranteed the Rhine frontier between Germany and Belgium and between Germany and France. Germany confirmed the demilitarization of the Rhineland and renounced its claim on Alsace-Lorraine. Germany also received support from Britain in case of French occupation of the Ruhr. *Ibid.*, pp. 96–98.

[55] *Izvestya*, 12 June 1925, cited by Kochan, pp. 98–99.

[56] Kochan, p. 101.

[57] *Ibid.*, p. 139.

[58] Thomas Weingartner, *Stalin und der Aufstieg Hitlers Die Deutschlandspolitik der Sowjetunion und der Kommunistischen Internationale 1928–1934* (Berlin, 1970), p. 275. The author calls it "eine Linkswendung des Kominterntaktik." Needless to say, Bukharin, Rykov, and Tomsky were still Bolsheviks, thus to the left of Stalin, who by 1928 had become much less a Bolshevik and far more a traditional Big Russian chauvinist.

[59] *Ibid.*, p. 276. Weingartner agrees with Kochan, in this respect.

[60] Kochan, pp. 145–146. My emphasis.

[61] *Ibid.*, pp. 146–147.

[62] Gustav Hilger and Alfred Meyer, *The Incompatible Allies* (New York, 1953), p. 253, cited by James E. McSherry, *Stalin, Hitler, and Europe*, 2 vols. (Cleveland and New York, [c.] 1968), I, 23.

[63] Kochan, p. 165.

[64] McSherry, I, 23. Robert C. Tucker, *Stalin in Power: The Revolution from Above, 1928–1941* (N.Y. c. 1990) documents Stalin's pursuit.

[65] *Ibid.*, p. 24, of a pact with Hitler almost from the moment the latter assumed power.

[66] *Russia and the Weimar Republic*, p. 174.

[67] Weingartner, pp. 276–278. The author has but one reference to Trotsky (Trotzki) in the Index (p. 115), but on this page Trotsky fails to appear.

[68] V. I. Lenin, *Toward the Seizure of Power* (New York, 1932), Book 1, p. 24; Leon Trotsky, *The History of the Russian Revolution*, 3 vols. (New York, 1932–1934), III, Appendix Two, p. 392; J. V. Stalin, *Foundations of Leninism*, 2nd ed. (Peking, 1957), p. 39; N. Bukharin and E. Preobrazhensky, *The ABC of Communism: A Popular Explanation of the Program of the Communist Party of Russia* (Ann Arbor, 1966), p. 138.

Chapter 4

From the Internationale to the Marseillaise: Jean Bruhat, Communist Historian of the Great French Revolution

James Friguglietti

In a speech delivered on May 19, 1919, a year and a half after he seized power in Russia, V. I. Lenin paid his respects to an earlier political upheaval. "Take the Great French Revolution," he told his audience.

> It is with good reason that it is called a great revolution. It did so much for the class that it served, for the bourgeoisie, that it left its imprint on the entire nineteenth century, the century which gave civilization and culture to the whole of mankind. The great French revolutionaries served the interests of the bourgeoisie although they did not realize it, for their vision was obscured by the words "liberty, equality and fraternity." In the nineteenth century, however, what they had begun was continued, carried out piecemeal, and finished in all parts of the world. . .

> Everyone who studies history seriously will admit that although it was crushed, the French Revolution was nevertheless triumphant because it laid down for the whole world such firm foundations of bourgeois democracy, of bourgeois freedom, that could never be uprooted.[1]

Not content with words of praise, Lenin ordered the erection of a statue of Maximilien Robespierre in Moscow, the first such monument ever put up anywhere. In Petrograd streets were renamed for such French revolutionaries as Jean-Paul Marat and Robespierre.[2]

In France itself, the historiography of the Great French Revolution was transformed by the events that occurred in Russia, less by the overthrow of Tsar Nicholas II in March, 1917, than by the establishment of a Communist regime under V. I. Lenin. When the French Communist Party was created at Tours in September, 1920, it enrolled historians who would view the Revolution of 1789 through the lens of the Bolshevik Revolution.

This essay will examine two closely interrelated questions. First, how did the French Communist Party view the French Revolution during the period from its creation until its dissolution in 1939? Second, how did its historians interpret the French Revolution exerting their scholarly abilities to serve their party? It will concentrate on a single historian, Jean Bruhat (1905-1983), whose career exemplifies Communist historiography during the later 1930s. Bruhat remains little known outside France because none of his books was ever translated into English and he never visited America or even England. Nonetheless, his work deserves to be examined closely, for it amply demonstrates how the historiography of the Revolution served partisan ends.

Let me begin with the question of how the French Communists perceived the Great Revolution during the interwar period. The French historian François Hincker, himself a loyal member of the Party, has suggested that its views developed in three distinct phases. First, from 1920 through 1923, Party historians actively sought to link the French and Bolshevik revolutions.

Most important of these scholars, Albert Mathiez (1874-1932), published a small brochure entitled *Le Bolchévisme et le jacobinisme*. In it he compared the Bolshevik and Jacobin regimes. They were, he declared,

> two dictatorships, born of civil and foreign wars, two class dictatorships, operating by the same means "terror, requisitioning, price controls" and in the last analysis, setting forth similar goals, the transformation of society, and not only Russian or French society, but universal society.

The Bolsheviks, in his words, had only "perfected" the methods of the Jacobins.[3]

In addition, during the early 1920s, under the auspices of the Communist Party newspaper *L'Humanité*, Mathiez published a new, annotated, eight-volume edition of Jean Jaurès's study on the Revolution published in the first four volumes of the *Histoire socialiste*. By reprinting this Marxist but scholarly account of the Great Revolution, the Party both appropriated and canonized Jaurès's work, thereby providing its historians with a reliable model to emulate.[4]

According to Hincker, the second phase of Communist Party attitudes began in 1923. That year the increasing Bolshevization of the Party drove many historians like Mathiez from its ranks. Dictation from Moscow greatly reduced the need to exalt the "Great" Revolution. Now it was the October Revolution and the accomplishments of the Bolsheviks led first by Lenin and then Stalin that took center stage. The French Revolution was increasingly viewed as a "bourgeois" affair, having little relevance for French Communists. As the Party's Paul Vaillant-Courturier remarked: "Our holiday is March 18, 1871 [date of the proclamation of the Paris Commune]. It is the anniversary of the October Revolution."[5] According to one scholar publications dealing with the Revolution of 1789 fell to a low level: between 1925 and 1934 only twenty-six articles and no books on the period appeared from the Communist Party press.[6]

Beginning in 1934, according to Hincker, the third and most important phase opened. The establishment of the Nazi regime in Germany as well as a growing threat from the far right in France, evidenced by the Stavisky riots of February 6, convinced Stalin to draw closer to the West in foreign affairs. Accordingly, the French Communist Party shifted from attacks on the Socialists and Radical-Socialists to a rapprochement that would culminate in the formation of the Popular Front and its victory in the national elections of May, 1936. From internationalism and enthusiasm for the October Revolution, the Party's leadership began to stress patriotism and glorify the Revolution of 1789.[7] The Communists' new policy sought not only to commemorate a major historical event but also to create a counterweight to fascism by emphasizing the democratic tradition born of the "Great" Revolution.[8]

Party spokesmen, notably its leader Maurice Thorez, now began to display enthusiasm for that national event. In a lengthy speech delivered at the seventh congress of the Communist International on August 3, 1935, he declared:

> In the name of the working class, we lay claim to the intellectual and revolutionary heritage of the Encyclopedists of the eighteenth century, who, by their writings and works, prepared the great Revolution of 1789. We proclaim that their materialistic doctrine, deepened, developed and enriched by the genius of Marx, Engels, Lenin and Stalin, has become dialectical materialism, Marxist-Leninism, the theory and practice of the revolutionary proletariat,

the great builder of socialism, which already controls over one-sixth of the globe. . . In the name of the working class, we lay claim to the heritage of revolutionary audacity and energy of the Jacobins.

Thorez then added: "Lenin often said: 'The Bolsheviks are the Jacobins of the proletarian revolution.'"[9]

With such encouragement, party-line historians began to produce a torrent of publications that glorified the achievements of and participants in the Revolution. By 1939, during the sesquicentennial celebrations, the Communists draped themselves in the tricolor flags and loudly intoned the *Marseillaise*. This new-found patriotism reached its climax with the Bastille Day festivities of July 14, 1939.

Yet little more than a month later, the signing of the Hitler-Stalin Pact, which brought Germany and Russia into a non-aggression agreement, prompted the government of Édouard Daladier to suppress the French Communist Party, suspend all its publications, and effectively reduce its historians to silence.[10]

No historian better exemplifies the outlook of the Communist Party during this period than Jean Bruhat.[11] He served as the Party's most talented and prolific scholar. But in the words of the English writer David Caute, Bruhat was "perhaps the most stalwart Stalinist among the professional historians."[12] A brief survey of his life and career is necessary to explain how he became so prominent a specialist on the "Great" Revolution within the Party's ranks.

As Bruhat reveals in his autobiography *Il n'est jamais trop tard*, published in 1983 shortly before his death, he sprang from modest origins, being the grandson of a carter and a miller, as well as the son of a postal worker. A native of the Gard Department in southwest France, he early showed considerable intelligence and rose through the public school system, winning numerous prizes for his excellent knowledge of French and geography. On his own Bruhat read such authors as Émile Zola, Romain Rolland, and the Russian Maxim Gorky. These writers stimulated his sympathies for the idea of revolution and the cause of labor.[13]

Admitted to the prestigious École Normale Supérieure in the autumn of 1925, he soon joined the Communist Party. Many years later, in 1947, Bruhat would connect his interest in history with his membership in the Party.[14] He spent three years studying intensely and took a class at the Sorbonne on the French Revolution taught by the noted historian Albert Mathiez. Bruhat also threw himself into Party activities that included participating in anti-government demonstrations and distributing leaflets. Meanwhile he read widely in Marxist texts to deepen his understanding of ideology.[15]

In 1929 Bruhat passed his examination for secondary-school teachers (*agrégation*). Then, after completing his military service, he took a teaching post at the *lycée* in Nantes. There he began what he later described as the "double life" of a teacher and Party activist. In addition to giving history lessons to his students, he engaged in Communist agitation in the large port city. In the process of Party work, he made the acquaintance of such party luminaries as Maurice Thorez and Jacques Duclos when they visited Nantes. Thanks to their influence, Bruhat in 1933 began contributing to *L'Humanité* a regular column entitled "Doctrine et Histoire." He regularly reviewed the latest books in modern history, particularly those written by members of the Party.[16]

As the Communist Party shifted towards a policy of cooperating with rather than denouncing Socialists and Radical-Socialists, Bruhat grew increasingly disconcerted. "I belong to a generation that was profoundly marked by internationalism," he recalled in his memoirs:

> Uniting the red flag and the tricolor flag, the singing of the *Internationale* with the *Marseillaise*, agreed! But it required that we uproot deep-seated convictions. . . The *Marseillaise* had sounded at too many chauvinist demonstrations for us to adopt it without difficulty. . . The embarrassment with which we sang the *Marseillaise* was followed by the profound joy we felt for the *Internationale*. Those who joined the Communist Party in the years 1934-36 did not sense this contradiction. But we old-timers, whose hatred of war and who internationalism had led us to Communism, did.[17]

Moving to Paris in 1937, Bruhat continued his "double life." While teaching history at the *Lycée* Bouffon, he assumed an increasingly important role in promoting the study and celebration of the French Revolution. Bruhat employed his historical knowledge in four different ways: first by enthusiastically supporting the policies of Stalin; second by assisting in the production of a major film dealing with the Revolution; third by creating an historical museum; and finally by helping to organize the sesquicentennial observances of 1939. These efforts demonstrate both his loyalty to the Communist cause and his expertise in Revolutionary history.

As a regular contributor to *L'Humanité*, Bruhat wrote a series of articles dealing with the punishment of traitors and spies during the French Revolution, comparing them with the recent trials of Old Bolsheviks and army officers in Stalin's Russia. At the behest of Party chief Thorez, Bruhat collected them into brochure form. Entitled *Le Châtiment des espions et des traîtres sous la Révolution française*, it demonstrated his complete fidelity to the Party line.[18]

Using his erudition, Bruhat justified Stalin's elimination of party and military figures in terms of similar events that took place during the Terror of 1793-94. Indeed, most of his 63-page brochure simply recapitulated familiar episodes of Revolutionary corruption and treason when politicians like Danton and generals such as Houchard paid with their heads for their sins.

In comparing these cases with the Russian purge trials, Bruhat drew the appropriate lesson. "Our readers have studied the trials of the Trotskyites," he observed. "They have seen how [General] Tukhachevsky and his accomplices have been unmasked. It is clear that the history of our revolution presented identical cases and quite comparable circumstances."[19] Just as "Old Jacobins" had perished because they betrayed the Revolution, so too the "Old Bolsheviks" merited execution for their crimes. If the "feudal" states sought to undermine the Republic in 1793, fascist powers were attempting to destroy the "first workers'" and peasants' republic in 1937. But whereas Robespierre and his Jacobin followers were ultimately defeated, it was because they had lost touch with the poorest levels of society. In contrast, Bruhat declared, the "Bolshevik party, under the leadership of Stalin, constantly elevates the condition of the masses."[20] Unlike the Dantonists, however, the Trotskyites proved no true revolutionaries but rather the "champions of capitalism in its decadent form—fascism."[21] Bruhat quoted the Austrian Communist writer Ernest Fischer who accused Grigori Zinoviev and Lev Kamenev of betraying the masses and the Revolution, of working for the kulaks, expelled capitalists and international counter-revolution. The struggle against traitors during the French Revolution had not weakened its material strength, Bruhat contended. So, too, the Russian Revolution had not weakened its own material strength because of the Moscow trials. He concluded by quoting Albert Mathiez's comment that in the Year II the corrupt "lived in constant fear that their escapades would be exposed and calmed their fears by denouncing their accomplices while denouncing themselves at the same time."[22]

Bruhat expected that these comparisons would help the friends of the Soviet Union, who were also admirers of the French Revolution, better to understand what had occurred in Russia. Undoubtedly, he was loyally serving the needs of the Communist Party. When he published his memoirs in 1983, however, Bruhat displayed considerable embarrassment about this publication. "I attempted to make the incomprehensible comprehensible," he confessed.

> O, history! What crimes are committed in your name! It was as if my membership in the Communist Party had dulled the critical spirit of the historian. . . But where the Soviet Revolution and its future were concerned, sentimental attachment won out over reason.[23]

Far more significant than writing this rather minor brochure was Bruhat's involvement in two projects intended to popularize the French Revolution among the general public. The two enterprises also helped to stimulate the spirit of the Popular Front that was sweeping France during the late 1930s. At the urging of Party leaders, Bruhat served as the historical advisor to Jean Renoir's film *La Marseillaise* as well as aided in organizing a museum in the Parisian suburb of Montreuil. Both represented a concerted effort by the Party to associate itself closely with France's revolutionary past. Both also offered Bruhat the opportunity to display his scholarly expertise.

In his autobiography Bruhat reports that Jacques Duclos personally summoned him to Paris during his summer vacation in 1937 to assist director Jean Renoir in producing his motion picture *La Marseillaise*. It was apparently Duclos himself who suggested that it focus on the march of a battalion of soldiers from Marseille to Paris where it participated in the overthrow of King Louis XVI on August 10, 1792.[24] Bruhat claimed to have served as the technical director to Renoir, who was preoccupied with achieving historical authenticity. "He bombarded me with questions, demanding in particular that the dialogue be directly inspired by conversations that historians had recorded," Bruhat recalled. He plunged into the memoirs left by French émigrés as well as works concerning aristocratic emigration in order to gather authentic dialogue. "Are you certain, absolutely certain, that this was actually said?" Renoir would ask him. Bruhat, for his part, watched the film being shot in old neighborhoods of Paris and was sometimes pained to see the camera trained on some anachronistic detail.[25] Today it is impossible to know exactly what Bruhat actually contributed to the film to ensure its historical accuracy. His name does not even appear among the credits.[26] But Renoir, who flirted with the Communist Party during the Popular Front era, certainly wrote the final shooting script himself. Mingling fact and fiction, he contrasted émigré nobles plotting intrigues at Coblenz with an enthusiastic battalion of volunteers marching toward Paris while singing the *Marseillaise* (hence the title of the film). Joining crowds from the Parisian sections, the soldiers are shown assaulting the Tuileries Palace, and at the conclusion of the film, marching confidently to do battle with the Prussians at Valmy. The volunteers, true men of the people, constantly display their rough sense of humor, good common sense, genuine courage, and love of equality.

Though it is infused with the spirit of the Popular Front and glorifies the common people, *La Marseillaise* never degenerates into agitprop like historical films produced in the Soviet Union during the 1930s. It has, in the words of director François Truffaut, "more than anything the look of newsreels culled from the French Revolution."[27] Thanks to Renoir's directorial skill (and perhaps Bruhat's research), a human drama rather than an exercise in ideology unfolds.

According to Bruhat, the premiere of the film, held on February 9, 1938, proved a triumph.[28] But as one critic has commented, *La Marseillaise* received an "unenthusiastic reception" and "commercially it was a failure."[29] Critical opinion was in fact divided. Naturally the Left hailed it as a triumph. Writing in *L'Humanité*, Louis Cheronnet lavishly praised the film and its director: "Nothing is more beautiful, more moving than the moment when a people becomes conscious of itself, of its rights and its duties, of its strength and hopes. This is the moment in the history of our nation that the film of Jean Renoir. . .shows us. An historical film? A political film? No, a human film."[30] Commenting in *Ce Soir*, Communist author Louis Aragon called it "Jean Renoir's greatest miracle" and exclaimed that "he has made a film so current and powerful, so human, that you are taken, carried away, swept off for more than two hours, as though it were our own life that was at issue. And, in fact, it is."[31]

For its part, the Right excoriated *La Marseillaise*. In *L'Action française*, for example, Lucien Rebatet assailed the "Communist Jean Renoir" for his production, which offered "Thorze-style patriotism" and "French war-like virtues carefully cultivated to the greater advantage of the U. S. S. R."[32]

Nonetheless, the film represents one of the Party's (and Bruhat's) most enduring accomplishments not to mention one of Jean Renoir's enduring successes.

A second, far less known and appreciated project in which Bruhat became deeply involved was the creation of an historical museum. In his autobiography he recalled that Jacques Declos, who lived in the eastern suburb of Montreuil and felt passionately about history, requested him to help organize a museum "devoted to the history of popular struggles in France."[33] For this purpose, a private society was formed to lease the château of Montreau, a three-story building located in a wooded park. Working with Joseph Billiet, a museum curator, and Albert Soboul, a fellow historian of the Revolution, both men Communists, Bruhat assembled an impressive variety of artifacts. In March, 1939, the institution opened to the general public.

At a press conference Bruhat declared that

> we have sought to create, not a partisan museum, but a French museum where Napoleon has his place beside the Jacobins. We have thus remained faithful to our scientific method, which does not suppress facts, but sets them in the development of history.[34]

In an article he wrote, Bruhat discussed the purpose of the museum.

> We want. . .to enable the visitor to contemplate documents that are not reproductions, but which are authentic ones. One small example: here is a yellowed paper with the tiny but firm signature of Robespierre. In examining it, the visitor imagines Robespierre reading this same sheet of paper and signing it. He thus find himself before an historical reality. It is an impression that he would not experience with a reproduction.[35]

Soboul himself provided a detailed description of the exhibit shortly after it opened. He called it a museum that was "above all, popular," with artifacts that were organized "scientifically." The originality of the institution, he explained, "lay expressly in the fact that, for the first time, a scholarly collection that does not aim to please a few collectors of rare souvenirs, but rather to educate a very wide public."[36]

The museum's collection, intended to be permanent, encompassed the development of French social history from the eighteenth century to the present. To commemorate the sesquicentennial, it concentrated on the Revolution "in its full historical meaning."[37] On the top floor of the château, a room was devoted to the *philosophes* and Encyclopedists "whose intelligence prepared the way for the Revolution." Included among the displays was a complete set of the *Encyclopédie* as well as other significant volumes, pamphlets, and engravings from the Enlightenment. In a corner near the main staircase, documents provided evidence of the repressiveness of the Old Regime monarchy.

On the second floor, a large room dealt with the events of the Revolution. Glass cases held items concerning the royal family, the fall of the Bastille, the festival of the Federation of 1790, the republican army, and revolutionary publications. Numerous autographs and medallions were also displayed. Finally, as Soboul put it, "the Napoleonic Era is evoked in an objective fashion, which fully explains the significance of the period of the consolidation of bourgeois power that followed Thermidor."[38]

Finally, on the ground floor two large rooms honored the famed Socialist deputy, orator, and historian Jean Jaurès. Installed in them were his writing desk, chair, and volumes drawn from his personal library, donated by the newspaper that he had long edited, *L'Humanité.*[39]

The museum demonstrated Bruhat's expertise as an historian of France. But perhaps even more important, it manifested the Communist Party's desire to use French history as a means to demonstrate its nationalism as well as to illustrate Karl Marx's well-known dictum that the "history of all hitherto existing society is the history of class struggles."

But the creation of a history museum in Montreuil played only a minor role in the Party's overall efforts to commemorate the one hundred and fiftieth anniversary of the Revolution. At its annual conference, held at Gennevilliers in January, 1939, Bruhat had declared to his comrades that Communists should "put forth the maximum effort" to celebrate the one-hundred-and-fiftieth anniversary of the Revolution.[40] He then suggested a program of events for local party activists to organize. These included the organization of popular festivals on July 14, lectures in schools, and even a "pilgrimage" to Valmy, the site of a republican victory over the invading Prussians in 1792.[41] How many towns, particularly those controlled by Party officials, actually followed his suggestions is difficult to determine.

Paris, however, remained the center of the Party's program of celebration. On June 25, 1939, a crowd of some 60,000 spectators gathered at the Buffalo Stadium in suburban Montrouge. There Maurice Thorez delivered a speech that defended the ideals of 1789 against the rising threat of fascism both abroad and home. "The fascists in France, agents of foreign powers and mercenaries of capital, naturally feel. . .hatred for the work of the Great Revolution, for the idea of progress, of justice, of liberty that it expressed and spread throughout the world."

Thorez went on to state that the working class of France needed to accomplish not a 1789, but a "1939, a 1940, a 1945 or 46, which would be the 1917 of the people of France, the taking of power, the installation of the dictatorship of the proletariat. . .."[42] Following Thorez's speech, tableaux retracing the history of the Revolution made their appearance. A battalion of marchers dressed like the Marseillais volunteers who in 1792 had traveled to Paris paraded before the spectators. Finally, floats paying tribute to the Soviet Union and the Red Army passed by the reviewing stand where the Party's leaders sat. Cries of "Long live the Soviet Union!" rose to greet them. Once again French Patriotism and Communist Party ideology merged.[43]

The most impressive display took place in Paris on Bastille Day. Rivaling the official military parade held earlier on the Champs Elysées, the Communist-inspired procession composed of some 250,000 marchers filled the streets between the Place de la Bastille and the Place de la Nation. "For hours," *L'Humanité* exulted, "marching along the entire route, which was decorated with red and tricolor flags, the descendants of those who took the Bastille proclaimed their will to bar the way to war and social reaction."[44]

Such manifestations enabled the Communist Party to pose as the legitimate heir of the Revolution, as well as to appear as the principal defender of the Revolutionary legacy of liberty, equality and fraternity. It had, in effect, returned with renewed vigor to its celebratory view of the "Great" Revolution that Lenin had proclaimed twenty years earlier.

Little more than a month later, the Party was profoundly shaken by news of the signing of the Hitler-Stalin Pact on August 23. The outraged government of Daladier moved first to suppress all its publications, notably *L'Humanité*, and then outlaw the Party itself. Ironically the dramatic shift in Soviet foreign policy, intended to protect Russia against possible Nazi aggression, led to the silencing of the most ardent defenders of France's Revolutionary heritage.

To prevent the government from confiscating the collection at the historical museum, Bruhat supervised the clandestine removal of the precious documents and artifacts to a secure site near Fontainebleau. These remained safely hidden throughout the war and were restored to their proper place afterward.[45]

After his mobilization for war service, Bruhat no longer had the opportunity to express his views freely in print. He could not, as he had planned, publish the compilation of texts that Marx and Engels had written about the Revolution. (Under the title *Les Grands texts du marxisme sur la Révolution française*, the volume had already been advertised as being "in preparation" by the Communist publishing house Éditions sociales internationales.)[46] Bruhat had to be satisfied with providing a brief introduction to the collection, which appeared under the pseudonym "Jean Montreau" in the last prewar issue of *La Pensée*.[47] Entitled "La Révolution française et la pensée de Marx," it closely examined how the French Revolution influenced the thought of Karl Marx. From a close reading of the German ideologue's writings, Bruhat concluded that it was the class struggle that took place in France beginning in 1789 which inspired his political ideas. The bourgeois class, born in the feudal world, sprang from basic changes in production and communication. During the Revolution the bourgeoisie overthrew the monarchy and aristocracy, but also brought the proletariat into the political arena, thereby preparing the social conflicts that marked the nineteenth century. Bruhat maintained that the "influence of the French Revolution on the development of Marxist thought was considerable."[48] In effect, he confirmed what Lenin had declared in his speech of May 19, 1919. The revolutionary movement that began with the capture of the Bastille in 1789 culminated in the storming of the Winter Palace in 1917.

Between the formation of the Popular Front and the suppression of the French Communist Party, a dramatic shift had taken place in Communist historians' views of the "Great" Revolution. As they transferred their allegiance from internationalism to patriotism, from the red flag to the tricolor, from the *Internationale* to the *Marseillaise*, they strove to educate both the party rank-

and-file and general public about the Revolution. Bruhat in particular became extraordinarily active in this cause. Contributing his extensive knowledge of Revolutionary history to the Party press, advising Jean Renoir concerning the filming of *La Marseillaise*, and creating an historical museum devoted to the Revolution, and helping to organize the celebration of 1939, he played a significant role in familiarizing his countrymen, especially Party members, with the events of the Revolutionary decade.[49]

Yet, as his now-forgotten pamphlet on the punishment of spies and traitors during the Terror amply demonstrates, Bruhat consistently subordinated his scholarship to the needs of the Party. As a recent scholar has remarked, Bruhat "particularly distinguished himself during the Stalinist Era by his unswerving adhesion to the party line."[50] True, when he eventually published his memoirs, Bruhat did express his sincere regrets for having been so naïve. Bruhat, however, never deserted the Party, and when he died in February, 1983, *L'Humanité* hailed him as a "plebeian intellectual."[51] Just as Lenin admired the "Great" Revolution, his French disciple returned the favor by expressing his reverence for the Bolshevik one. In all his historical writings published during the 1930s, Bruhat faithfully serve not Clio but Stalin.

Endnotes

[1] Speech delivered at the First All-Russian Congress on Adult Education, in V. I. Lenin, *Collected Works, 29, March-August 1919*. (Moscow: Progress Publishers, 1965), pp. 371-72.

[2] Victor Daline, "Historique de l'étude de la Révolution française en URSS," A. Narotchnitski, ed., La Révolution française et la Russie (Paris: Editions Librairie du Globe, 1989), p. 101.

[3] Albert Mathiez, *Le Bolchévisme et le jacobinisme* (Paris: Librairie du Parti socialiste et de l'*Humanité*, 1920).

[4] Jean Jaurès, Histoire socialiste de la Révolution française, 8 vol. Albert Mathiez, ed. (Paris: *L'Humanité*, 1922-24).

[5] Quoted in François Hincker, "La Lecture de la Révolution française par le Parti communiste français," *Communisme: revue d' études pluridisciplinaires*, 20-21 (1988-1989), p. 105.

[6] Catherine Bensadek, *La Révolution française dans l'édition communiste (1920-1989): Bibliographie* (Paris: Bibliothèque marxiste de Paris, 1989).

[7] Hincker, op. cit., 102-03.

[8] Roger Martelli, "Héritiers de la Révolution française," in Jean-Pierre Azéma, Antoine Prost and Jean-Pierrre Rioux, *Le Parti communiste française des années sombres, 1938-1941* (Paris: Éditions sociales, 1967), pp. 163-64.

[9] Maurice Thorez, *Œuvres choises en trois volumes*, 1 (*1924-1937*) (Paris: Éditions sociales, 1967), pp. 163-64.

[10] Hincker, op. cit., 103.

[11] For details of Bruhat's life and career, see the following obituaries: Jean Bouvier, "Jean Bruhat, 1905-1983," *Revue d'histoire moderne et contemporaine*, 30 (1983), pp. 322-23; Pierre Chambon, "Jean Bruhat," *Annuaire de l'Association amicale des anciens élèves de l'Ecole normale supérieure*, 1984, pp. 73-75; François Hincker, "Jean Bruhat (1905-1983)," *Annales historiques de la Revolution française*, 55 (1983), pp. 188-92; Claude Willard, "Jean Bruhat (1905-1983)," *Cahiers d'histoire de l'Institut de recherches marxiste*, 12 (1983), pp. 3-5. Willared calls Bruhat "the first Communist to have examined [*défriché*] history in the light of Marxism."

[12] David Caute, *Communism and the French Intellectuals* (London: André Deutsch,

1964), p. 276.

[13] Jean Bruhat, *Il n'est jamais trop tard* (Paris: Albin Michel, 1983), pp. 22-32.

[14] "As an historian I very early became certain that Communism was not only the hope of the world, but also the final stage of human development and that it was possible to hasten this development by strengthening the Communist Party, which, in my view, is the Party of History." Jean Bruhat in *Pourquoi je suis communiste* (Paris: Éditions du Parti communiste français, 1947), p. 13.

[15] Bruhat, *Il n'est jamais trop tard*, p. 19.

[16] Ibid., 70.

[17] Ibid., p. 72.

[18] The first article in the series, "La Révolution française et la conspiration de l'étranger," appeared in *L'Humanité* on April 13, 1930. It became chapter one of his brochure *Le Châtiment des espions et des traîtres sous la Révolution française* (Paris: Éditions Bureau d'éditions, 1937).

[19] Ibid.

[20] Ibid., p. 58.

[21] Ibid., 59.

[22] Ibid., p. 62.

[23] Jean Bruhat, *Il n'est jamais trop tard*, p. 86.

[24] Ibid., p. 98.

[25] Ibid., 98-99. In an interview published in *L'Humanité* on Aug. 11, 1937, Renoir outlined his approach to the film, but made no mention of any role that Duclos might have played in its inception.

[26] See the detailed credits for the film given in André Bazin, *Jean Renoir* (New York: Simon & Schuster, 1974), pp. 249-51. Bazin mentions N. Martel Dreyfus and Mme. Jean-Paul Dreyfus as the "historical consultants." For a detailed analysis of the film, see Geneviève Guillaume-Grimaud, *Le Cinéma du Front populaire* (Paris: Lherminier, 1986), pp. 99-106. Guillaume-Grimaud also reproduces numerous stills from it.

[27] Bazin, *Jean Renoir*, p. 252.

[28] Bruhat, *Il n'est jamais trop tard*, p. 99.

[29] Chantal Thomas, "La *Marseillaise* de Jean Renoir: naissance d'un chant," in Jean-Claude Bonnet and Philippe Roger, eds., *La Légende de la Révolution au Xxe siècle* (Paris: Flammarion, 1988), p. 124.

[30] Quoted in Célia Bertin, *Jean Renoir: A Life in Pictures* (Baltimore and London: Johns Hopkins University Press, 1991) pp. 145-46.

[31] Ibid.

[32] Quoted in Thomas, La *Marseillaise* de Jean Renoir, p. 124.

[33] Ibid.

[34] Bruhat, *Il n'est jamais trop tard*, p. 99. It might be noted that the municipal council of Montreuil later succeeded in having a new Métro station that was located in the suburb named for Robespierre. See *L'Humanité*, Oct. 14, 1937.

[35] Jean Bruhat, "Le Musée de l'histoire à Montreuil-sous-Bois," *Cahiers du Bolchevisme*, 16, no. 4 (April, 1939), p. 553.

[36] Pierre Vilar and Albert Soboul, "La Révolution française vue à travers les expositions historiques," *La Pensée: revue du rationalisme moderne*, no. 2 (July-Sept. 1939), p. 114.

[37] Ibid., p. 115.

[38] Ibid., p. 118.

[39] Bruhat, *Il n'est jamais trop tard*, 100. According to Bruhat, he personally typed the explanatory notices accompanying the items in the museum collection.

[40] *L'Humanité*, Jan. 25, 1939. For the complete text of Bruhat's speech, see Jean Bruhat, "Le Peuple de France célébrera le 150e anniversaire de la grande révolution," *Cahiers du bolchevisme*, 16, no. 2 (Feb. 1939), pp. 190-96. As he informed his audience: "It is necessary this year that democrats, with the Communists in the lead, celebrate the French Revolution. It is necessary that, after the diplomatic Munich, we have no historical Munich."

[41] Ibid. Cf. Jean-Marie Goulemot and Jean-Jacques Tatin, "Le Parti communiste et le cent-cinquantième anniversaire de la Révolution française: l'année 1939," in *Communisme: revue d'études pluridisciplinaires*, no. 20-21 (1988-89) ,pp. 88-100, which compares the official ceremonies with those organized by the Communist Party.

[42] *L'Humanité*, June 26, 1939.

[43] Ibid. Pictures of the marchers appeared on the front page of the issue, more on the next day.

[44] *L'Humanité*, July 15, 1939.

[45] Bruhat, *Il n'est jamais trop tard*, p. 100, 106.

[46] See in *La Pensée: revue du rationalisme moderne*, no. 2 (July-Sept. 1939), an advertisement for publications of Éditions sociales internationales located opposite page 1.

[47] Jean Montreau [Jean Bruhat], "La Révolution française et la pensée de Marx," *La Pensée: revue du rationalisme moderne*, 3 (Oct.-Dec. 1939), pp. 24-38. cf. Jean Bruhat, "La Révolution française et la formation de la pensée de Marx," *Annales historique de la Révolution française*, 38 (1966), pp. 125-26: "In 1939, during the one-hundredth-and-fiftieth anniversary of the Revolution, I was requested by a publisher to assemble all the writings of Marx and Engels concerning the Revolution of 1789. The task was far from complete when war broke out. I had only the time to jot down a few notes intended as a possible introduction to the collection. They appeared under a pseudonym in the fall of 1939." (Montreau was the name of the château in Montreuil where Bruhat had helped to install the historical museum earlier that year.)

[48] Montreau, op. cit. p. 24.

[49] Bruhat's wife Yvonne (1906-95) also contributed to the commemoration by publishing a small brochure discussing the role that women played during the Revolution: *Les Femmes et la Révolution française* (Paris: Édition du Comité mondial des femmes, 1939).

[50] Sudhir Hazareesingh, *Intellectuals and the French Communist Party: Disillusion and Decline* (Oxford: Clarendon Press, 1991), 232. Hazareesingh also characterizes him as "a typical Stalinist stalwart" (256n).

[51] For the Party's final tribute to Bruhat, see Arnaud Spire, "Un 'intellectual plébéien,'" *L'Humanité*, Feb. 12, 1983.

Chapter 5

The I.W.W. and the Akron Rubber Strike of 1913[1]

Roy T. Wortman

> Of course there is no need to jettison a fundamental commitment
> to social change. Equally dangerous, however, is a commitment to
> political judgments that have been surpassed by history.—Stanley
> Arnowitz

"Akron remains, to this day, the supreme mistake of the I.W.W.," declared the *One Big Union Monthly* in 1920. "Never in the history of the I.W.W. has a strike that opened with such alluring prospects led to such a crushing disillusionment."[2] The supreme mistake was Akron's rubber strike in 1913.

Akron's industrial development in the early twentieth century took place at top speed.[3] In addition to incentives offered by the city to the rubber industry, an extra resource was present in the form of a readily available labor pool. Seventy percent of this pool were native-born Americans who were "internal migrants" hailing from rural Ohio, West Virginia, and Pennsylvania; an immigrant workforce from central and eastern Europe, lured to the United States by promotional agents' glowing pictures of wealth, comprised the remainder.[4] This polyglot labor pool satiated the burgeoning industry's demand for employees, and by 1913 eight corporations—Goodrich, Firestone, Goodyear, Star, Swinehart, Buckeye, Miller, and Diamond—were the main employers in Akron.

"We really were a big family," said Harvey Firestone as he looked back to 1902, when he had twelve employees.[5] A paternalistic sense of community marked his early years in the industry, a community that would, by 1913, become fragmented and torn by strife. By 1913, however, Firestone's 1,800 employees were subject to industrial regimentation and discipline, the cult of efficiency, and the diminution of individual status. As "family" transmogrified into corporation, the once-familiar bond between employer and employee was lost. "I don't even know the names of my foremen," Firestone lamented. "It used to be different."[6] *India Rubber World*, the industry's trade journal, noted a similar problem: production efficiency and accelerated growth made the industry a depersonalized one in which foremen were removed from the problems and grievances of wage earners.[7] And, on the other side, the Industrial Workers of the World noted the shift in Akron's development from community to impersonal industry when Wobblies noted that "Akron has become a city of furnished rooms," with a turnover of eight hundred workers moving in and out of the city monthly.[8]

Workers attempted to better their situation through organization. In 1906, five hundred rubber workers organized a union but it was short-lived: the union's office was burglarized, its records stolen, and union members lost their jobs in the rubber industry.[9] Yet as of 1913 Akron's chamber of commerce was still blind to a problem between labor and management and smugly asserted that the "oppression of labor is so uncommon as to be almost unknown" and declared that rubber factories had modern, fireproof buildings with ample sanitation, ventilation, and light.[10] Workers in Akron and State Senator William Green of Coshocton, a trade unionist and vociferous opponent of labor radicalism, disagreed with the assessment offered by the chamber of commerce. Green argued that the rubber industry, coddled by protective tariffs from the government, made "enormous profits from the American people." In a populistic vein, he added, "Notwithstanding the favors extended to them by the people's government, these corporations have assumed an autocratic and arrogant attitude, refusing to meet with employees to hear grievances and to settle differences."[11] Green specified such grievances as the Taylor speed-up system, which granted employees bonuses if they produced more than their fellow workers. Proponents of Taylorism, the new gospel of efficiency in Progressive life, maintained that speed-up rewarded employee initiative and efficiency. Yet rubber workers countered that Taylorism, the gospel of the "world of the factory," forced them to work faster, causing exertion and injuries to health.[12] Moreover, the length of the workday was contested by workers. With the exception of Goodyear's eight-hour shifts in its tire-building department, hours for male workers in the industry ran between ten to eleven for day work and thirteen for night work. Women employees worked a fifty-four-hour week. Rubber workers complained that they would be discharged if they voiced their problems to management.

These findings came from the Green Committee, appointed in February 1913 to investigate the background causes of the strike. The committee documented many of the workers' fears that complaints would lead to reprisals by management, and noted the rubber industry's general inability to deal with employee problems that led to worker discontent in the factories.

Related to this issue was the workers' fear of the blacklist system. The Green Committee found no conclusive evidence that a list formally existed but noted that each company's employment department maintained "a minute description" of each worker which, in essence, constituted a surveillance dossier. Workers reacted adversely to the system and with good reason: "They seemed to regard the minute description of them taken upon the employment card as an unfair and humiliating espionage." Management argued that these measures were needed to protect the industry from workers with bad backgrounds, but rubber workers saw it as a de facto blacklist. The committee found that prior to the strike, rubber industry wages were comparable to other industries, but that was not the real issue. At issue was the piecework system, the corollary of Taylorism, which made for wide disparities in wages in some cases.[13]

These complaints, coupled with unsanitary conditions and wage cuts in 1912, led to worker frustration and resentment,[14] a situation that was ripe for the I.W.W. The Wobbly campaign began in the summer of 1912 when organizer Elizabeth Gurley Flynn spoke in Akron, urging organization from "cellar to roof."[15] "What was done in the Lawrence textile mills," she declared, "may be done in the Akron rubber shops."[16] Six months later the I.W.W. in Akron burgeoned into an angry, albeit awkward, union. Organization was rationalized as a means of countering the corporate structure. Wobbly organizer Walter Knox considered Akron's rubber industries as a huge trust that demanded the counter-organization of workers into a "labor trust." The I.W.W. seized the moment.

Thus, in 1912, I.W.W. organizers from Cleveland established Akron's Rubber Workers' Industrial Union No. 470. They attempted to maintain secrecy because of an effective labor spy organization that had six years earlier destroyed an embryonic union group.[17] At first the Wobblies managed to recruit only a few members. Then an innovation at Firestone's works sent workers running to the I.W.W. New machines were introduced that enabled workers to produce more tires, but a new, reduced pay scale also was introduced.

On February 11, 1913, protesting Firestone's policy, a group of twenty-five tire finishers walked off the job. Three hundred other Firestone workers followed.[18] Firestone refused to negotiate with the workers and instead gave notice that "all tire makers and. . . finishers who leave the building. . . and who do not return for work this afternoon, we will consider as having given up their positions. . . ."[19] The announcement did not halt the spread of the strike. Other departments in the Firestone plant and then other companies in Akron quickly joined in. Governor James Cox ordered the State Board of Arbitration to visit Akron and attempt a settlement, but the companies refused the board's services.[20] With the possibility of arbitration rejected by the rubber companies, angry, unorganized workers went to the I.W.W.

Events moved so rapidly that the strike came as a surprise even to the Wobblies. Prior to the strike, the I.W.W. was weak in Akron and Cleveland, and local issues were neglected in favor of the famous Wobbly strike in Paterson, New Jersey, then in full swing. Seeing the possibility of a new radical stronghold in Ohio, however, allies from the Socialist party were soon supporting Wobbly efforts to capture the organization of the Akron strike. Socialists also urged public support for a nonviolent struggle.[21]

On February 13, an I.W.W. strike committee representing the rubber workers announced that it would post pickets and intercept men going to work on the morning shift.[22] As organizational strength grew, and as the momentum of the strike increased, I.W.W. veterans from other strikes and free speech struggles throughout the United States converged on Akron.[23] Arturo Giovanitti, one of the leading Italian-language Wobbly spokesmen, noted the climate of the city when he stated that "Akron is shaken. . . . All creeds, colors, and flags are represented in the strike." Yet there was a calmness about the strikers that prompted the *Beacon Journal*, a Progressive party newspaper, to note that "not a single address was made which in any way could be calculated to inspire hatred or violence."[24] A nonviolent stance was maintained, consistent with Wobbly policy in other strikes.

Membership in the Akron I.W.W. local quickly swelled to more than 2,000. With glee a Wobbly wrote: "Haven't seen a cop since I have been here. . . and everybody says it's the most peaceful strike ever heard of. All hail the rebel proletaire! Hurrah for the strike! Less booze for the bosses! More bread for the workers!"[25] By the strike's fourth day over 12,000 workers were staying home. Strikers maintained their peaceful ways, but Akron's mayor, Frank W. Rockwell, telegraphed Governor Cox: "Situation here alarming. . . . Local authorities will be unable to cope with it if it breaks loose. Request two companies ONG [Ohio National Guard] with more available."[26] Rockwell knew from Ohio's adjutant general that guard units from Cleveland, Youngstown, and Warren were within a one-hour railroad trip of the strike.[27] Yet Governor Cox did not jump into the situation. He refused Rockwell's request for troops and offered instead the State Board of Arbitration "to establish amicable relations" in Akron. The offer was refused by the rubber industry.[28]

Despite its rejection, the board attempted to use moral suasion on the parties in the strike. One member of the board, D. H. Sullivan, a former miners' organizer with a reputation for being fair-minded, met with Akron's police chief, who told him that no trouble was expected.[28] On February 17, with I.W.W. membership now estimated at 6,000, board members met with organizers George Speed and Walter Glover, who assured arbitrators that strikers would "remain quiet." "We believe your assurances," replied the board, and "we find you a good natured crowd, not intent on violence." Such assurances were borne out by speeches made earlier in the day by Speed and Glover:

> It is not the laboring classes who resort to violence and rioting . . . It is the so-called upper classes, the capitalists, who resort to such means; they have robbed the working man and all their wealth was gained by violent, unscrupulous means. What chances has an honest man in such an age?. . .
>
> No, use no violence, boys; show the bosses that the laboring men have the brains to stand together and organize; show them that you do not depend on violent methods to gain your purpose and you are sure to win out in this strike.[29]

By February 18, the I.W.W. claimed 12,000 members out of a total of 20,000 rubber workers.[30] The situation was still peaceful and the sheriff saw no reason to act.[31] Wobblies could thus far claim control of the situation, and they paraded triumphantly with an eighteen-piece marching band followed by strikers holding signs reading "We are the I.W.W." and "Thirteen Hours Killed Father." From an exuberant atmosphere heady with momentary triumph, the I.W.W., after consulting with strikers, presented a list of grievances. The forty-two grievances touched on three areas: all employees fired because of strike participation had to be rehired; work schedules were to be an eight-hour day and a six-day week; and attention was to be given to wage increases. But despite the enthusiasm and élan, the I.W.W. had already passed its zenith. In the third week of the strike, fewer and fewer strike badges could be seen in the street. Cold weather reduced the number of pickets, and workers returned to the job. Ben Williams, Wobbly editor of *Solidarity*, had high hopes for a sustained strike, but his aspirations never materialized.[32]

When the I.W.W. strike committee called for 5,000 pickets at the Goodrich plant on February 25, only 200 showed up, met by as many police officers and deputies. The temper of the strike now changed; police, for the first time, arrested one of the strike leaders, Frank Midney, for allegedly "promoting disorder."[33]

By this time a schism had developed between workers who wanted compromise with management and the more militant strike position espoused by the I.W.W. A spokesman for workers stated that the I.W.W. alienated the strikers. Perhaps Wobbly unwillingness to make concessions disturbed some workers. On that same day, William D. Haywood visited Akron in an effort to bolster sagging morale by urging unity and nonviolence. Significantly, Haywood recognized that the strike was lagging, and thus he looked to future tactics rather than to the present condition of the strike. "If the boss starves you back to work then you. . . win this strike on the inside of the factory. Don't use the speeding-up, but the slowing-down process."[34] Despite this attempt to regroup the strike force, the rubber workers continued to lose interest in the issue. By March 3, even while the Green Committee probed the causes and grievances of the strike, workers were returning to the factories in large numbers. The emergency period was over. Mayor Rockwell, who had earlier feared the potential of the strike, now relaxed and allowed saloons to reopen.[35]

For workers, getting back to the job was more important than the goals of the I.W.W. Haywood no doubted recognized this when he spoke again in Akron on March 6. "Do not depend on the Senate Probe committee to help you," he said to an audience of 1,000. "Get out on the picket line. . . I know how anxious you are to get back to work. You are like an old horse which has been on a treadmill. It doesn't know what to do. But hold out a little longer. Don't give in." Haywood's appeal fell on deaf ears as Wobblies signed up only thirty-seven members that day. Nearly everybody had returned to their jobs.[36]

On the evening of March 7, as the strike peaked, the first serious clash occurred between police and strikers. The disorders were repeated on March 8 when, against city orders, 350 strikers picketed the Goodrich plant. To disperse the illegal picketers, sheriff's deputies charged the crowd and made seven arrests. The use of force was significant: it indicated the strong desire of those in authority to destroy the strike and showed as well their contempt for Governor Cox's conciliatory position, which insisted on the preservation of free assembly and speech.[37] Two Socialist city councilmen protested police interference, but the remainder of the council defeated their resolution.[38] When police-striker confrontation over picketing flared up again on March 11, the sheriff warned against gatherings of three or more people on streets: in short, the right to picket was denied. By now police had a new ally when prominent residents of Akron formed the Citizens Welfare Association, a deputized vigilante group led by the Reverend George P. Atwater, "Bible in one hand and a wagon spoke in the other." This mobile force of well-to-do vigilantes, with sixty automobiles at its disposal, feared the radicalism of the

I.W.W. as disruptive to the hegemony of Akron's ruling classes and forced forty to fifty Wobblies to leave the city, thus contributing to the breakup of the local union.[39] Governor Cox was asked by strikers to stop this "mob of the rich," but this time Cox had lost interest in harmony and conciliation. He refused to act.[40]

In addition to worker desertion and resistance from the Citizens Welfare Association, the Wobblies also faced opposition from the more conservative AFL, as the strike lost the support of Akron's Central Labor Union (CLU).[41] Cal Wyatt, AFL organizer who had competed with the I.W.W. for membership at earlier strikes in Little Falls, New York, and Lawrence, Massachusetts, now tried to take over the Akron strike. Under his aegis a rubber workers' local was formally organized, and its AFL members wore small American flags in contrast to the red-ribbon strike badges of the I.W.W.[42] Wyatt tried to influence public opinion against the I.W.W. by raising the issue of "radicalism." Indeed, when the Green Committee entered Akron, Wyatt stated, "I do not see how these I.W.W. people can be very anxious for such an investigation. . . as up to this time they have been stating that they cared nothing for government, and they were not expected to favor having the legislature take up this matter."[43] Wyatt's efforts at AFL organization, however, were not successful. Momentum for worker organization was destroyed with the strike and the AFL rubber workers' local had a "poorly attended" meeting. Wobblies estimated AFL membership at about 100.[44] Nonetheless, Wyatt succeeded in convincing the CLU to withdraw its support of the strike.[45] Ironically, the anti-Wobbly AFL did not endear itself to manufacturers. Goodrich and Goodyear declined negotiation even with the conservative CLU.[46]

By the third week in March, three-quarters of the striking rubber workers had returned to work. Rubber companies refused to hire Wobbly activists for fear of sabotage. The I.W.W. organization suffered another blow when the rented meeting hall closed its doors on the grounds that the place needed plastering. Moreover, Wobblies claimed that Roman Catholic priests duped their foreign-born congregants by stating that the strike was already over. On top of this, public attention was diverted to another, more pressing problem: a sudden, massive flood. By March 25, 1913, the strike came to a halt and did not flare up again.[47]

A postmortem reveals a variety of factors that caused the strike's failure and, with that failure, also the demise of the I.W.W. in Akron. The strike was spontaneous, while industry was established and well prepared with funds and law enforcement allies. Akron's chamber of commerce, rubber manufacturers, police, and two of the city's three newspapers posed formidable opposition to the I.W.W.[48] Management, reluctant to accept the State Board of Arbitration's services, vitiated whatever bargaining power the I.W.W. might have had. A minor irritant was contributed by strife between two I.W.W. organizers who had personal differences.[49] Moreover, as the strike's demise was reviewed, another factor was alleged—the use of provocateurs who worked to instigate police action against the I.W.W. Industrial espionage was not unique to Akron. It was, as federal investigators asserted, a nationwide trend used by segments of industry to infiltrate and destroy union organization. What Selig Perlman said of the Lawrence strike applied to Akron: "Hand in hand with the system of blacklisting goes a system of espionage."[50]

This was borne out when, shortly after the strike, J. W. Reid, an employee of Diamond Rubber Company, admitted that he was an operative for the corporation's auxiliary company, an industrial police group. At the same time, Reid served as the I.W.W.'s secretary-treasurer in Akron and helped keep Local No. 470 alive. Reid admitted that some officials of the local acted as industrial spies who sabotaged strike efforts. For instance, I.W.W. membership rolls were taken by industrial spies from union headquarters to the Portage Hotel, where stenographers recorded the names of union members. Another time, Reid, told to abscond with the union's treasury, had qualms of conscience and confessed all in a public affidavit.[51] It was no small wonder, then, that management and other opponents of the I.W.W. in Akron knew in advance the moves the union would make. Industrial spies were the intelligence network for the rubber industry, and law enforcement officers and the Citizens Welfare Association were its janissaries who received ample thanks: after the strike the industry trade journal reported that F. C. Shaw, vice-president of Goodrich, sent a gift of $2,000 to Akron's police department "as a slight token of. . . appreciation for services rendered, not so much to ourselves as to the city generally."[52]

More to the point, the Akron rubber workers were usually ignorant of or indifferent to I.W.W. ideology; the union offered an escape valve for immediate frustrations and tensions, but that was as far as the I.W.W. reached. The overwhelming majority of strikers who joined the I.W.W. during the strike did so without any real knowledge of Wobbly doctrine. One worker epitomized this sentiment when he told the Green Committee that he signed up with the Wobblies without even reading its constitution. The worker simply believed that the I.W.W. would secure better working conditions.[53] The I.W.W., as it looked back on its failure in Akron, attributed defeat to the strikers themselves. "The American striker," noted an I.W.W. writer, "is unschooled. . . in picketing and unamenable to the mass enthusiasms which mean so much to the success of the strike. The American temperament is too phlegmatically individualistic."[54] In short, the issue in Akron was the creation of union organization to respond to local and immediate issues in the rubber factories. The Akron strike magnified the difficulties of union organization and bargaining in an environment that lacked a tradition of worker solidarity.

The I.W.W.'s last stand in Akron consisted of a letter both angry and sarcastic from Frank Dawson, Wobbly publicity director, to Mayor Rockwell:

> This day is April Fool's day. That is why I write to the man who, holding the highest political office, has proven himself the biggest ass since the poor animal died, that Jesus rode into Jerusalem on. I have adhered to the motto, "Appropriateness is the first of virtues."[55]

Aside from his obvious frustration, Dawson's letter also revealed a misreading of the rubber industry's workers. Not only were many of them too "individualistic," as the I.W.W. observed, but many were deeply rooted as well to traditional values that enabled them to accept, stoically, life on this earth devoid of the quest for the radical and visionary long-range goals of the I.W.W. The Akron rubber workers' apparent radicalism in 1913 seemed more of a consequence of specific grievances against the rubber industry than a radical alienation from deeply rooted values. That, even more than the vigilantes and police, destroyed the Wobbly effort at organization in Akron. Mayor Rockwell refused, after the end of the strike, to grant the Wobblies a permit for street meetings;[56] Akron's I.W.W. remained dormant until prodded and harassed by the federal government during the Great War.

Yet, the Wobblies were not a failure in Akron. Despite their apparent defeat, achievements were gained by the rubber workers. Between 1914 and 1920 rubber workers, without union support, gained the eight-hour day, voluntary factory sanitary regulations, and "the big money" from lucrative war contracts. With the exception of Goodyear's "Industrial Republic," a company union, Akron rubber workers remained unorganized until the advent of the New Deal.[57] Though rubber workers secured the eight-hour day and higher wages, the fact remained that without unionization the rubber companies refused to respond to the problems caused by industrial poisoning from lead, analine coal-tar, benzol, naphtha, carbon disulphide, and phenol poisoning.[58]

The I.W.W. impulse was, in a limited vein, successful over twenty years after the strike. Industrial union democracy came to partial fruition in the 1930s through the CIO and the modest success of the Wobblies themselves; for in the 1930s the Wobblies—or at least a rebellious faction of the Wobblies—*did* succeed in organizing within the I.W.W. fold as Metal and Machinery Workers Industrial Union No. 440 and made gains in Cleveland's metal-fabricating shops. Yet, for every gain there was a loss: in making collective bargaining a reality for the I.W.W. in Ohio in the 1930s, and in signing contracts with the employer class, No. 440, by virtue of its tactics (which tried to synthesize long-range revolutionary goals with pragmatic job unionism), was forced to disaffiliate from the I.W.W.[59] The "rebel proletaire" of the rubber strike had, by the 1930s, come a long way via a circuitous route. But the 1930s were long removed from the rubber strike of 1913, which was short-lived. Almost four months after the end of the strike, Akron's feeble local made a plea for direct action and the inevitability of the historical process:

> If you dam up the river of progress, at your peril and cost let it be.
> That river will seaward without you; Twill break down your dam and be free.
> And we heed not thy pitiful barriers/That you in its way have downcast;
> For your efforts but add to the torrent/Whose flood must o'erwhelm you at last.[60]

But the dam did not break, nor did the apocalypse occur. For in the 1930s New Deal NRA codes, the Wagner Act, and organized labor eventually secured many of the specific demands of the Wobblies, but in the process the I.W.W. program was stripped of its radical implications.

Endnotes

[1] "The Story of the I.W.W.," *One Big Union Monthly* 2 (April 1920), 46 (reprinted New York, 1968).

[2] Harold S. Roberts, *The Rubber Workers: Labor Organization and Collective Bargaining in the Rubber Industry* (New York, 1944), p. 8.

[3] *Solidarity*, March 1, 8, 1913; letter from Paul Sebestyen to Roy T. Wortman. Sebestyen was a Hungarian I.W.W. organizer in Ohio.

[4] Harvey S. Firestone, *Men and Rubber: The Story of Business* (New York, 1926), p. 13.

[5] Alfred Leif, *The Firestone Story* (New York, 1951), pp. 67–70.

[6] *India Rubber World*, 57 (April 1913), 365–66.

[7] *Solidarity*, March 8, 1913.

[8] Selig Perlman and Philip Taft, *Labor Movements*, in John R. Commons, ed., *History of Labor in the United States, 1896–1932* (New York, 1935), 4, p. 277.

[9] *India Rubber World*, 57 (March 1, 1913), 301–02.

[10] Senate Resolution No. 29, in Ohio, Eightieth General Assembly, Senate, *Journal* (1913), 103, p. 247. Green's resolution to investigate the strike and to subpoena witnesses for testimony was adopted in the state senate by a vote of 30 to 3. Green (1870–1952) served as secretary-treasurer of the United Mine Workers, 1912–1924, and became president of the AFL in 1924.

[11] "Majority and Minority Reports of the Senate Select Committee appointed to investigate causes and circumstances of the strike of employees of the Akron Rubber Industries," in ibid., appendix, pp. 207–8. Hereafter cited as the Green Committee Report.

[12] Ibid., pp. 208–9, 211.

[13] *Akron Beacon Journal*, February 13, 1913. For an individual case of a wage cut, and for complaints on unsanitary conditions, see O. S. Miller's testimony to the Green Committee, *Akron Beacon Journal*, March 5, 1913. Discontent over the piecework system is best seen in the testimony of A. E. Mapes and Elizabeth Bryan, ibid., March 10, 1913.

[14] *Solidarity*, August 17, 1912.

[15] Ibid., February 8, 1913.

[16] "The Story of the I.W.W.," 44.

[17] *Akron Beacon Journal*, February 12, 13, 1913; *Solidarity*, February 22, 1913.

[18] *Akron Beacon Journal*, February 13, 1913.

[19] Green Committee Report, p. 207; *Solidarity*, February 22, 1913; *Akron Beacon Journal*, February 15, 1913.

[20] "The Story of the I.W.W.," 44–45.

[21] *Solidarity*, February 22, 1913; *Akron Beacon Journal*, February 13, 1913.

[22] Letter from Paul Sebestyen to Roy T. Wortman.

[23] *India Rubber World*, 47 (March 1, 1913), 301; *Akron Beacon Journal*, February 13, 1913.

[24] *Solidarity*, February 12, 1913.

[25] *Akron Beacon Journal*, February 15, 1913.

[26] Ibid.

[27] *Akron Beacon Journal*, February 15, 1913; *Solidarity*, March 1, 1913; Green Committee Report, p. 207.

[28] *Akron Beacon Journal*, February 17, 1913.

[29] Ibid.

[30] Ibid., February 18, 1913.

[31] Ibid., February 19, 1913.

[32] *Solidarity*, March 1, 1913.

[33] *Akron Beacon Journal*, February 26, 1913.

[34] Leslie H. Marcy, "800 Percent and the Akron Strike," *International Socialist Review*, 13 (April 1913), 723.

[35] *Akron Beacon Journal*, March 3, 1913.

[36] Ibid., March 6, 1913.

[37] Ibid., March 7, 8, 1913; Marcy, "800 Percent," 724.

[38] *Akron Beacon Journal*, March 11, 1913.

[39] Ibid., March 12, 13, 1913; *India Rubber World*, 47 (April 1, 1913), 365; *Solidarity*, March 22, 1913; Hugh Allen, *The House of Goodyear: Fifty Years of Men and Rubber* (Akron, 1949), p. 172.

[40] *Akron Beacon Journal*, March 13, 1913.

[41] Ibid., March 15, 1913.

[42] Ibid., March 1, 1913.

[43] Ibid., February 26, 1913.

[44] Ibid., February 25, 1913; *Industrial Worker*, March 6, 1913.

[45] Ibid., February 20, 1913; March 15, 1913.

[46] Ibid., March 20, 1913.

[47] *India Rubber World*, 47 (April 1, 1913), 366; *Akron Beacon Journal*, March 22, 25, 1913; *Industrial Worker*, April 3, 1913.

[48] Letter from Paul Sebestyen to Roy T. Wortman.

[49] "The Story of the I.W.W.," 46.

[50] Selig Perlman, "Preliminary Report on an Investigation of the Relations between Labor and Capital in the Textile Industry of New England," (1914), United States Industrial Relations Commission, unpublished report, Wisconsin Historical Society; Daniel O'Reagan, "Memoranda and Reports on Field Investigation of Private Detective Agencies, May 17, 1914," in USIRC, unpublished reports, National Archives and Records Service, Record Group 174, contains recommendations for curbing professional strikebreaking agencies; letter from Paul Sebestyen to Roy T. Wortman; for an illustrative document giving methods of operation in Ohio, see *United Mine Workers' Journal*, 25 (April 1, 1915).

[51] *Solidarity*, January 17, 1914; "The Story of the I.W.W.," 46.

[52] *India Rubber World*, 47 (June 1, 1913), 480.

[53] *Akron Beacon Journal*, March 10, 1913.

[54] "The Story of the I.W.W.," 45.

[55] *Akron Beacon Journal*, April 1, 1913.

[56] *Akron Beacon Journal*, May 27, 1913.

[57] Howard and Ralph Wolf, *Rubber: A Story of Glory and Greed* (New York, 1936), p. 507.

[58] Alice Hamilton, "Industrial Poisons Used in the Rubber Industry," U.S. Bureau of Labor Statistics, *Bulletin* No. 179 (October 1915), p. 9; Rey Vincent Luce, "Analine Poisoning in the Rubber Industry of Akron, Ohio," in ibid., appendix pp. 57–58; Rey Vincent Luce and Alice Hamilton, "Industrial Analine Poisoning in the United States," U.S. Bureau of Labor Statistics, *Monthly Review*, 2 (June 1916), pp. 1–12; and Emery R. Hayhurst, *A Survey of Industrial Health—Hazards and Occupational Diseases in Ohio* (Columbus, 1915), pp. 206–29.

[59] Roy T. Wortman, "The Resurgence of the I.W.W. in Cleveland," *Northwest Ohio Quarterly*, 47 (Winter 1974–1975), 20–29.

[60] *Solidarity*, July 12, 1913.

Chapter 6

Walter F. White[1]

Robert L. Zangrado

Walter Francis White (1 July 1893–21 Mar. 1955), civil rights leader, was born in Atlanta, Georgia, the son of George Washington White, a mail carrier, and Madeline Harrison, a teacher. His middle-class, African-American family took seriously its obligations to the black community, even though they all shared features and skin color that made them appear white. After graduating from Atlanta University in 1916, White worked for the Standard Life Insurance Company for almost two years.

When the Atlanta school board threatened to discontinue seventh-grade classes for black students (who already were barred from public high schools), White helped to mount a community protest and to found the Atlanta branch of the National Association for the Advancement of Colored People (NAACP). In 1917 James Weldon Johnson of the NAACP's headquarters staff came to assist the local effort and took an immediate liking to White and secured his appointment as assistant executive secretary in the NAACP headquarters in January 1918. White held that post until 1929, when he became the acting—and in 1931 the permanent—executive secretary.

White was an outgoing and energetic leader and exhibited a fierce attachment to the NAACP's program for racial justice. His Caucasian-like features facilitated his courageous investigation of over forty lynchings and numerous race riots. Given the widespread racism and hatred of the time, the NAACP could hardly reverse racial discrimination in education, housing, employment, voting, and public transportation. Instances of mob violence, however, forced some white Americans at least to realize the need for reform. Driving the message home with press releases, conferences, exhibits, and public rallies, the NAACP lobbied Congress for an antilynching law. White and Johnson, who became executive secretary of the NAACP in 1920, were central to this campaign. The antilynching bill passed the House of Representatives on three occasions (1922, 1937, and 1940) but failed in the Senate each time because of actual or threatened filibusters.

Along with his senior NAACP colleagues Johnson and W. E. B. Du Bois, White encouraged and promoted the careers of the black writers, artists, and performers of the Harlem Renaissance. Moreover, White was part of it himself as the author of two novels, *The Fire in the Flint* (1924) and *Flight* (1926), and the classic study of lynching *Rope and Faggot: A Biography of Judge Lynch* (1929), written while on a Guggenheim Fellowship.

When White assumed leadership of the NAACP in 1931, the depression had eroded membership fees and contributions. Furthermore, the association faced intense competition from the Communist Party–USA, which was competing openly with the NAACP for African-American support. The two organizations clashed publicly over the 1931 Scottsboro case, when both tried to secure the exclusive rights to represent the defendants in court. White's animus toward the party and its tactics never receded, and he maintained a relentlessly anti-Communist posture, especially during the Cold War of the late 1940s and the 1950s.

It was during the New Deal years, however, that White began allying the NAACP with other progressive forces in the quest for equal rights. The 1930 Supreme Court nomination of John J. Parker, who had made racist remarks early in his career, prompted White and the NAACP to join the American Federation of Labor in defeating the appointment. When the Senate narrowly rejected Parker's nomination by two votes, White's stature and that of the NAACP rose accordingly. During the 1930s White, as executive secretary, also oversaw the implementation of the NAACP's plan for systematic litigation against discrimination, a campaign formulated by the NAACP Legal Defense and Educational Fund, Inc., and executed in the courts by Thurgood Marshall. At the same time, White wed the association to a number of liberal, labor, ethnic, women's, church, and civil liberties organizations in a shared pursuit of social justice. This coalition flourished under his guidance and shaped the goals and strategies of the civil rights movement into the 1990s.

White had a global perspective as well. In 1921 he attended the Second Pan-African Congress in London, Brussels, and Paris, which put him in direct contact with black leaders from Africa, the Caribbean, and the United States. All his life he worked for greater home rule and economic investment in the Caribbean. During and after World War II, he was a steady advocate of independence for India. Anxious to investigate the treatment of African-American troops, he went to England, North Africa, and Italy as a war correspondent in 1944. His findings were published in *A Rising Wind* (1945). A similar trip took him to Australia, the Philippines, and the South Pacific in 1945. On his return, he served as a consultant to the U.S. delegation at the founding conference of the United Nations in San Francisco and the 1948 General Assembly sessions in Paris.

After World War II White used his weekly columns in the Chicago *Defender* and in several major metropolitan dailies to argue that the war against fascism and America's competition with the Soviet Union for Third World allies only underscored the urgency of racial justice at home. White's prescriptions included desegregation of the military, fair employment practices, elimination of poll taxes, antilynching legislation, and voting rights for the District of Columbia. He helped to convince President Harry S. Truman to endorse them during his 1948 campaign.

White's final years were busy but not problem-free. An autobiography, *A Man Called White* (1948), was well received, but while working on the book he suffered the first of several heart attacks. In June 1949 White and his wife of twenty-seven years, Leah Gladys Powell, with whom he had two children, divorced. His second marriage within a week to Poppy Cannon, a successful white public relations consultant and food editor, provoked a storm of protest, not the least among African-American journalists and some NAACP board members, who worried about middle-class sensibilities and the NAACP's reputation.

Matters within the NAACP were further complicated in the early 1950s by personality and policy disagreements between White and two colleagues, Roy Wilkins, the assistant executive secretary who succeeded White as executive secretary in April 1955, and Thurgood Marshall. These were reminiscent of the more public and explosive clashes that White had had with Du Bois in 1934 (over the latter's advocacy of a separate African-American economic system) and in 1948 (when Du Bois openly championed the third-party candidacy of Henry A. Wallace for president). Such conflicts with his NAACP associates added to White's reputation among detractors as arrogant and self-serving. White died in his New York City home. His sixth book, *How Far the Promised Land?*, appeared posthumously in 1955.

BIBLIOGRAPHY

White's papers and those of Poppy Cannon White are in the James Weldon Johnson Collection at the Beinecke Rare Book and Manuscript Library at Yale University. The files of the NAACP at the Manuscript Division of the Library of Congress are indispensable for any evaluation of White's career. No scholarly and comprehensive biography currently exists, but one may consult Poppy Cannon, *A Gentle Knight: My Husband, Walter White* (1956); Edward E. Waldron, *Walter White and the Harlem Renaissance* (1978); and Robert L. Zangrando, *The NAACP Crusade Against Lynching, 1909–1950* (1980). Helpful as well are E. J. Kahn, Jr., "Profiles: The Frontal Attack," *New Yorker*, 4 Sept. 1948, pp. 28–32 and 34–38, and 11 Sept. 1948, pp. 38–40 and 42–46. Nathaniel Patrick Tillman, Jr., "Walter Francis White: A Study in Interest Group Leadership" (Ph.D. diss., Univ. of Wisconsin, 1961). Obituaries are in the *New York Times*, 22 Mar. 1955; *Crisis*, Apr. 1955; and *Journal of Negro History* (July 1955). *Phylon: The Atlanta University Review of Race and Culture* published a series of eulogies in its Sept. 1955 issue.

Endnotes

[1] This article originally appeared in *American National Biography*, vol. 23. Eds. John A. Garraty and Mark C. Carnes. New York: Oxford University Press, 1999: 246–48. Reprinted by permission of the author, the publisher, and the American Council of Learned Societies.

Chapter 7

Planning Parks in the Seventies: Federal and Provincial Parks in the Gaspé

Howard Reinmuth Jr.

The "Quiet Revolution" of the 1960s in Québec inaugurated a passion for planning that matched, if indeed it did not surpass, that of concurrent federal planners in Ottawa. Both teams of planners were particularly interested in using their professional skills to bring marginalized areas like Québec's Gaspé region into the mainstream of economic development. Under the Bureau d'amanègement de l'est du Québec (BAEQ), the Gaspé became a pilot region, a kind of human laboratory for economic planning. Meanwhile, as the planners did their work, 82,000 Gaspésians emigrated in the decade 1961–71 in search of employment.

The Gaspé is a distinct region despite being linked by the Québec government for administrative purposes with the Lower St. Lawrence (Bas St Laurent) and its capital, Rimouski. Geographically the Gaspé is a peninsula jutting into the Gulf of St. Lawrence, a region redolent with associations with Jacques Cartier, yet little settled until the nineteenth century. Then a pattern developed: francophones settled the north coast; anglophones, especially from Jersey and Ireland, the south coast.

In modern times a highway and railroad cut across the base of the peninsula from Mont Joli to Matapédia, connecting the ends of the coastal road that traverses the periphery of the Gaspé. In 1911 a railway was completed from Matapédia to Gaspé, connecting at the former with the line from Halifax to

Montreal of what became in the 1920s the Canadian National.[1] The interior of the peninsula has always been nearly devoid of population.

Along the coast, however, a distinctive way of life developed similar to that in other areas of Québec and elsewhere in eastern Canada. This subsistence mode of living combined seasonal fishing (above all for cod, which was then salted and dried), cultivation of root crops (potatoes, carrots, turnips), collection of berries, and tapping of maple syrup, hunting, and cutting timber, chiefly in winter.[2] This pattern developed most commonly in isolated settled areas or in regions of Québec newly opened to colonization. It was a way of life not suited to production for markets nor to providing twentieth-century standards of education and social services.

Within the Gaspé region, two areas exemplified this mode of existence: Forillon peninsula and Bonaventure Island. By combining them, the ethnic and religious composition of the Gaspé can be discerned. Forillon, on the north coast, consisted mainly of francophone Roman Catholics living in scattered fishing villages with a few Protestant anglophones, usually storekeepers, among them. Bonaventure Island was, like the south coast, inhabited mainly by anglophone Irish and Jerseyites, usually Roman Catholics.

Historically, Bonaventure Island had attracted worldwide attention in the early twentieth century when an international convention was signed to protect the migratory birds there.[3] A federal statute to implement this convention was subsequently enacted in Ottawa in 1919. Henceforth the island was divided into three parts: the rookeries on the east side, under federal protection; an intermediate, uninhabited zone of woods; and a small area facing Percé on the mainland, where the island's inhabitants lived. A few visitors came to the island in the summer to observe the birds. After World War II artists also came. Some of the visitors, mostly Americans, purchased property there as the islanders gradually moved to the mainland.

Only in 1950 was there accommodation for visitors in an inn.[4] But by that date the island had been linked with Percé by telephone, postal service, and small boats. Meanwhile, Forillon peninsula had remained in isolation, devoid of a road around the peninsula, with fishing villages linked by boat and trails only.

I

The defeat of the Union Nationale in the 1960 Québec election and the return of the Liberals under Jean Lesage ended the long era of *Duplessisme* marked by frequent clashes between Québec and Ottawa. Then in the 1962 federal election Diefenbaker's Progressive-Conservatives were defeated and the Liberals were returned to power for a long period during the ministries of Lester Pearson and, after 1968, of Pierre Trudeau. An era of federal cooperation with Québec replaced an era of confrontation. The new Québec government was willing to accept federal money for joint projects such as parks. Planners in both Ottawa and Québec conceived new projects aimed at rapid economic development of previously remote and economically neglected areas.

The creation of the two parks required a degree of cooperation between Ottawa and Québec. In the case of Bonaventure Island, this cooperation already existed because of shared jurisdiction but, nevertheless, could lead to conflict as well. In the founding of Forillon Park a greater degree of cooperation was required because the issues there were more complex.

In 1961 the Diefenbaker government passed an act to further regional development, generally known by its acronym, ARDA (Agricultural and Regional Development Act). This act became the basis for the creation in 1963 of BAEQ, a private non-profit corporation. Young, enthusiastic, university-educated planners were among the first to propose a park for the Gaspé, specifically for the Forillon peninsula.[5] They were also among the first to discuss creating a provincial park on Bonaventure Island.[6] Planners saw these parks as part of a larger project to develop this neglected region.

In doing so, the strategists of the BAEQ were taking a contrary approach to one earlier recommended by the Gordon Commission Report of 1958. The concept in this report was to move people to jobs, specifically to move workers in the declining coal-mining industry in the Maritimes to industrial centers like Montréal and Toronto. On the contrary, the BAEQ reports projected instead creating jobs where the people lived through government and, to some extent, private investment, and by providing training or retraining of workers at government expense. As well, BAEQ saw relocation for those in remote parishes they proposed to close or those who were expropriated as very small in both spatial terms and concerning the numbers involved—hundreds of families at Forillon Park, dozens at Bonaventure Island. They failed to appreciate that a move of even a few miles could prove profoundly unsettling to people whose world was so circumscribed.

The planners' task was as daunting as the need for action was urgent. In 1963 the income per person in Québec was 87% of the national average, or C$1,310. But that of the Gaspé was only 41% of the national average, or C$623 per person.[7]

The BAEQ proposed three successive five-year plans: 1967–1972, 1972–1977, and 1977–1982. They expected Percé to play "un role moteur pour l'ensemble de la région."[8] This supposed that tourists would make a complete circuit of the Gaspé peninsula. They also projected that the 225,000 tourists of 1964 (one-third of whom were in fact visiting relatives and friends) would increase to between 500,000 and 600,000 by 1977, thereby creating 700 permanent and 2,300 temporary new jobs.[9] The large number of temporary jobs reflected the reality that almost all of the tourists came in about ten weeks, from late June to Labor Day. (The BAEQ planners hoped to extend the season in June and September.) They expected the average tourist to spend at least one week in the Gaspé. The planners foresaw the need for a variety of new facilities to serve tourist needs more adequately: more hotels and better restaurants; camping facilities; youth hostels.[10]

In order to establish parks like Forillon, the BAEQ expected to use expropriations to clear part of the land.[11] This would prove to be one of their most controversial recommendations. In general, they expected to make of tourism "une activité dynamique nouvelle," provided that more tourists came to the Gaspé and that they prolonged their average length of stay.[12] Of course the BAEQ made many proposals about other sectors of the economy—fishing, for example—but tourism was the principal area to affect the creation of new parks.

The planners also suggested that the government of Québec buy Bonaventure Island "en tout ou en partie" as a bird sanctuary and as part of the development of the Percé zone.[13] The planning by the BAEQ has been described by Prof. Jean-Claude Robert as "la plus pousée au Canada."[14] The total amount to be expended in the first phase, more than C$250 million, seemed at the time a very large commitment. The full text of the plan, 2,500 pages plus 40 technical annexes, appeared in 1965. Not until 1968 did the governments in Ottawa and Québec agree in principle to implement the plan. By this time a new "dynamique" had entered the picture: Jean Chrétien was now Minister of Indian Affairs and Northern Development (1968–1974), a ministry that included Parks Canada. He saw parks, hitherto almost exclusively a western phenomenon, as one means of bringing the federal presence closer to the people of Québec. In short, parks were part of the Trudeau government's policy of bilingual federalism. Chrétien was instrumental in obtaining a federal park in the Mauricie near his home in Shawinigan. He also decided to realize the project for Forillon Park.[15]

In 1969, in pursuance of the 1968 accord, the Caisse de Financement pour l'Est de Québec was established with 75% federal and 25% provincial funding. That action paved the way for the final agreement between Ottawa and Québec in October 1970, which included plans for both Forillon and Bonaventure Island. By October 1971 the first provisional plan for Forillon had been prepared by Parks Canada, pursuant to which public hearings were held in Gaspé and Rimouski on November 17 and 19. In that same year the expropriations began. The 1970 agreement had provided that the Québec government would expropriate the necessary lands to create Forillon Park and compensate the private owners. The lands would then be deeded at no cost to the federal government with a clear title.[16] The requisite Québec statute, law 29 of July 17, 1970, gave the provincial government its authority.[17] Thus the expropriations could begin at Forillon as they did in the same year on Bonaventure Island.

In contrast to the BAEQ's plan to bring jobs to people was the fact that, between 1961 and 1971, some 82,000 people emigrated from the Gaspé, mainly to Montréal. According to a survey made in 1967 by the Québec newspaper *Le Soleil*, 75–80% of young Gaspésians who had finished a course of work or in technology left the region to seek work elsewhere.[18]

II

At Forillon, the expropriations were originally projected to cost C$850,000–1,000,000. They were subsequently described by Guy Dorion, president of the expropriation tribunal, as virtually without precedent in the history of Québec, for they involved 59,000 acres of land (about 92 square miles), 205 families, 2,500 parcels of land.[19] Most of the families came from small, isolated fishing villages. At the time these expropriations were proposed to Jean Chrétien, a minority report was submitted by Bernard Major (now administrator of Bonaventure Island) proposing that instead of expropriations, the local people be used for interpretation and permitted to remain in their homes. M. Major pointed out that some of the people at Grand Grève had never been anywhere except by boat. He claimed, indeed, that of those relocated at Cap Rosier and Gaspé, some had died within a year or two as a result of being uprooted.[20]

The situation on Bonaventure Island was different. There, the inhabitants had no warning of the impending expropriation. Sydney Maloney, the island's chief entrepreneur and proprietor of its only inn, was stunned by a letter from the Ministry of Public Works in Québec in September 1971 announcing the expropriation without appeal. When the evaluators came, according to a francophone guest at Mr. Maloney's inn, they began to cheat him because he didn't understand French. So she asked to act as an interpreter on his behalf in order to protect his interests.[21]

There is disagreement concerning a related matter: the alleged threat posed by Americans acquiring land on the island. In the official 1985 booklet concerning Bonaventure Island issued by the ministry of Loisir, Chasse et Pêche, it is stated that over a period of thirty years, more than one-half of the island had been acquired by Americans. In 1968, therefore, a search of titles revealed "le danger criant de l'appropriation en trangère d'un element très significatif du patrimoine national québécois."[22] But M. Bernard Lavergne of Loisir, Chasse et Pêche told me in 1987 that American ownership only became apparent through title searches *after* the government decision to acquire the island had been made.[23]

The most important influence on the payment of expropriations was totally unforeseen—the first OPEC oil embargo and the sudden onset of double-digit inflation. When the impact of these developments began to be felt, those expropriated claimed they should have been paid more money. Lawsuits in the courts by those expropriated at Forillon followed, made possible by the creation of a new tribunal to hear them, and a political decision was made by the Bourassa government to increase the amounts awarded. William Tetley, later a professor of law at McGill University, was then Minister of Public Works (1975–76). He flew to Gaspé, where he was met by a hostile crowd clamoring for increased compensation. In the end an additional C$1,000,000 was appropriated, double the original amount: more, Professor Tetley thinks, than the lands in Forillon were worth.[24]

The Gaspésians then took their revenge in the 1976 election by throwing out the Liberal deputy for Gaspé and electing a member of the Union Nationale instead. It was, however, the Parti Québécois that won the election and formed its first government. That party subsequently won the Gaspé seat in the 1981 election.[25]

Concerning Bonaventure Island, there was disagreement about compensation. Sydney Maloney received C$100,000 for his property. In inflationary conditions, this amount did not suffice to purchase his present inn at Le Coin-du Banc and furnish it, yet M. Lavergne of Loisir, Chasse et Pêche told me that Mr. Maloney had been "très grassement payé."[26] The fundamental problem was the rapid rise of inflation subsequent to the initial fixing of compensation.

III

The development of Forillon Park proceeded so that by 1977 there were more than 500,000 visitors just as the BAEQ had originally projected. Of these, 87% were Québécois and nearly one-third came in July. According to the *Plan Directeur* of 1978, the capacity of the park was then to have been 1,418 campers and 6,732 visitors per day in summer, and 1,125 visitors per day in winter. By 1985, the park was to have been completed. Its theme was "l'harmonie entre l'homme, la terre et la mer."[27]

During the same years in the 1970s, there was discord between the federal government and Québec concerning Bonaventure Island. Initially, the island was given the curious status of a hunting preserve; only in 1975 did it become a park. Most of the buildings on the island, including Sydney Maloney's inn, were burned to the ground. Only 14 of 47 structures remained.[28] One thing the closure of the island had ensured was additional traffic for Percé in terms of accommodations, meals, and souvenirs.

Part of the federal-provincial conflict was finally resolved in 1981 by an accord concerning migratory birds. Before this date visitors to Bonaventure Island and the interpretation center near Percé had been confused by the two uniforms of employees of Parks Canada and Loisir, Chasse et Pêche. Subsequent to the agreement federal employees withdrew both from the island and from the Visitors' Center.

In 1985, there was an additional agreement concerning the wharf on Bonaventure Island, which had been under federal jurisdiction. The federal government spent more than C$100,000 to repair the wharf and then turned it over to Loisir, Chasse et Pêche.[29] That ministry then integrated Bonaventure Island in its entirety into its system of parks by decree 148-85 of January 23, 1985.[30]

IV

The aftermath of the establishment of Forillon Park and of the Bonaventure Island Park saw reaction against certain aspects of the planning for the parks, above all the expropriations. In some respects, this negative reaction concerned the human cost and the feeling that the mainly youthful, university-educated planners were abstracted from reality, and even that they were guilty of arrogance toward the vulnerable people whose lives they caused to be uprooted. One must also remember that it was the politicians against whom people directed their greatest anger. The electors could remove the politicians from office, whereas they could not dismiss the bureaucrats in Québec and Ottawa.

The people whom I interviewed who participated to some degree in the process of establishing the parks generally shared negative opinions from several points of view. William Tetley, then Québec Minister of Public Works, told me he felt Ottawa had been indifferent both to the rights of the people affected and to provincial rights. He considered the policy of expropriation to have been wrong and its implementation to have been a disaster.[31] M. Bernard Lavergne of Loisir, Chasse et Pêche told me that the experience had made politicians more sensitive in these human matters. There are no longer any expropriations.[32]

The effects on individuals expropriated were often devastating. Sydney Maloney told me that after expropriation his sister Agnes had purchased a mobile home rather than a house so that she could move if the government again confiscated her property. And Lise Deguire said that not a day goes by without his thinking about the island.[33]

In the same vein, Jules Bélanger related a story about an old man who was expropriated from Forillon Park. Although he was relocated only three miles from his former home, he longed to return. He spoke feelingly about watching his brother's home being burned. (Mr. Tetley explained to me that this was done because the park was legally "dead" once the people had been relocated.[34]) One of his fellows also expropriated at Forillon told the old man, "on vivra pas vieux icitte."[35]

In a related matter, as M. Bélanger pointed out, much money was spent preparing citizens for jobs that did not exist in the region. In fact, he considered that much of this money was little more than disguised social assistance. There had been a hope—vain in the event—that the Gaspé would cease to export workers and export instead the products of their labor.[36] Young people nevertheless continued to leave the region to seek employment in the cities.

If one takes broader contexts than those of the parks into account, one finds a growing opposition in this period to some kinds of planning that had been taking place in Canada for decades. One such project that affected the Gaspé was the closure of remote areas, outlying farms, and villages, and the removal of people to more populated places where education and social services could more easily be provided. These closures had begun pursuant to proposals of the BAEQ and were provided for in the 1968 accord between Ottawa and Québec. Entire parishes were closed; buildings were burned and people relocated. Among the "victims" there was much disillusionment and anger. By 1976 there were evident electoral implications.[37]

The same policies had been implemented by the Smallwood government in Newfoundland after Confederation. Large areas on the thinly populated south shore of the island, and many isolated islands and villages elsewhere, were closed and the people relocated to larger communities where roads to the outside world were built and social services provided. In the process, the previous way of life based upon seasonal fishing, growing of root crops, and winter cutting of timber was eliminated. As a result, many people had only seasonal, if any, employment and existed on welfare from Ottawa the greater part of the year.

Professor Jean-Claude Robert told me he did not know of a single instance anywhere in the transatlantic world where comprehensive planning like that of the BAEQ has succeeded in bringing an area like the Gaspé up to the same level of economic development as a more advanced area.[38] Perhaps the most striking postwar example, admittedly a special case, is Italy's Mezzogiorno, where the central government poured billions of dollars into the economy, as a result of which the Mafia became wealthy and remained powerful and millions of people migrated to northern Italy in search of employment.

V

Nowadays, the parks at Forillon and on Bonaventure Island require modest amounts of planning but receive substantial amounts of competent administration. For hundreds of thousands of people annually, a visit to the parks is a great pleasure. Summer employment has afforded thousands of young people marvelous experiences over the years. Yet the broader hopes of the BAEQ planners have not been realized. There has been no significant increase in permanent jobs in tourism, for example, and most of the temporary jobs with Parks Canada in Forillon and with Loisir, Chasse et Pêche on Bonaventure Island have been filled by university students on summer holiday. For those in the tourist business, the high season remains June 24 (St. Jean Baptiste) to Labor Day with only modest numbers of visitors in May–June and in September. I have seen for myself that Percé is virtually a ghost town in winter, a very depressed and depressing place.

The fishing industry is still small and local. Since virtually all major matters concerning fishing are now international, the principal responsibility for them is at the federal level. One interesting project in the Gaspé involves raising salmon commercially and smoking them for the nearly insatiable market in northern Europe, especially Germany. As of 1988, this project had substantial support from the Québec government.

The Bourassa government in Québec followed a policy of privatization and also of devolving control of some facilities outside the parks to local units.

For example, the hotel and cooking school at Ft. Prével were privatized, while the camping ground at Carleton was turned over to the municipality.[39]

Thus the planning of Forillon Park of Parks Canada and Bonaventure Island Park of the government of Québec resulted in well-conceived, much-frequented facilities. How does one weigh in balance the advantages of this planning for the many against the costs in human suffering to the few? Was Bernard Major correct in saying that the planning could have been done so that the human costs could have been avoided? Such questions will probably always be raised without definitive answers.

Endnotes

[1] Bélanger, Jules, Desjardins, Marc, and Frenette, Jean-Yves, *Histoire de la Gaspésie* (Montréal, 1981), p. 466.

[2] Parcs Canada, Région du Québec, Planification, Parc Forillon, *Plan Directeur* (1978), 2.1.2.2.

[3] Québec: Ministère de Loisir, de la Chasse et de la Pêche, *Le Parc de l'Ile Bonaventure et du Rocher Percé* (1985), p. 10.

[4] Thibeault, Lucie, "L'Ile Bonaventure au temps des Indulaires," *Gaspésie* XXIII no. 2 (1985), p. 17.

[5] Prof. Jean-Claude Robert, a former minister of Indian and Northern Affairs, said that there was a "Conseil d'Orientation Economique en Gaspésie" before 1960 and that the Québec Liberal Party (PLQ) platform of 1960 contained proposals for economic development in the Gaspé. Interview with Jean-Claude Robert, March 8, 1984.

[6] For planners see *ibid*. For BAEQ: *Plan de Développement*, cahier 5 (4) 123.

[7] Bélanger, *Histoire de la Gaspésie*, 774 n. 1.

[8] BAEQ, *Plan*, cahier 5, ch. 3, 39.

[9] *Ibid.*

[10] *Ibid.*, 14.

[11] *Ibid.*, 49.

[12] *Ibid.*

[13] *Ibid.*, 123.

[14] Interview with Jean-Claude Robert, March 8, 1984.

[15] Interview with William Tetley, March 6, 1984.

[16] Québec: Ministère des Travaux Publics, Projêt du Parc Forillon, Acquisition des Terrains, Prôjet d'Entente Féderale-Provinciale art. 55 (26 mai 1968).

[17] Lois du Québec 1970 ch. 32.

[18] BAEQ: *Plan de Développement*, cahier 7, ch. 4, 2. Bélanger, *Histoire de la Gaspésie*, 774 n.1.

[19] *Les Recueils de Jurisprudence du Tribunal del'Expropriation* (decisions de la Règie des services publics) Tom I (1973), publié 1975.

[20] Interview with Bernard Major, June 3, 1987. Parks Canada proposed Grand Grève to illustrate the life of the fisherman-cultivator—without, of course, any of the people! Parcs Canada, Parc Forillon, *Plan Directeur*, 2.2.2.2.5.

[21] Interview with Lise Deguire, May 27, 1987.

[22] Québec: Loisir, Chasse et Pêche, *L'Ile Bonaventure*, 10–11.

[23] Interview with Bernard Lavergne, June 11, 1987.

[24] Interview with William Tetley, March 6, 1984.

[25] Bélanger, *Histoire de la Gaspésie*, 738.

[26] Interview with Lise Deguire, May 28, 1987, and Bernard Lavergne, June 11, 1987.

[27] Parcs Canada, Parc Forillon, *Plan Directeur* 4.4.1. and 1.3.3.

[28] Thibeault, "L'Ile Bonaventure," 22.

[29] Most of this material came from an interview with Bernard Major, June 3, 1987.

[30] Thibeault, "L'Ile Bonaventure," 22.

[31] Interview with William Tetley, March 6, 1984.

[32] Interview with Bernard Lavergne, June 11, 1987.

[33] Interview with Lise Deguire, May 28, 1987.

[34] Interview with William Tetley, March 6, 1984.

[35] Bélanger, *Histoire de la Gaspésie*, 722.

[36] *Ibid.*, 696.

[37] *Ibid.*, 698–700.

[38] Interview with Jean-Claude Robert, March 8, 1984.

[39] Interview with Bernard Lavergne, June 11, 1987.

Chapter 8

The Manifesto of the Communist Party and Its Contemporary Relevance

Louis Patsouras

I. The Manifesto of the Communist Party

The Manifesto of the Communist Party (*Manifesto*), by two young German revolutionary Communists, Karl Marx and Friedrich Engels—the first, twenty-nine years old; the second, twenty-seven—was published in 1848 by the Communist League (of which they were members), and is now celebrating its sesquicentennial.

My favorite edition is the 1948 centennial one, by International Publishers, consisting of forty-eight pages. It included the five-page 1888 classic "Preface" by Engels, which explained that the term "Communist" in the title signified a strictly proletarian movement, not middle-class "Socialist" as understood at the time. The arresting opening page, beginning with "A specter is haunting Europe—the specter of Communism," was followed by four basic sections: (1) "Bourgeois and Proletarians," thirteen pages; (2) "Proletarians and Communists," ten pages; (3) "Socialist and Communist Literature," eleven pages; (4) "Position of the Communists in Relation to the Various Existing Parties," two pages; and notes of just over three pages, most by Engels.

From a theoretical perspective, the first two sections contained the basic essentials of Communism; the third was a critique of earlier and contemporary socialist movements; and the fourth was on tactics, with the Communists supporting progressive movements, while simultaneously keeping in mind the "hostile antagonism between bourgeoisie and proletarians," ending with the battle cry, "Workingmen of all countries, Unite!"

The first run of the work was only eight hundred copies, but since then, it has been read by many hundreds of millions of people in both Communist and capitalist nations, rivaling the Bible in popularity. But without the Communist states of the twentieth century, it is doubtful that the work would be celebrated today.

The *Manifesto* itself, from a historical perspective, was published on the eve of the 1848 revolutions in Europe, themselves part of a revolutionary tide sparked by the two great social revolutions of the late eighteenth century, American and French, and the European revolutionary waves of 1820–21 and 1830–32, working-class insurrections in Lyon in 1831 and 1834, uprisings in Silesia in 1844, and intense working-class activity in Britain, which saw the formation of the Grand National Consolidated Trades Union of Great Britain in 1833 (destroyed in 1834) and the Chartist Movement of the 1830s and '40s—all of which contributed to the *Manifesto*'s appearance.

In Paris, from 1843 to 1845, Marx met Engels—who influenced Marx's becoming a Communist—and was deeply impressed by Paris's many socialist clubs. He himself joined the *Droits de l'homme*, a group of approximately three thousand workers whose elected officers were middle-class students and intellectuals.

After his expulsion from Paris in the winter of 1845, Marx spent three years in Brussels, where, with Engels, he formed the Communist Correspondence Committee in 1846 to engage in both practical politics and preparation for revolution. In February 1847, Marx and Engels joined the London-based League of the Just, which by June of that year became the Communist League, a clandestine organization, with Marx president of the Brussels branch. The Brussels German Working Men's Society was soon founded by Marx and Engels as a front for their League. Marx himself contributed a substantial portion of his inheritance from his father's estate to arm League members for future working-class uprisings.

The 1848 revolutions began with the toppling of the monarchy in France, spreading to Germany, Austria, and Italy their basic thrust for nationalism and democracy principally led by the bourgeoisie. But the proletariat and socialism were especially influential on the French scene. When Louis-Philippe was overthrown in France, the Provisional Government had four socialist ministers—Louis Blanc, Alexandre Martin (Albert), Ferdinand Flocon, and Alexandre Ledru-Rollin, the last a left-wing Jacobin close to socialism. This was the first time that socialists formed part of any government.

But the mainly bourgeois government, opposed to any basic social reform, quickly terminated the workshops established in Paris for unemployed workers, a slap at the socialists. The workers responded with an insurrection, the "June Days" (the first working-class socialist uprising in history) of June 23–26, under the red flag of socialism, instead of the French tricolor, with the battle cry of "bread or lead." The insurrection was mercilessly suppressed by the forces of order, precluding any further socialist participation in the 1848 French events.

When Marx was expelled by the Belgian government in early 1848, he was welcomed by a revolutionary Paris, but he and Engels soon left for Germany to participate in the German Revolution. Marx served as editor of the *Neue Rheinische Zeitung* (published from June 1, 1848 to May 19, 1849, in Cologne)—a radical working-class newspaper of social democracy backed by Communists and progressive bourgeois elements—and was president of the Cologne Workers' Association. Engels contributed articles to the newspaper and engaged in military action. After Marx and Engels endorsed the "June Days" in Paris, bourgeois support for the newspaper evaporated. With the failure of the revolution in Germany, Marx and Engels soon went to England, hoping for another imminent revolutionary wave.

As active promoters of a Communist working-class revolution/dictatorship, Marx and Engels followed in the footsteps of François-Noël (Gracchus) Babeuf, Sylvain Maréchal, Philippe Michel Buonarotti (a descendent of Michelangelo), and others in the Society of Equals, the first Communist organization spawned by the French Revolution. In May of 1796, the Society of Equals staged an uprising in Paris for a temporary dictatorship of the masses against the bourgeoisie, but the uprising was suppressed by the Directory. This revolutionary Communist current is called Babouvism, after Babeuf.

Buonarotti, a survivor of the repression, was involved, along with other French socialists such as Louis Blanc and Louis-Auguste Blanqui, in the 1830 French Revolution in Paris, passing on the Babouvist torch to Blanqui. The last participated in the 1848 events in Paris, attempting a failed working-class revolutionary seizure, and was the first socialist to propose that a revolutionary elite establish a working-class dictatorship. To be sure, Marx and Engels had the highest regard for Babeuf, Buonarotti, and Blanqui.

Before reviewing the main body of the *Manifesto* or its first two sections, commentary is in order for the third section, which critiqued other socialisms of the period. For instance, it lampooned "Feudal Socialism," including its Christian variant, viewing it as a reliquary of the past: "Christian Socialism is but the holy water with which the priest consecrates the heart-burnings of the aristocrat." Then, it condemned "petty bourgeois socialism," although this socialism's principal proponent, Jean Charles Leonard Sismondi, was praised for criticizing many of the ill consequences of capitalism: the "disastrous effects of machinery and division of labour, the concentration of capital and land in a few hands; overproduction and crisis[,]. . . inevitable ruin of the petty bourgeois and peasant, the misery of the proletariat, the anarchy in production, the crying inequalities of wealth, the industrial war of extermination between nations." But the *Manifesto* opposed its solutions, "corporate guilds for manufacture" and "patriarchal relations in agriculture," on the basis of their retaining the "old property relations." It also attacked "German or 'True' Socialism" for wishing to preserve the German petty bourgeoisie, and "Conservative or Bourgeois Socialism," especially one of its practitioners, Pierre-Joseph Proudhon, whose anarchism, emphasizing worker ownership of production in their workshops, fostered accompanying socioeconomic parochialism. Finally, it commented on the "Critical-Utopian Socialism and Communism" of François Charles Fourier, Robert Owen, Etienne Cabet, and others. Although the *Manifesto* acknowledged the great value of their critical views toward bourgeois society and their aims, such as the "abolition of the family, of private gain and of the wage-system," it opposed their running away from society to establish their utopian colonies.

In general, the *Manifesto* asserted that while utopian visions and scathing criticism of existing bourgeois society were useful for the realization of socialism, the emancipation of the working class could come only through its own rigorous political struggle against the bourgeoisie.

Section I began with the historical materialist approach relating historical progression to technology interacting with "class struggle" between "oppressor and oppressed," exploiters and exploited, master and subaltern classes. The class struggle itself always existed, both "hidden" and "open," manifesting underlying tensions/conflicts: in "ancient Rome" among "patricians, knights, plebeians, journeymen, apprentices, serfs"; in the modern period, between the working class and bourgeoisie. Within classes themselves, there were "subordinate gradations" or status groups. The modern class struggle between the working class and bourgeoisie arose from the overriding fact that capital itself created the modern urban working class: "In proportion as the bourgeoisie, i.e., capital, is developed, in the same proportion is. . . the modern working class developed."

This new class dynamic occurred in the context of the rise of the bourgeoisie that gradually replaced the nobility as the ruling class and expanded the means of production, more so "than all the preceding generations together," with the introduction of the new "manufacturing systems," of "giant, modern industry" such as "steam manufacture," "constantly revolutionizing the instruments of production, and thereby the relations of production, and with them the whole relations of society." These developments accelerated the rise of the city, encouraged colonization and world trade, and brought about a "universal interdependence of nations" or "world market" through "free trade," lessening "national one-sidedness and narrow-mindedness" in both the "material" and "intellectual" spheres. And: "In place of the old wants, satisfied by the production of the country, we find new wants, requiring for their satisfaction the products of distant lands and climes."

The bourgeoisie through these developments and "cash payment" produced an ethic that was corrosive to the past, of "venerable prejudices and opinions": "All that is solid melts into air, all that is holy is profaned." All the while, the bourgeoisie was constantly strengthening itself by enriching itself; it "concentrated property in a few hands," in tandem with "centralized means of production."

The new class alignments and class struggles resulting from these revolutionary developments deepened the divide between the proletariat and upper bourgeoisie, although the peasantry and lower middle class were still numerous. The working class itself was handicapped by the excessive poverty of its lower layer, the "lumpenproletariat," or "that passively rotting mass thrown off by the lowest layers of the old society," which, although at times it might join a "proletarian revolution," was more likely to become a "bribed tool of reactionary intrigue."

The most significant thesis of the *Manifesto* was the horrific capitalist oppression borne by the working class. It was best exemplified at work, for "cash payment" signified that workers were simply a cost of production, their time belonging to capital, which disciplined them under the "command of a perfect hierarchy of officers and sergeants." The machine, allowing for an almost endless division of labor, reduced workers to "appendage[s] of the machine," ever more exploited with speed-ups and more hours of work, themselves related to new technologies, which required less physical strength to perform work, thus lessening age and gender differences. (When the *Manifesto* was written, the labor of women and children in British factories and mines was common.)

These developments occurred when the "lower strata of the middle class, the small tradespeople, shopkeepers and retired tradesmen, the handicraftsmen and peasants—all these s[a]nk gradually into the proletariat," as large capital overwhelmed small capital. Indeed, in volume three of *Capital*, Marx specifically argued that this advancing technology would invade the white-collar part of the lower-middle-class workforce of his time, those involved in lower mental labor, would proletarianize it as general education became more prevalent and as "increased division of labor in the office" prevented workers from employing the full range of their skills, which could be "more rapidly, easily, universally, and cheaply reproduced with the progress of science and industry." These passages presaged the proletarianization of the lower middle class remarked by C. Wright Mills in *White Collar* (1951) and by others, confirming Marx's thesis of an ever-larger working class.

The *Manifesto* asserted that these basic socioeconomic differences between the proletariat and the bourgeoisie, in the context of the increasing globalization of capital, would lead ultimately to the internationalization of the class struggle between them, compelling workers to cooperate internationally, a condition facilitated by "improved means of communication which are created by modern industry."

There was also comment on the importance of working-class struggles for reform within capitalism, such as the "ten-hour bill in England," spurring on more reform. But was there a danger, then, that too much reform would "embourgeoisify" sections of the working class? Not in the long run as capitalist contradictions become ever more acute.

The problem of capitalist depressions was also covered cursorily but cogently (see Marx's *Capital* and the *Grundrisse* for detailed exegeses on this), employing the term "commercial crises." The basic cause for these phenomena is the systemic imbalance between production and consumption—or "over-production"—related to bourgeois property relations being simply "too narrow to comprise the wealth created by them"; "the productive forces at the disposal of society no longer tend to further the conditions of bourgeois property." But the bourgeoisie would overcome these depressions by "the enforced destruction of a mass of productive force," or by escalating bankruptcies and unemployment "by the conquest of new markets, and by the more thorough exploitation of the old ones," i.e., through new technologies, imperialism, and so forth.

Another subject considered in the first two sections was imperialism and its usual concomitant of war, related to the existence of class societies, of the "exploitation of one part of the society by the other." But: "In proportion as the exploitation of one individual by another is put to an end, the exploitation of one nation by another will also be put to an end. In proportion as the antagonism between classes within the nations vanishes, the hostility of one nation to another will come to an end."

To be sure, the critique of imperialism was not yet fully developed. In asserting, for instance, that the bourgeoisie "draws all nations, even the most barbarian, into civilization," its Eurocentrism did not recount the barbarities perpetrated by the Western conquerors on indigenous people in Africa, the Americas, and Asia, which, however, were clearly noted in Marx's *Capital*.

These views relating the proletarian class struggle against the bourgeoisie to the one against chauvinism and its corollary of imperialism were of the utmost profundity, workers invariably being the cannon fodder of ruling national nobility/bourgeois and bourgeois elites. In this context, "the workingmen have no country." Although this section praised the bourgeoisie for despoiling nature—as in these passages: "Subjection of nature's forces to man" and "clearing of whole continents for cultivation"—Marx's *Capital* mentioned the deleterious effects of soil erosion, deforestation, and industrial pollution, making Marx one of the founders of ecosocialism.

Near the end of the first section, the *Manifesto* observed that the cumulative problems of working-class social misery and alienation, intensified by periodic depressions and enlargement of the working class by the dynamism of capital and technology that proletarianized an ever-larger part of the population, made a working-class revolution imminent. In this critical period, a "portion of the bourgeoisie goes over to the proletariat," especially a "portion of the bourgeois ideologists, who have raised themselves to the level of comprehending theoretically the historical movement as a whole." Presumably they would lead the revolution. This scenario thus also indicated the importance of ideas to bringing about socialism.

Section II delineated the means and ends Communists employed to bring about socialism in a bourgeois world replete with contradictions, some of a positive nature. To begin, it emphasized cooperation between Communist and "other working-class parties," with the "immediate aim" being the "overthrow of bourgeois supremacy [and] conquest of political power by the proletariat" in the various nations, while pursuing the common bonds of international working-class solidarity. Since the heart of bourgeois power was productive private property obtained through exploiting labor, Communists would abolish it for socialized property so as not to "subjugate the labour of others," a condition more easily made possible as capitalism inexorably concentrated property into ever-fewer hands.

Although the *Manifesto* had the bourgeoisie significantly involved in making the modern nation-state (economic centralization resulting in "one government, one code of laws, one national class interest, one frontier and one customs tariff"), it also observed the countertendency of a "world market," related to freedom of "commerce," leading to the diminution of "national differences and antagonisms between peoples"—all of this to accelerate the "supremacy of the proletariat."

This prophecy has had mixed success. In the first half of the twentieth century, internecine capitalist wars, especially World Wars I and II, weakened capitalism to allow for Communist revolution in the former Russian Empire and China. But this happening was followed by a capitalist counteroffensive, which aided in the implosion of Soviet Communism and the weakening of Chinese Communism. Thus, by the year 2000, global capitalism is basically triumphant, but working-class parties in almost every nation exist to challenge its hegemony—more on this later.

The *Manifesto* then analyzed the nuclear patriarchal family, which under capitalist arrangements continued, in varying degree, men's general domination of women since the dawn of written history. When the *Manifesto* argued for a "community of women," bourgeois ideologues were outraged, forgetting to mention, as it pointed out, that bourgeois men had numerous affairs outside marriage. At this time, because of working-class social misery, working-class relationships between men and women were usually of short duration.

Significantly, the broad outlines for the first stage of a future socialist society—with the "proletariat" being the ruling class employing "democracy"—were also presented, involving (1) a gradual expropriation of bourgeois property, "to centralize all means of production in the hands of the state" (as "credit" through a "national bank," "communication and transport," "extension of factories and means of production owned by the state") and "to increase the total of productive forces as rapidly as possible"; (2) abolishing "property in land" and "rent" payments; (3) "a heavy progressive or graduated income tax"; (4) "abolition of all rights of inheritance"; (5) confiscating property of opponents of the revolution; (6) full employment; (7) "combination of agricultural with manufacturing industries" to end the "distinction between town and country"; (8) "free" and universal public-school education; (9) "abolition of child labor"; and (10) "combination of education with industrial production."

The second or higher stage of "Communism" (not named here) would arrive with the end of "class distinctions," when "public power will lose its political character" and "production has been concentrated in the hands of a vast association of the whole nation." The last quotation was later refined in Marx's *The Civil War in France* to "united cooperative societies are to regulate national production upon a common plan."

The *Manifesto* itself believed that socialism was realizable in a basically pre-industrial society (V. I. Lenin and Leon Trotsky, among others, at times thought otherwise), for it envisaged the distinct possibility that a bourgeois revolution in Germany would be immediately followed by a proletarian one. This was because Germany already had "a more developed proletariat than what existed in England in the 17th century [1650's Revolution] and in France in the eighteenth century [1789 Revolution and subsequent events]." Although their writings in general indicated that socialism could come about only after a well-developed industrial capitalism had been established, Marx and Engels were utopian revolutionaries well into the 1850s.

As observed, the *Manifesto* encompassed all the essentials of Marxism, although in abbreviated form: (1) historical materialism, with its mixture of technology and class struggle propelling history forward, which in the contemporary period basically pitted the workers against the bourgeoisie, ending in the triumph of the former over the latter, gradually ushering in a classless society; (2) the progressive role in history of the bourgeoisie in its destruction of feudalism/manoralism and expanding productive forces; (3) the suffering/alienation of the proletariat at the hands of the bourgeoisie; (4) the increasing contradictions of capitalism, including economic downturns and greater concentration of production/capital; (5) the sexism in the capitalist patriarchal family; (6) growing working-class militancy as capitalism progressed; and (7) the general outlines of a future society under working-class hegemony.

The *Manifesto*'s analysis of bourgeois society and desire to change it had many transcendent passages. Several examples: "Communism deprives no man of the power to appropriate the products of society; all that it does is to deprive him of the power to subjugate the labor of others by means of such an appropriation," and the new society is one "in which the free development of each is the condition for the free development of all." Were not these quotations and other mentioned of the highest spiritual—i.e. human—quality, signaling the end of exploitation/antagonisms of various kinds, including those of class and war? Indeed, they extended and deepened the progressive religious/philosophical traditions as enunciated by Buddhism; by the great Hebrew prophets, of Amos, Micah, Isaiah, and Jesus of Nazareth in protosocialist or socialist modes; by the Communism of Greek humanism, intertwined with the mysticism of Pythagoras, Socrates, and Plato; by the materialistic humanism of Democritus, Aristotle (Marx's great philosopher of the classical world), Protagoras, and Greco-Roman Stoicism. These traditions of humanism then appeared in the progressive elements of the Enlightenment, the French Revolution, utopian socialism, English Radicalism, German philosophy (especially by Georg Hegel), Romanticism, and the advanced sections of the working class. To be sure, Marx and Engels added the necessity for proletarian revolution; the revolutionary Spartacus was Marx's favorite hero.

Who can deny the grandeur and daring sweep of the *Manifesto*'s profoundly materialistic and humanistic vision, based on technology and prior class struggles, which proclaims that the nineteenth-century working class, in horrific socioeconomic misery, half-starved and scarcely educated, will quickly overthrow the bourgeoisie and usher in the good society of socialism? This humanistic and rationalistic Marxist hope, with its semi-"religious" millenarianism, has inspired large sections of the working class and other progressive forces, making it a formidable movement for human emancipation.[1]

II. Contemporary Validity of *The Manifesto of the Communist Party*

A. Political and Socioeconomic Matters

The *Manifesto*'s critique of capitalism has much contemporary validity, but its prophecy of socialism's rapid rise has had mixed results. To begin, the two great Communist revolutions of the twentieth century—Russian and Chinese—have failed or are failing, although their impact on twentieth-century history is of great consequence. To be sure, these revolutions occurred in economically backward nations on the capitalist periphery whose reactionary elites were sufficiently weakened by imperialist invasions to allow for Communist success.

The distortion and disregard of Marxist values in the Soviet Union and China resulted from many factors. Most important were their economic backwardness and capitalist hostility to socialism, along with capitalism's higher levels of technology and social capital, which ultimately proved decisive in influencing "Communist" bureaucracies to further catapult themselves above farmers and workers by embracing capitalism.

These bureaucracies under "socialism" ruthlessly dominated workers and farmers, denying them democracy at work and in civil life, any dissent being rapidly and ruthlessly squashed. Within the ruling Communist parties, changes of policy or conflicts over power were often decided by purges involving much bloodshed. Underlying this process was the sharp dichotomy between manual and mental labor in economic milieux of scarcity attempting to modernize. But some aspects of socialism remained, such as the abolition of private property in the means of production and exchange, much general socioeconomic equality, and extensive social welfarism.

Although these two failures of socialism cannot be denied, there are now large socialist and Communist parties throughout the world. For instance, almost every EU nation has a ruling social democratic party, often backed by Communists, as do Canada, Australia, and New Zealand. A large Communist Party exists in Russia, with former Communist Parties in Eastern Europe and in the former Soviet Union nations usually calling themselves "socialist." In Latin American, strong socialist parties are in place in almost every nation;

and, of course, there is Cuba. In Asia, China, North Korea, and Vietnam are ruled by Communist Parties, and India has a longstanding socialist and Communist tradition, while in Indonesia the Communist Party was destroyed by General Suharto. Arab socialism also has a powerful presence, especially in Iran, Libya, and Algeria. In Israel, the Labor Party is now in power. In sub-Saharan Africa, socialist and Communist parties play a major role in South Africa, Angola, and the Congo, among other nations. Even in the United States, the left wing of the Democratic party, representing approximately half of it, is not far from social democracy, and some small left-wing parties, principally the Greens, have made their presence known locally.

The *Manifesto*'s prophecy—that as capital increases, so should the working class—is essentially correct. When the *Manifesto* was written, only a small part of the world's population was composed of workers, but today, approximately a third are workers. By 2025 another two billion people will enter the cities, making it a majority.

Another generalization of the *Manifesto* saw increasing social misery for workers in the form of lower living standards. But workers in the First World, especially in the past fifty years, have experienced rising standards of life as a result of more social capital, intertwined to a dynamic technology and working-class political and strike activities, including general strikes lately in Greece, France, Italy, Portugal, and South Vietnam. But any slackening of working-class activity, as in the United States, generally results in lower real wages for many workers. Furthermore, the Marxist concept of increasing relative misery, as enunciated in *Capital* (that higher living standards for workers do not prevent increasing wealth difference between them and the wealthy), is more valid than ever.

Global capitalism is more entrenched today than ever as the world's economy is characterized by more interdependence among nations, although there is uneven economic development among them. After thirty or so good years for Western and Japanese capitalism following World War II, the inherent contradiction within capitalism of overproduction affecting profit margins has brought about these results today: (1) Unemployment in the economically advanced and developing nations is very high. In the United States, it is now officially just over 4 percent, but in actuality, according to Lester C. Thurow and other economists, it is at least twice as high. In the EU alone, unemployment is approximately 12 percent, and 25 percent in Russia. In Brazil, Mexico, and Indonesia, along with underemployment, it affects one-third to one-half of the workforce. (2) Economic stagnation is evident in East Asia, including Japan, and in Russia, where, since Communism imploded, the gross domestic product (GDP) has fallen by half in the past ten years. But even where the GDP is rising, as in the EU and the United

States, the bourgeois offensive in the former results in higher unemployment for workers, but no great loss yet in social-welfare benefits; in the latter, the effects of capitalism have led to lower wages and more hours of work for most workers, in addition to loss of health-care coverage and other benefits

A case study of the American workforce experiencing these and other difficulties as a result of intensified capitalist exploitation will now be considered. The average workweek was 40 hours in 1973, but 51 in 1997. Real median weekly wages for the bottom 80 percent of the workforce declined by 18 percent from 1973 to 1995, but rose 4 percent from 1995 to 2000. Weekly leisure time decreased from 26 hours in 1973 to 20 hours in 1999. The retirement age for Social Security recipients will rise from the present 65 to 67, then to 70. Americans are now living longer, but with the elimination of the costs of alienation and conspicuous consumption inherent under capitalism, the retirement age should be much lower than the present one; indeed, a six-hour workday, with higher living standards, is also realizable in this context.

The socioeconomic savaging of the American working class may be attributed to the failure of the working class itself to develop a social democratic party to challenge capitalist hegemony. Although the working class comprises more than three-fifths of the population, it still lacks a cohesive class consciousness, riven as it is by racism against blacks and Hispanics and by other divisions, especially economic, between upper and lower halves, the latter heavily black and Hispanic. Many of the more favored workers, including many union members, vote Republican, while the less favored have a poor voting record or are "illegals."

Thus, American political conservatism has led to labor's decline, with hostile anti-labor legislation, such as the Taft-Hartley Act, and unfavorable court decisions, abetted by a neo-liberal free-trade policy that invites capital to invest in low-wage nations such as Mexico and China. Not surprisingly, while a third of the workforce was unionized in the 1950s, only a seventh is in 2000.

This triumph of conservatism over labor in the United States can be seen in big-business control of the political process and the mass media, both of which profoundly influence public opinion. Today, approximately 70 percent of political contributions to both the Democratic and Republican parties come from the wealthy and corporations, outspending labor by a six-to-one margin. Of course, without a critical mass of money, it is almost impossible to win an election. This advantage is reinforced by the approximately 20,000 lobbyists in Washington, the overwhelming majority representing the interests of large corporations.

In the significant area of the mass media—newspapers, television, magazines, and radio—whose influence on the general culture, including politics, is undoubtedly immense, corporate ownership is becoming more concentrated, with accompanying interlocking directorates forming a "new communications cartel" in which fewer than twenty corporations "control most of the business in daily newspapers, magazines, television, books, and motion pictures."

The *Manifesto*'s insistence that only by waging an incessant class struggle against the bourgeoisie can the proletariat improve its socioeconomic circumstances may be accurately measured today by comparing the social gains of EU workers, who vote for social democratic parties and parties to the left of them, with those of their American counterparts.

These social benefits are now common in EU nations: universal and comprehensive health insurance, mandated annual vacations of from four to seven weeks for the workforce (an important element in why the average annual hours of work are now 1,966 in America, 1,656 in France, and 1,560 in Germany), maternity leave with pay for many months, extensive community childcare services in some (as in France), subsidies for housing and for children, minimally tolerable unemployment insurance of unlimited duration in many of them, and somewhat adequate old-age pensions.

But in a conservative United States, the social reality is quite different. Unlimited welfare involving the federal government working directly with the states was abolished in 1996, with the federal government now giving block grants of money to the states, which impose their differing time limits of no more than five years for welfare recipients, but usually much less. Vacation time is not mandated by law, averaging two weeks. Furthermore, with no universal health insurance, 45 million workers are without health insurance, and for most women, there are no paid maternity leaves/benefits.

These conditions are part of a social structure that characterizes the dire social misery of the lower half of the working class. Its worst aspects include the up to three million homeless—half of whom are working, but living in automobiles—many of them severely mentally ill; and 300,000 penniless and abused children ("street kids"), either abandoned or runaways. As for hunger, two 1980s studies by the Physician Task Force on Hunger in America, chaired by Dr. J. Larry Brown of Harvard University, a two-year urban and rural probe, and the Citizens Commission on Hunger in the United States, an 18-month study by Harvard physicians, reported that 20 million people experienced hunger for at least part of every month; an update by Dr. Brown in 1992 estimates this number at 30 million. Food banks are now widespread.[2]

Contemporary class alignments in the United States confirm that Marx's view of class, of the growing class polarity, stoppable only by working-class action between the bourgeoisie and proletariat, is essentially correct. The richest 1 percent of households (two-fifths of whom are managers/executives, more than a fifth physicians, an eighth lawyers, and a fifth salespersons) own 40 percent of all private wealth, including half the stock and three-fifths of the bonds. Their minimum wealth in the early 1990s was 2.3 million dollars, doubling from 1979 to 1992 and at least doubling again from 1993 to 2000 with the dizzying upward spiral of the stock market in the past eight years— there are now almost six million millionaires in the nation, the poorer ones in the upper reaches of the upper middle class. In the past two decades, this group has acquired more than 70 percent of the new wealth.

This group is followed by the next 9 percent of households (almost all of the upper middle class) with 30 percent of the wealth, and the next 10 percent (largely the upper half of the lower middle class) with 15 percent of it. The bottom 80 percent of the people have the remaining 15 percent of the wealth. They make up the lower half of the lower middle class (the lower middle class is between a fifth and a fourth of the total) and the working class, the approximately two-thirds at the bottom.

The top two classes are almost exclusively composed of mental labor, as is approximately half of the lower middle class. Approximately a fourth of adults today have at least a four-year college degree, while a similar number attend college but do not graduate. College graduates may be roughly divided into two broad groups of mental labor, or Rifkin's "knowledge class"—20 percent in the higher category (scientific researchers, graduate-school graduates, physicians, lawyers, and so forth), 80 percent in the lower one or the mass professions (teaching, nursing, engineering, and computer specialists). The remainder of the class chain is ensconced in the working class. Its upper half is composed of skilled workers/technicians and semi-skilled ones in the mass unionized industries; its lower half is lodged in the non-unionized semi-skilled and unskilled workers (many self-employed), the long-term unemployed, the welfare-dependent, and deeply alienated petty-criminal elements. As industrial workers decrease in numbers, the working class is increasingly represented by clerical, retail/wholesale, service, and transportation workers.

An examination of this class model shows that the upper working class— skilled and union workers, along with clerical workers and technicians—is not socioeconomically far from lower mental labor lodged in the mass professions. Indeed, universal primary and secondary education and now mass college education, related to rapid technological change and desire for upward social mobility, do not relatively change the class position of many educated individuals; lateral, not upward, social mobility is the lot of many of them.

Some statistics help us better understand this class picture: The estimated wealth of the Forbes 400 (the richest four hundred families in the United States) rose from 477 billion dollars in 1996 to a trillion in 1999. The deepening wealth polarity may also be expressed in the following median worth of families in dollars adjusted for inflation in 1989 and 1998, respectively: age under 33—9,900 and 9,000, down 9 percent; ages 35 to 44—71,800 and 63,400, down 12 percent; ages 45 to 54—125,700 and 105,500, down 16 percent. In ethnic terms, in 1995 the median family wealth in dollars was 61,000 for whites, 7,400 for blacks, and 5,000 for Hispanics.

This wealth inequality itself comes from inherited wealth (from half to three-fourths of wealth is from inheritance and income generated by it) and rising income inequality (the propensity to consume/save formula that allows high-income families to consume/save more than others). In 1998, the average annual compensation (salary, bonuses, stock options, and perquisites) for chief executive officers (CEOs) of major American corporations was 10.6 million dollars, while the worker's average salary was 21,000 dollars—an approximately 500 to 1 ratio. Two sets of percentage income are presented for population quintiles from lowest to highest for 1967 and 1996 respectively—5, 10, 17, 24, and 44; 4, 9, 15, 24, and 49. Changes in after-tax family income from lowest to highest population quintiles from 1977 to 1999 are as follows: minus 9, plus 1, plus 8, plus 14, and plus 43. The slight gains noted for the fourth and third quintiles are a result of a longer workweek and of more women entering the workforce. In comparison with other nations in after-tax income equality between the lowest and highest population quintiles, the United States has double that of France and Germany and triple that of Japan.[3]

The *Manifesto*'s prophecy that capitalism has "concentrated property into a few hands" is now more valid than ever as monopolistic competition reigns. This occurs when five or so firms have more than a 50 percent share of any market, thus allowing them to fix prices.

Transnational corporations (TNCs)—companies with plants in two or more nations and in which at least a fourth to a third of profits come from other nations—now have monopolistic control in leading economic sectors in both national and international markets. This monopolization in the 1990s was 70 percent in consumer durables, 60 percent in automobiles and trucks, and 55 percent in airline, aerospace, steel, and electrical/electronic components. Not far from monopoly advantage are oil, the media, and personal computers at 40 percent market share, and somewhat further away are chemicals at 35 percent and insurance at 25 percent.

By the mid 1990s, the top five hundred TNCs (approximately a third from the United States, another third from the EU, with Germany, France, and Britain in the lead, and slightly more than a fifth from Japan) made up more than a third of the GDP of the economically advanced nations and conducted 70 percent of the world's trade, about two-fifths intra-firm. This economic globalization of general free trade results in imports and exports together being a large part of the GDP—a fourth for the American, and half for the French, British, and German.

This capital concentration is also evident in the top thousand American corporations' generating at least 60 percent of American GDP income, the remaining 11 million businesses the other 40 percent. Yet another index for this is the Standard and Poor's 500, representing 85 percent of the value of publicly traded companies. To be sure, this economic concentration has been accelerated by the great flurry of mergers/acquisitions in motor vehicles, pharmaceuticals, communications, aviation, and banking, among others: In 1997–98, for instance, it totaled 3.5 trillion dollars within the orbit of American companies, including global acquisitions by or of them.

One of the consequences of this monopolization, according to Senator Philip Hart of Michigan, is that price fixing annually gouged the American public of more than a trillion dollars in higher costs for consumer goods in the early 1990s.

Finally, global capitalist hegemony is also well observed in the three trillion dollars traded daily internationally, 85 percent in currency, the remainder in stocks and bonds, much of it conducted for the six trillion dollars in off-shore tax havens in Hong Kong, the Cayman Islands, Bermuda, the Isle of Man, and other places, two-fifths held by American citizens.[4]

B. The Horrors and Costs of Alienation

The multiple walls separating individuals from one another, or alienation, and its devastating consequences, are of course mainly borne by the workers/ working class, but no person or class can escape it entirely because of the overarching socioeconomic, political, and cultural realities of class society with its inherent conflicts and tensions. To be sure, work, the principal human activity, is most involved with the problem of alienation.

We begin contemporary analyses of alienation, following Marx's treatment of it in the *Manifesto* and other works, with *Labor and Monopoly Capital* by Harry Braverman. His principal Marxist thesis is that the wondrous technological advances since the 1950s have intensified worker dissatisfaction in the workplace because the technology is designed to magnify workers' powerlessness, condemning most workers to doing work requiring little or no intellectual challenge, as well as chaining them to a "round of servile duties." Indeed, as the technology advances, most workers become ever more inconsequential because they do not "own the machine and the labor power."[5] Another source is Bertell Ollman's *Alienation: Marx's Concepts of Man in Capitalist Society*, which holds that Marx's theory of alienation represents "the devastating effect of capitalist production on human beings, on their physical and mental states and on the social processes of which they are a part."[6]

These views are buttressed by two socialist academics who write about their experience as workers in factories: *La Condition ouvrière* by Simone Weil, a noted French anarchist and lycée professor in the Paris area during the 1930s; and *Working for Capitalism* by Richard M. Pfeffer, a professor at Johns Hopkins in the Baltimore area during the 1970s. Both unsparingly indict the capitalist factory system for its horrid treatment of workers, viewing them as things or objects to be manipulated. Thus, workers are rigidly caged in an environment controlled by an authoritarian bureaucracy, imposing almost endless job gradations and unbending rules and regulations whose aim is to exploit, divide, and disempower them as much as possible. At the shop floor itself, the work is repetitive and at maximum speed in a hellish environment, with foremen treating workers like children and using harsh language to discipline them, further eroding their dignity. Also, since workers have a limited education, the mysteries of the machine process further magnify their alienation, exacerbated by the possibility of their being dismissed at any moment from work, either singly or *en masse*, thrown into the darkness of unemployment, of helplessness and despair.[7]

That work basically defines a person's life, itself associated with status and class divisions and all they entail, is poignantly described in Studs Terkel's *Working*, a magnificent tome of oral history in which more than a hundred Americans recount how work affects their lives in general. In covering the continuum of work/class, this study affirms the obvious, of more losers than winners in the race for success: For most workers, jobs are physically exhausting and psychologically stressful, in a hierarchic cage characterized by humdrum work routines. But for the fortunate few, work is generally creative and often accompanied with great financial rewards. To be sure, there are a few socialists, an insignificant minority, who question the status quo.[8]

Terkel's observations are confirmed by Barbara Garson, a well-known social activist, in *All the Livelong Day*, a brilliant report of the lives of blue- and white-collar workers stripped of all dignity and autonomy as labor division increasingly multiplies, ever more fragmenting work and accelerating its pace. In *The Electronic Sweatshop*, Garson indicts the new and spreading computer technology for subjecting white-collar workers to a new work slavery, the aim being to "restrict their autonomy" and "to make people cheap and disposable." She also observes the deleterious effects of electronic surveillance at work, which records and evaluates every second of it. In this critique, Garson follows Braverman's objections to Taylorism.[9]

Another major study on work is *The Hidden Injuries of Class* by Richard Sennett and Jonathan Cobb. In addition to describing the wasteland of work for most workers, they trace the social psychology of a ferociously competitive society that divides people between the successful and the failures (especially blue-collar workers) who usually blame themselves for their shortcomings, exploring the relationship between work and class, with its built-in cultural values that favor the dominant bourgeoisie over the workers.[10]

Yet another well-regarded study, *Personality and Organization*—a synthesis of many other studies and of original research by Chris Argyris at Yale—concludes that workers at the lower end of the work/class continuum experience more feelings of powerlessness and frustration than do those performing mental labor. Thus, for instance, assembly-line workers faced with keeping up with the rapid pace and repetitive nature of their work, along with long work hours, often succumb to psychosomatic and related illnesses such as high blood pressure and heart disease, and are more prone to accidents.[11]

The problems caused by unremittingly boring/repetitive work at high speed, now often electronically monitored, have recently been examined in three studies: a United National International Labor Organization report, "Job Stress: The Twentieth Century Disease" (1993); Mitchell Marks's *From Turmoil to Triumph* (1994); and Jeremy Rifkin's *The End of Work* (1995). The first insists that the annual cost to the American economy in the form of illness, absenteeism, lower productivity, job turnover, and so forth is approximately 200 billion dollars. The second, by a psychologist and consultant to business, laments lower worker morale and disenchantment with management in the wake of recent mergers and downsizing, which have increased unemployment and work time (the latter resulting in "burnout") but decreased real median wages. The third, by a labor economist, reiterates in great detail the problems posed by the first two studies and recommends a 30-hour work week.[12]

The American workplace itself is not only an arena of strife between labor and capital, but also one of individual competition and those of race, ethnicity, religion, and gender. Not surprisingly, these antagonisms at times spill over into violence. For instance, a 1996 report by the National Institute for Organizational Safety and Health reports a million crimes annually occurring in the workplace (11 percent of total crime), including 1,100 murders (4 percent of the total), three-fourths of which occur during robberies. A survey conducted by the Northwestern National Life Insurance Co. of six hundred workers in 1993 obtains similar results to those of the Justice Department: one-sixth claim to have been physically attacked and one-fifth threatened by physical harm. (The "workplace avenger" who runs amuck killing fellow workers is well known.) Also, out of a workforce of approximately 130 million in the early 1990s, the average annual toll of the unhealthful and dangerous workplace was a hundred thousand deaths, with four hundred thousand illnesses and ten million injuries, of which seventy thousand were permanent, two million necessitated absence from work, and eleven thousand resulted in fatalities.

To be sure, the annual death rate for blue-collar workers is invariably higher than that of their middle-class counterparts. In Indiana, for instance, the average construction worker dies at age 60, about ten years below the national average. A recent study conducted by General Motors and the United Auto Workers at its Lordstown plant near Youngstown, Ohio, concludes that in its two assembly plants, the cancer mortality rate among workers is "40 percent higher than normal," and in its fabrication plant, "50 percent higher." Of course, other factors are probably involved in this, such as the stress of working-class life in general. Annual costs in the early 1990s for workplace injury and illness (excluding cancer) were 140 billion dollars.

When Ronald Reagan reduced the staff of the Occupational Safety and Health Administration (OSHA) by 400 inspectors, citations for violations were cut by half. In 1987, OSHA had just over 300 safety inspectors to look after six million private workplaces. But by 1997, there were 2,000 inspectors, although this was still an insufficient number.

Tensions and conflicts at work are now exacerbated by downsizing, with lifetime jobs becoming ever more scarce. Since most workers identify themselves closely with their work, intimately related as it is with economic security and psychic self-worth, unemployment often results in feelings of shame and worthlessness, which in turn adversely affect family relations. When debts cannot be repaid and family possessions dwindle, the psychological health of all family members is imperiled. Not surprisingly, the long-term unemployed have a 30 percent higher rate of divorce than average and abuse their children and spouses more often and more severely than others. From a general perspective, a 1-percent increase in unemployment results in a rise of 4 percent in suicide, almost 6 percent in murder, and 4 percent for men and 2 percent for women in state psychiatric hospitals.[13]

Middle and upper management, too, cannot completely escape alienation at work, especially its extremely competitive part. Although workers in unionized corporations have some job protection from arbitrary dismissal, there is much less protection for middle and upper management. Furthermore, the rewards of money and power are so great for managers that they spend not only much of their working lives, but also their social ones in networking and politicking for promotion. In this labyrinth, uncertainty reigns. Middle management is now being ravaged by recent trends in corporate downsizing and introduction of new technologies, leading not only to mass layoffs and correspondingly lower salaries, but also to increased work loads and inexorably to greater job stress and burnout. This group is also losing its favored status in the workforce because mass higher education has increased its numbers.

In the contemporary Darwinian jungle of middle and upper management, the supposed rationality and efficiency of merit in the business world is largely mythical. For instance, more than half of middle managers readily admit that promotions are made on a "largely subjective evaluation and arbitrary decision." Even top executives are concerned with recent downsizing and the increased work loads accompanying them. In a 1991 survey of senior executives in the largest thousand American companies, 54 percent feared losing their jobs and 26 percent feared "burnout," the two leading anxieties. Of course, senior executives usually have clauses in their contracts to compensate them for a number of years in case of dismissal.

There is also inherent economic waste in the American corporation because of its conflict/alienating model in the workplace. Respected economist David Gordon in *Fast and Mean* convincingly indicates this by contrasting the American corporation with the more cooperative German and Japanese ones: in the early 1990s, the former had 13 percent of its workforce in management, while the latter two had only 4 percent each.[14]

There are many other consequences of alienation/oppression, such as obesity, bulimia and anorexia, compulsive gambling, extensive use of injurious drugs (legal and illegal), and crime in its three manifestations. The following paragraphs cite the average annual costs of such consequences from the early to mid 1990s, with some exceptions where indicated, in the United States.

Eating disorders undoubtedly hasten the death of millions and incur economic costs of 250 billion dollars from illness, absence from work, and early death. Compulsive gambling heavily engages 5 percent of the people, with more than 500 billion dollars wagered legally and many tens of billions illegally. Its socioeconomic ravages include child and spousal abuse, divorce, and job loss estimated at 90 billion dollars. Legal and illegal drugs inflict especially high human and material burdens. The two most deadly legal drugs are nicotine and alcoholic drinks. The former causes 400,000 deaths and costs 110 billion dollars; the latter, 150,000 deaths, including half of the almost 40,000 killed in automobile accidents, and 130 billion dollars. Illegal drugs cause 17,000 deaths and cost a street value approaching 100 billion dollars.[15]

Crime within nations (war among nations as yet is not generally considered a crime) is tripartite in nature—street, business, and family. Such crime certainly denotes the lack of human solidarity, including love, trust, and empathy for others, widespread in economically competitive and class-bound societies replete with great economic insecurity and aggression and riven by deep individual and social antagonisms.

Street crime, involving burglary and robbery of motor vehicles, homes, and commercial establishments, consumes approximately 16 billion dollars and results in the priceless loss of human life, including 24,000 murder victims, and psychological and monetary damages to their survivors.

A recent United States Judiciary Committee report affirms that America is the "most violent and destructive nation on earth," with the highest per capita rate of homicide and robbery among First World nations. Statistics also reflect high rates of incarceration. In 2000, the prison population of two million is mostly men, of whom principally half are black (a third of black men ages 20 to 29 are in prison, on parole, or on probation), a third white, and a sixth Hispanic. Many are in prison for non-violent offenses, such as illegal trafficking in drugs. Four million are now on parole or probation.

Surely, crime and violence are associated with the ills of poverty and attendant psychological stresses. For instance, half of black men from ages 25 to 34 are either unemployed or earning wages below the poverty line. Psychological impairment affects a large portion of inmates and is exacerbated by horrid prison conditions. This lumpenproletariat is both victim and victimizer in the overarching capitalist-alienation horizon.

A comprehensive 1996 Justice Department report, "Victim Costs and Consequences: A New Look," asserts that the total annual cost for family and street crimes—including rape, physical injury and psychological trauma, and murder, with police and legal expenses and time lost from work—is 450 billion dollars. Furthermore, 38 billion dollars are spent on the prison system, with its half a million employees, and many billions of dollars more for 700,000 private guards and anti-theft devices.

The second type of crime, annual business crime—kickbacks, bribery, fraud, extortion, violating federal regulations, and tax evasion—robbed the public of approximately 300 billion dollars in the 1990s, not counting employee embezzlement of up to 40 billion dollars. In any given decade, approximately a fifth of the largest five hundred corporations are fined by the federal government.

Several of the most expensive frauds of the last decade include the following: (1) the Savings and Loan scandal, whose total cost to the taxpayers over forty years will be approximately more than half a trillion dollars; (2) Michael Milken's billion-dollar fine for insider trading; and (3) Archer Daniels Midland's hundred-million-dollar fine for price fixing. Then, there is the perennial waste of 25 billion dollars in military procurement. Furthermore, corporations annually cheat employees out of approximately 20 billion dollars in overtime pay.[16]

The third part of the crime triad consists of family violence. One in eight women is beaten by her husband, and as many as a fifth of men and a third of women are sexually abused in childhood, usually by a father and/or mother or near relative with an essentially compulsive personality, addicted to work, religion, power, and sex. A tragic consequence of this, according to the Centers for Disease Control and Prevention, is that 10 percent of teenagers attempted suicide in 1997, a statistic that is related to violence among spouses in a third of marriages. Violence often continues in the form of sibling rivalry, often violent, and in the battering of the elderly by their children, especially of the "weak, disabled, and female," involving up to three million cases annually.

Emotional and physical abuse (the two usually related) of children results in later neurotic and even psychotic behavior. According to Dr. Judith Lewis Herman, in *Trauma and Recovery*, up to 60 percent of psychiatric patients requiring hospitalization were physically and mentally abused in childhood. Genetic predisposition may be present in mental illness, especially in psychosis, but it is exacerbated by environmental factors, which are the decisive cause in most instances. More than a fifth of the American people today suffer from diagnostically recognizable neurotic symptoms, such as excessive anxiety and depression, pronounced phobias, obsessive-compulsive disorders, manic-depressive psychosis, and major depression, and a little more than 1 percent are psychotic or paranoid schizophrenic; indeed, over a lifetime, perhaps as many as 70 percent have some form of mental illness.

An alienated society also leads to widespread sexual dysfunction. According to the Center for Sexual and Marital Health at the Robert Wood Johnson Medical School in New Jersey, a fourth of women fail to achieve orgasm and from ages eighteen to thirty-nine, a third lack any interest in sex; for men, 30 percent have problems with premature ejaculation and 15 percent lack any sexual interest, because of various stresses such as sexual abuse and poverty. Women whose income declined more than 20 percent in the three years before being interviewed had a 60 percent chance of lower sexual desire than those whose income increased.

Family violence and other horrors just recounted confirm that gender relationships within the family, reflecting those of the general society, are deeply troubled. To achieve men's liberation, that of women is also axiomatic. In fact, Engels's *The Origin of the Family, Private Property, and the State*, which amplified the text of the *Manifesto* on women, called for women's liberation, appropriately relating it to women gaining employment outside the home. This work is important to socialist feminism, influencing works such as Simone de Beauvoir's *The Second Sex*, Shulamith Firestone's *The Dialectic of Sex*, and Ann Ferguson's *Sexual Democracy*.

Today, the traditional capitalist-patriarchal family is in crisis in the economically advanced nations. In the United States, for instance, half of first, three-fourths of second, and nine-tenths of third marriages end in divorce. This should be viewed in the context of women, including two-thirds of married women with children, now composing almost half the workforce. Especially economically ravaged in this scenario are poor women and children: approximately half of black, a quarter of Hispanic, and a seventh of white families are headed by women, with a fourth of children fatherless.

At work sexism, although less pervasive than before, still exists. In the United States, women on average today earn 76 percent of what men earn, significantly higher than the 55 percent average of the prior generation. But half the women now employed have left a job because of sexual harassment, although laws exist protecting them in this and other areas. For instance, the Civil Rights Act of 1964, which included gender, made it a federal offense for companies of more than 25 employees to discriminate in hiring women, and a 1991 law specifically protected women against sexual harassment at work. Since the latter law, the case load for sexual harassment increased from just above 6,000 in 1991 to 15,000 in 1996.

Furthermore, more women are now attending college—earning more than half of bachelor's and master's degrees—and branching out from teaching, nursing, and library work to law and medicine. As yet, there are few women CEOs, but they represent 10 percent in leading corporate positions and two-fifths in middle management. With women experiencing less discrimination, the working- and lower-middle-class combination should experience a diminution of status differences among men and women, allowing it to wage a more effective class struggle against the upper bourgeoisie.[17]

The social costs of alienation should also include at least some of those caused by pollution, which a socialist society in the First World should be able to reduce rapidly. In the United States alone in the 1990s, the approximate annual cost of pollution in human and economic terms was as follows: in the workplace, 23 percent of cancer deaths and 275 billion dollars; of air on health, more than 200 billion dollars, with damage to industrial and residential structures at another 30 billion dollars; of water on health, boats, and recreational facilities, another 12 billion dollars, and removing hazardous wastes from earth and water from 32,000 sites, another 20 billion dollars.

To these annual wastes, add 150 billion dollars for advertising, nearly 300 billion dollars consumed by the military, and almost 27 billion dollars for national intelligence agencies, such as the Central Intelligence Agency, National Security Agency, and Defense Intelligence Agency.

The validity of the *Manifesto*'s emphasizing increasing socioeconomic misery for the masses may be tested by works of contemporary economists and others who maintain that, contrary to popular belief, the actual GDP of First World and other nations is actually falling. In one such work, *For the Common Good*, Herman E. Daly and John B. Cobb Jr. assert that after factoring in the costs of economic growth/pollution—national advertising, air and water pollution, long-term illness caused by a deteriorating ecostructure, loss of topsoil and non-renewable natural resources, time lost in commuting, automobile accidents, and so forth—which they deduct from the accepted GDP, the standard of life actually falls in recent times. They aver that in the United States, although per capita income more than doubled from 1950 to 1986 in 1972 dollars, their "index of sustainable economic welfare," which subtracts the aforementioned negative costs, shows the real standard of life rising by a fourth, reaching its peak years from 1968 to 1979, then declining a tenth.

Daly and Cobb have been joined in this critique by Richard Douthwaite in *The Growth Illusion* and David C. Korten in *When Corporations Rule the World*. The *Manifesto* was a landmark work in beginning this line of socioeconomic reasoning, expanded by Marx in *Capital* and Thorstein Veblen in *The Theory of the Leisure Class*.[18]

In summary, the *Manifesto*'s basic theses, of the great power of capital to determine general national and global events and policies, of increasing class polarity between the proletariat and bourgeoisie intensifying the class struggle between them, of lower working-class living standards unless arrested by working-class activity, of the destructive effects of the business cycle on working-class life, and of the basic alienation of workers at work and outside of it in a capitalist society, are as relevant today as ever.

Indeed, the *Manifesto* presents a devastating critique of bourgeois social Darwinism, which glorifies the pitting of individuals, status groups, and classes against one another, in a world whose antisocial profit motive—associated with technologies destructive to the environment and continuing large-scale military expenditures, including the perfection of more lethal nuclear and other weapons—is now destroying the eco-structure and humanity along with it.[19]

Endnotes

[1] Karl Marx and Friedrich Engels, edited and annotated by Friedrich Engels, *The Manifesto of the Communist Party* (New York: International Publishers, 1948), pp. 3–48. *The Communist Manifesto Now*, eds. Leo Pantich and Colin Leys (New York: Monthly Review Press, 1998), has many excellent articles on Marx/Engels and the *Manifesto*, including proper background of its revolutionary views. On Marx's life, see Maximilien Rubel and Margaret Manale, *Marx without Myth: A Chronological Study of His Life and Work* (New York: Harper Torchbooks, 1976). On Engels, see David McLellan, *Friedrich Engels* (New York: Penguin Books, 1978). On the proletarianization of white-collar workers: Karl Marx, *Capital, III: The Process of Capitalist Production as a Whole* (Moscow: Progress Publishers, 1966). C. Wright Mills, *White Collar: The American Middle Class* (New York: Oxford University Press, 1956), pp. 289–314.

[2] On the failure of the Communism in the Soviet Union and Chinese People's republic, see, for instance, David Kotz and Fred Weir, *Revolution from Above: The Demise of the Soviet System* (London: Routledge, 1997). Robert Weil, *Red Cat, White Cat: China and the Contradictions of "Market Socialism"* (New York: Monthly Review Press, 1996). On the world's workforce in the 1990s and its rate of unemployment, see, for instance, Ray Marshall (former U.S. secretary of labor under Jimmy Carter and now a professor of economics at the University of Texas at Austin), "A World Out of Work," *Akron Beacon Journal*, Oct. 15, 1995, pp. G1 and G3. On increased hours of work weekly, fall in real wages, and less leisure time for U.S. workers, see, for instance, Merrill Goozner, "Long hours may add to flawed statistics," *Akron Beacon Journal*, July 5, 1998, pp. G1 and G9. On vacation time, see Jeremy Gaunt, "U.S. workers given no breaks on vacation," *Akron Beacon Journal*, Aug. 30, 1991, p. C9. On annual number of hours worked by U.S., German, and French workers, see Juliet B. Schor, *The Overworked American: The Unexpected Decline of Leisure* (New York: Basic Books, 1992), pp. 32–41. On real wages declining for the bottom 80 percent of the workers, see Lawrence Mishel, Jared Bernstein, and John Schmitt, *The State of Working America, 1996–1997* (Washington, DC: Economic Policy Institute, 1996), pp. 129–1937 (Hereinafter Mishel, *Working America*). Jeremy Rifkin, *The End of Work: The Decline of the Global Labor Force and the Dawn of the Post-Market Era* (New York: G. P. Putnam's Sons, 1995), pp. 165–72. On the wealthy controlling the political process, including lobbying, see Philip M. Stern, *Still the Best Congress Money Can Buy* (Washington, DC: Regnery Gateway, 1992), pp. 17–30 and 168–71. G. William Domhoff, *Who Rules America?: Power and Politics in the Year 2000*, third edition (Mountain View, CA: Mayfield Publishing, c. 1998), pp. 171–296. On the media, see Ben H. Bagdikian, *The Media Monopoly*, fifth edition (Boston: Beacon Press, 1997), pp. 3–45, 118–33, and 152 ff. On homelessness and hunger

in the U.S., see Joel Blau, *The Visible Poor: Homelessness in the United States* (New York: Oxford University Press, 1991), pp. 24 ff. On hunger, see Jonathan Yenkin, "About 30 million go hungry in the U.S.," *Akron Beacon Journal*, Sept. 10, 1992, p. A3; J. Larry Brown and H. F. Pizer, *Living Hungry in America (The Harvard Physician Task Force on Hunger in America)* (New York: Macmillan, 1987), pp. ix, 161 ff., 190–203.

[3] On class structure, see Harry Braverman, *Labor and Monopoly Capital: The Degradation of Work in the Twentieth Century* (New York: Monthly Review Press, 1974), pp. 293–449. Rifkin, *End of Work*, pp. 109–97 on the changing working class. On wealth, see Democratic Staff of the Joint Economic Committee (Based on Data, Analysis and Additional Assistance Provided by James D. Smith), *The Concentration of Wealth in the United States: Trends in the Distribution of Wealth among American Families* (Washington, DC: Joint Committee United States Congress, 1986), pp. 2–48. Mishel, *Working America*, pp. 273–92. Holly Sklar, "For CEOs, a Minimum Wage in the Millions," *Z Magazine*, July/August 1999, pp. 63–66. Holly Sklar, "Booming Economic Inequality, Falling Voter Turnout," *Z Magazine*, March 2000, pp. 37–41 on increasing family wealth and income gaps and the worth of the Forbes 400 in 1999. On inherited wealth, see Doug Henwood, *Wall Street: How It Works and for Whom* (London: Verso, 1998), pp. 68–70.

[4] On increasing concentration of capital in the productive and financial spheres or corporate mergers, nationally and internationally in transnational corporations, see David C. Korten, *When Corporations Rule the World* (West Hartford, CT: Kumarian Press, 1995), pp. 53–226. "A survey of Multinations," *The Economist*, March 27–April 2, 1993, pp. 5–20. William Greider, *One World, Ready or Not: The Manic Logic of Global Capitalism* (New York: Simon and Schuster, 1997), pp. 21–22. Richard J. Barnet and John Cavanagh, *Global Dreams: Imperial Corporations and the New World Order* (New York: Touchstone Books, 1995), pp. 385–423. John Cavanagh, "The Costs of Economic Liberalism," *Monthly Review*, May 1997, pp. 49–53. Tom Athansiou, *Divided Planet: The Ecology of Rich and Poor* (Boston: Little, Brown and Co., 1996), pp. 192–98. Steve Brouwer, *Sharing the Pie: A Disturbing Picture of the U.S. Economy* (Carlisle, PA: Big Picture Books, 1992), pp. 14–16. Paul Hawken, *The Ecology of Commerce: A Declaration of Sustainability* (New York: HarperCollins, 1993), p. 8. Leslie Wayne, "Wave of Mergers is Recasting Face of Business in U.S.," *New York Times*, Jan. 19, 1998, pp. A1 and A10. On the annual cost of monopoly pricing in the United States, see Ralph Estes, "The Public Cost of Private Corporations," *Advances in Public Interest Accounting*, VI, 329–51. On the six trillion dollars in off-shore tax havens, see Alan Cowell and Edmund L. Andrews, "Undercurrents at a Safe Harbor," *New York Times*, Sept. 24, 1999, pp. C1 and C4.

[5] Braverman, *Labor and Monopoly Capital*, pp. 95, 194, and 241.

[6] Bertell Ollman, *Alienation: Marx's Concept of Man in a Capitalist Society* (London: Cambridge University Press, 1976), p. 131.

[7] Simone Weil, *La Condition ouvrière* (Paris: Gallimard, 1951), p. 15 ff. Richard Pfeffer, *Working for Capitalism* (New York: Columbia Univ. Press, 1979), pp. 47–102.

[8] Studs Terkel, *Working: People Talk About What They Do All Day and How They Feel About Their Work* (New York: Pantheon Books, 1974); cf., for instance, Mike Lefevre, factory worker, pp. xxxi–xxxviii, with David Pender, factory owner, pp. 393–97.

[9] Barbara Garson, *All the Livelong Day: The Meaning and Demeaning of Routine Work* (Garden City, NY: Doubleday, 1975), pp. 38 ff., 58 ff., and 90 ff. Barbara Garson, *The Electronic Sweatshop: How Computers are Transforming the Office of the Future into the Factory of the Past* (New York: Simon and Schuster, 1988), pp. 40–114, 166–71, 175–263.

[10] Richard Sennett and Jonathan Cobb, *The Hidden Injuries of Class* (New York: Alfred A. Knopf, 1972), pp. 30 ff., 55 f., 72 ff., 92 ff., 121 ff., 147 ff., and 162 ff.

[11] Chris Argyris, *Personality and Organization: The Conflict Between System and the Individual* (New York: Harper Torchbooks, 1970), pp. 76–122.

[12] On the ILO Report, see David Briscoe, "Labor force reluctant lot, report says," *Akron Beacon Journal*, March 23, 1993, p. D6; and Frank Swoboda, "Employers Recognizing What Stress Costs Them, U.N. Report Suggests," *Washington Post*, March 23, 1993, p. H2.

[13] On recent downsizing and mergers of corporations, resulting in overwork, higher levels of violence, unsafe working conditions, and so forth, see: Rifkin, *End of Work*, pp. 182–97. William Greider, *Who Will Tell the People: The Betrayal of American Democracy* (New York: Simon and Schuster, 1992), pp. 111–22; *In These Times*, Nov. 14–20, 1990, p. 16. *Akron Beacon Journal*, Aug. 13, 1990, p. 4; Jan. 28, 1996, pp. A1 and A4; July 9, 1996, p. A3.

[14] On the job stress and higher unemployment rates for managers, see Mitchell Lee Marks, *From Turmoil to Triumph: New Life after Mergers, Acquisitions, and Downsizing* (New York: Maxwell Macmillan International, 1994), pp. 6–14. Earl Shorris, *The Oppressed Middle: Politics of Middle Management* (Garden City, NY: Anchor Press/Doubleday, 1981), chs. 6 and 7. Carl Hecksher, *White-Collar Blues: Management Loyalties in an Age of Restructuring* (New York: Basic Books, 1995), pp. 3–94. David Gordon, *Fat and Mean: The Corporate Squeeze of Working Americans and the Myth of Corporate Downsizing* (New York: Free Press, 1996), pp. 33–60.

[15] On drugs, see Steven B. Duke and Albert C. Gross, *America's Longest War: Rethinking Our Tragic Crusade Against Drugs* (New York: Jeremy P. Tarcher/Putnam Books, 1993), pp. 23–32 on tobacco, 33–42 on alcohol, pp. 54 ff. on heroin, etc. On gambling, see Marc Cooper, "America's House of Cards," *The Nation*, Feb. 19, 1996, pp. 11–19.

[16] On murder and suicide, see *Mother Jones*, Jan.–Feb. 1994, p. 40. On the "Victim Costs and Consequences" report, see *Akron Beacon Journal*, April 22, 1996, p. A4. On black males, see *U.S. News and World Report*, Oct. 16, 1995, pp. 53–54; David Remnick, "Dr. Wilson's Neighborhood," *The New Yorker* (*Black in America* issue), April 29 and May 6, 1996, p. 54. On the number of street murders and cost of white-collar crimes, see Russell Mokhiber, "Underworld U.S.A.," *In These Times*, April 1–13, 1996, pp. 14–16. Ralph Estes, "The Public Cost of Private Corporations," *Advances in Public Interest Accounting*, VI (1995), 339–45. Robert Sherrill, "A Year in Corporate Crime," *The Nation*, April 7, 1997, pp. 11–20.

[17] On the family, see, for instance, Blair Justice and Rita Justice, *The Abusing Family* (New York: Plenum Press, 1990), pp. 191 ff. On sexual dysfunction, see Peter J. Howe (*Boston Globe*), "Study finds not everyone enjoying sex," *Akron Beacon Journal*, Feb. 10, 1999, pp. A1 and A4. On women in college and so forth, the daily press is an excellent source. See, for instance, "Women at Work," *Akron Beacon Journal*, Nov. 9, 1992, p. D7.

[18] On pollution and other wasteful practices of capitalism, see Geider, *Who Will Tell the People*, pp. 121 ff. Matthew Alan Cahn, *Environmental Deceptions* (New York: Univ. of New York Press, 1993), pp. 15–120. Herman E. Daly and John B. Cobb Jr., *For the Common Good: Redirecting the Economy toward Community, the Environment and a Sustainable Future* (Boston: Beacon Press, 1989), pp. 1–84 and *Growth Has Enriched the Few, Impoverished the Many, and Endangered the Planet* (Tulsa, OK: Council Oaks Books, 1993), pp. 4–50 and 284–323. Korten, *When Corporations Rule the World*, pp. 25–50 and 229–47.

[19] See Richard Herrnstein and Charles Murray, *The Bell Curve: Intelligence and Class Structure in American Life* (New York: Free Press, 1994), pp. 269–340, for instance, on ethnic/racial differences in IQ. An excellent critique of this work is by Steven Fraser, ed., *The Bell Curve Wars: Race, Intelligence, and the Future of America* (New York: Basic Books, 1995). The classic on social Darwinism is by Richard Hofstadter, *Social Darwinism in American Thought* (Boston: Beacon Press, 1955), pp. 3–66, for instance.

Chapter 9

Paradise Sought, Paradise Found, Paradise Lost: The Three Phases of Plato's Thought

John F. Pepple

If you ask a mathematician if, say, the number of prime numbers is infinite, you will get a yes answer. You can ask this question of any mathematician and get the same yes answer. What is distinctive about mathematics is that those who specialize in it become true experts. All will give the same answers to your questions (assuming an answer has been found and proved), and there can be no intelligent dissent on that answer. Widely different are areas such as ethics, politics and aesthetics. In these areas, the specialists disagree on just about everything so that there are no true experts. If you ask if abortion is justified, the answer you get depends upon whom you ask. The same is true if you ask specialists in politics about the most just form of government or specialists in aesthetics about the nature of beauty.

All would agree that our lives would be substantially different if there were experts in these areas. If we were ever in doubt about a moral decision, we would simply ask an expert in order to get the true answer. Likewise, we would not have to argue about the best form of government, for any expert in politics would be able to tell us. Those who disagreed with the expert would be considered simply wrong by all decent and sensible people. In ethics and politics, our lives would be much different than they are now. In aesthetics, there would be fewer changes in our lives, it is true, but there would still be some. If there were aesthetic experts, then those who thought that works of art deemed beautiful by the experts were ugly would be encouraged to refine their tastes until they could see that such works were indeed beautiful.

I am going to call this collection of experts "moral experts" for short, and I am going to call a world in which moral experts actually exist "paradise" (even if not all would agree that such a world would be paradise). What I contend is that in his early period Plato searched for but failed to find such experts; that in his middle period he devised a way to produce such experts; and that in his late period he was confronted, to his disappointment, with a group of his own students who indirectly raised serious objections against such a project. Accordingly, I call the three phases of Plato's thought paradise sought, paradise found, and paradise lost.

I begin with what is generally accepted, that Plato's philosophical career can be divided into three periods: early, middle, and late. The early dialogues include *Apology, Hippias Minor, Crito, Ion, Euthyphro, Menexenus, Charmides, Laches,* the first book of the *Republic, Protagoras, Gorgias, Lysis, Hippias Major,* and *Meno.* The middle dialogues include *Euthydemus, Cratylus, Phaedo, Symposium,* books two through nine of the *Republic,* and *Phaedrus.* The late dialogues include the last book of the *Republic, Parmenides, Theaetetus, Timaeus, Critias, Sophist, Politicus, Philebus,* and *Laws.*[1]

This division was discovered in the late nineteenth century as a result of stylistic analysis, prior to which there had been a number of wildly speculative and divergent conjectures on the chronological ordering. Once style had given us that ordering, the nature of both the early and middle periods seemed fairly clear (though what I shall say in this article may be slightly different from what others have said). The nature of the late period has been elusive, however, and no consensus has been reached. In this article, I hope to offer a new and more compelling answer.

Paradise Sought

The early period begins with the *Apology,* which is Plato's account of the defense of Socrates. Since it reflects an actual historical speech, we cannot expect much in this dialogue to reflect Plato's own search for moral experts. Nevertheless, we do find Socrates saying that he had questioned three types of people: politicians, tragedians, and craftsmen (21b-22e). The politicians turned out not to have true wisdom, and as for the tragedians, he related that even the bystanders to his conversations were better at giving the meaning of tragedies than their authors were. The craftsmen, he discovered, had expertise in their crafts, but no expertise beyond that. Here, then, we see that Socrates had questioned two out of the three types of moral experts I have been talking about, the political and the aesthetic. More important is the conclusion: that there are no moral experts and that Socrates is wise because he is aware of his own ignorance in these matters.

The *Apology* was followed by a number of dialogues whose pattern provides the most obvious evidence that in his early period Plato was seeking moral experts. That pattern begins with someone claiming to have some sort of moral expertise, is followed by Socrates asking them hard questions about their expertise, and ends with the conclusion that they do not have the expertise that they have claimed. In the *Euthyphro, Charmides, Laches, Lysis, Hippias Major,* and the first book of the *Republic,* Socrates discusses a moral term with a character who either claims to have moral expertise or is presumed to have it. For Euthyphro the term is piety; for Charmides, temperance; for Laches, courage; for Lysis, friendship; for Hippias, beauty; for the characters in the *Republic,* justice. In each instance Socrates, through tough questioning, is able to show that they don't have the knowledge they claim to have.

In *Ion,* the question is what sort of expertise Ion, a reciter of Homer, has. (The same is true of Hippias in *Hippias Minor.*) The conclusion reached is that he has no expertise of any kind, but is merely divinely inspired. In the *Gorgias,* the questioning is no longer about the definition of moral terms (as it was in the *Euthyphro,* et. al.), but is instead about moral topics, and none of Socrates' interlocutors – Gorgias, Polus, and Callicles – proves to be a moral expert (although each claims to have knowledge on moral issues). Accordingly, out of the fourteen early dialogues, the first (*Apology*) contains a small section in which Socrates describes his attempt to find moral experts, and nine others have a pattern showing that Plato was looking for, and failing to find, true moral experts.

That leaves just four early dialogues. In the *Crito,* it is true, there is no evidence that Plato was searching for moral experts. In it, he portrayed Socrates as defending a particular moral claim, which contradicts his claim in the *Apology* that he was ignorant. But since the contradiction between the *Crito* and the *Apology* presents a problem for every interpreter, I am going to ignore it. I will also ignore *Menexenus,* since it is not a philosophical dialogue and so should not be expected to exhibit a search for moral experts. This leaves *Protagoras* and *Meno,* and both of these ask the same question: Can virtue be taught? That Plato asked this question shows that Plato was at this time searching for moral experts, for if there were such experts, then it is likely that they would pass on their knowledge. Likewise, if virtue can be taught, then it is reasonable to believe that there are moral experts. The answer in both dialogues is, however, that there are no teachers of virtue. So, out of fourteen early dialogues, twelve of them show that Plato was at that time seeking but not finding moral experts.

In his early period, then, Plato looked for but failed to find true experts in ethics, politics, and aesthetics. The only person who could conceivably be considered a moral expert would be Socrates, but as he usually professed ignorance, he could hardly be what Plato was looking for.

Paradise Found

This situation changed radically in Plato's middle period, and the reason seems to have been his becoming acquainted with some of the Pythogoreans, especially Archytas. Gregory Vlastos has given us a vivid description of what Archytas meant to Plato:

> Here is a new model philosopher for Plato, giving him everything he might have missed in his old one: Socrates had recoiled helplessly from Athenian politics, convinced it was irremediably corrupt. Archytas enters with stunning success the political fray in his own city. And Socrates had recoiled from metaphysics, while Archytas was a master metaphysician in the Pythagorean tradition. Socrates . . . advised against the study of advanced mathematics, while Archytas was at the forefront of mathematical discovery.[2]

By acquainting Plato with mathematics, Archytas gave Plato a much better example of experts than he had previously been using. Prior to this, Plato would often use as his examples of experts people such as physicians and ship pilots,[3] but physicians and ship pilots can and do disagree on things, while mathematicians rely on proofs, on which there can be no intelligent disagreement. In addition, after becoming acquainted with metaphysics, Plato was led to ask new questions. The most important question he asked was, "What is the nature of the things that Socrates was trying to define? What is the nature of things like courage, piety, and justice?" One obvious answer was that these things were unchanging. Courage in Plato's day was no different from courage at the Battle of Marathon a century earlier, and the same could be said of piety and justice. From there it was a short step to saying that these things are neither created nor destroyed. Moreover, we don't detect these things with the senses (at least not directly), yet we somehow have a dim understanding of them. It must be the case, then, that these things exist in another realm, a realm that transcends our physical realm and which requires thought and not the senses to understand. Plato further believed that we had had a previous existence in which we were in this realm and had become acquainted with these things, which scholars commonly call the forms.[4]

Now Plato believed that in this life we could come to know these forms if we trained ourselves properly. In the *Phaedo*, he talked of how the true philosopher must ignore the body as much as possible in order to know the forms. In the *Symposium*, he spoke of a process of how we could know about the form of beauty, a process that began with loving another person's body, but which involved the contemplation of ever more abstract things, finally ending with the contemplation of the form of beauty. Finally, in the *Republic* he detailed a long and arduous period of training that would eventually allow people with the right potential to contemplate important forms like those of justice and goodness.[5]

Now what is important for the middle period is that Plato believed that anyone who could "see" one of these forms with his mind's eye was then an expert on that feature of the world. The person who could contemplate the form of beauty had a standard to which earthly beauties could be compared; the same was true for anyone who could contemplate the forms of goodness and justice. Accordingly, Plato thought he had hit upon a method to train people to become true experts in ethics, politics, and aesthetics.

The result is that the dialogues of this period are quite different from the early dialogues. In the early dialogues, Plato had Socrates talk about his ignorance, but in the middle dialogues, Plato had Socrates expound on all sorts of doctrines. In fact, the Socrates of the middle period is so different from the Socrates of the early period that Vlastos suggested they are as different from each other as each is from any third philosopher one could think of.[6] That is perhaps going too far, but it is surely true that the middle dialogues are quite different from the early ones.

Let me make several comments before going on to the late period, when Plato's whole program unraveled. First, whatever the form of justice tells us about justice here on earth, Plato did not exactly use it to tell us what a just form of government should be like. Instead, he reasoned that if there were true experts in politics, then those experts ought to rule. After all, why allow anyone else to rule? Anyone who was not a true expert would make decisions that were not just, and why bother having such a ruler if people were available who would make the right decisions? So the form of government that Plato opted for was rule by the political expert. This won't happen, he told us at *Republic* 473c-d, unless either philosophers become kings or kings become philosophers. As a result of this slogan, the term that has grown up around Plato's ideal form of government is the philosopher-king, though a more accurate description of such a person is that he or she is a political expert.

Second, the existence of these experts depends very clearly on the existence of the forms. What if they don't exist? And what proofs did Plato give for their existence? Obviously, if the forms do not exist, then there can be no moral experts of the sort that Plato was envisioning. As for his proof for the forms' existence, it is true that he gave a (rather clumsy) proof of their existence at the end of Book V of the *Republic*, but very early in the middle period he began talking of them as if it were obvious that they existed. Accordingly, he must have had an earlier proof for their existence, but no such proof has been found. This has befuddled scholars, who cannot quite imagine that such an important point would not have been argued for at some definite passage in those dialogues. It will take us too far afield to get into these matters, but I believe that scholars have been looking at this matter in the wrong way. Plato's early proof for the forms consisted of nothing other than indirect proofs against all rival metaphysical positions. (In this article I merely announce this without proof, though I have demonstrated it elsewhere.[7]) This series of proofs occurred in a number of separate passages of the dialogues of the early middle period, so it is no wonder that scholars have not found *the* passage containing the proof for the existence of forms.

The third comment I want to make about the middle period is that Plato seemed to know of no strong arguments against his position at this time. Throughout the middle dialogues, no respectable anti-form arguments are given or discussed. Indeed, at the end of Book V of the *Republic* he talked about a group of people he described as the lovers of sights and sounds who do not believe in forms, but who appear to have no grounds for their belief. At least, Plato imputed none to them. A consequence of the absence of such arguments is what previously seemed to me to be some of the most arrogant attitudes I have found in any philosopher. Most philosophers talk as though philosophy is a discipline shot through with opposing positions of equal or near equal intellectual respectability. But not Plato. He talked of philosophy as *his* philosophy. He talked of philosophy as the study of the forms, which he had instituted. How arrogant could one get? However, his arrogance doesn't seem so misplaced if we consider that no one had a good argument against the existence of the forms at this time and that what he was attempting to do with the forms – namely, use them to help us train true moral experts – was such a spectacular achievement to aim at. For perhaps a good fifteen or twenty years (from about 387 to 367), Plato serenely believed in the existence of forms and churned out dialogues that used the existence of forms as their basis. But then everything changed.

Paradise Lost

What changed everything was the invention of an argument traditionally known as the "Third Man argument." This argument is mentioned in

Aristotle and appears in Plato's own dialogue the *Parmenides* (at 131e-132b). The Third Man argument points out that if there is a set of large things, then by standard Platonic procedure one assumes that there exists a form of largeness in which they all participate, thus coming to be large. But, asks the character Parmenides, what if one considers a new set containing the original set together with the form of largeness? Then another form will emerge in which the new set participates. And if one then includes that second form with the other large things, a third form will emerge, and so on. There is thus an infinite regress of forms of largeness, with the result that there is no form which is *the* form of largeness.

How, then, did this argument change everything? It was the first time Plato had seen an intelligently constructed argument against his beloved forms. Moreover, there is evidence that it was accepted as valid by many people including his own students, particularly his own nephew.

Before getting into that, however, let me observe that not many accept such an interpretation. Instead, scholars are divided into two camps, the unitarians and the revisionists, and the question for them is, Why did Plato present an argument against his own theory? The unitarians believe that once Plato had invented the theory of forms, he never had any doubts about or felt any need to revise this theory. Accordingly, the Third Man argument cannot be a valid argument against the forms, and so Plato's purpose in presenting it was, for example, to provide an exercise for the reader to discover its flaws. And such scholars have looked at this argument and have immediately found its flaw, for they say that this argument implies that the form of largeness is itself a large thing, which they regard as absurd. As one scholar so colorfully put it:

> Oddness is not odd; Justice is not just; Equality is equal to nothing at all. No one can curl up for a nap in the Divine Bedsteadity; not even God can scratch Doghood behind the Ears.[8]

But there are at least two problems with this interpretation. One is that such a view imputes a modern understanding of what we now call universals to Plato and ignores the possibility that Plato had his own reasons for wanting to say that largeness is large. The most obvious such reason is that forms weren't intended to be just what philosophers today call universals. They were also intended to be objects that highly trained people could contemplate, after which they would understand the essence of each form and become moral experts. If the form were nothing but a universal, then it would have no features distinguishing it from any other universal, and so knowledge of beauty and justice would not be obtained.

The other problem is that Aristotle took the Third Man to be valid against Plato's forms,[9] and if the argument depended upon a premise that was clearly rejected by Plato, Aristotle would have never said such a thing.

The other group of scholars, the revisionists, claims that Plato regarded the Third Man as valid and was forced to revise his theory of forms in the light of this flaw. I was a revisionist for many years, but gave it up because the evidence for Plato's having revised his theory in response to the Third Man was negligible. In addition, the revisionists must tinker with the accepted chronology of the dialogues in order to eliminate some damning evidence against their theory.[10]

Why, then, did Plato present an argument against his own theory? Plato's intention was expressed clearly enough in an overlooked sentence that appears almost immediately after the Third Man and other objections have been raised. It is in this passage that we expect an explanation, and Plato didn't fail us. Plato's explanation, as I said, is clear, but it is also the sort of thing that apparently one needs to be prepared to hear, for no scholar has seen it before now. I myself read this passage for twenty years without seeing what Plato was so obviously getting at. It seems to be like a message from a spy that only the intended recipient will understand or a subtle bribe that only those expecting a bribe will notice. I do not mean to say that Plato deliberately tried to hide his information, but rather that he was writing for his contemporaries, who knew things that we do not.

What, then, did he say? At 135a3-4, he had Parmenides say, "The result [of hearing these objections] is that the hearer is perplexed and contends that [the forms] do not exist." The first thing to notice is that nothing is said here of fallacies to look for or revisions in the theory of forms that need to be made. Instead, Plato talked of the hearer's reaction to the Third Man and the other objections. Notice that the hearer reacts by accepting the Third Man and concluding that forms do not exist. However, subsequent sentences (135a7-c) make it clear that Plato continued to believe in the forms. Apparently, what is important here is the clash between what most people thought about the Third Man (that it was valid against the forms) and what Plato thought (that it wasn't valid). As I said above, what the Third Man represents for Plato is the first intelligently constructed objection (not necessarily a valid one) directed against his forms, one that persuaded many others that forms do not exist. For the rest of this article, I'm going to assume that Plato spent his last decades on earth arguing with people about the existence of forms.

Now let me ask, Who is the hearer? Plato spoke of the "hearer" in the singular, but he said it as though he were talking of a nearly universal reaction (as we might say that the tiger is a dangerous animal and mean by this not a particular tiger but all tigers). Nevertheless, there is one hearer in particular whom I believe Plato had in mind. The sentence at 135a3-4 suggests (perhaps not very strongly) that this person had initially believed in the forms, but had then turned away, contending that the forms do not exist. Is this Aristotle? No. Scholars have long thought that Plato's chief philosophical antagonist was Aristotle, and so have wanted to attribute the Third Man to him. But the dates don't work. The *Parmenides* is thought to have been written about 370-367,[11] and Aristotle entered the Academy, at age 17, in 367. It is of course possible that when Aristotle entered the Academy, he immediately made a very telling criticism against the forms. But we hear no rumors to this effect, and even if he had done so, Plato probably wrote the *Parmenides* a year or more after first having the Third Man presented to him. Moreover, we are told at 135a3-4 that the "hearer" rejects the existence of forms, and this was not exactly true of Aristotle.

If it was not Aristotle who presented the Third Man to Plato, then who was it? We are fortunate to have enough information to figure this out. The person in question was old enough to have achieved the philosophical maturity to make a criticism against Plato. He was a member of the Academy and so probably had believed in the forms initially. He was also known for rejecting them. This person was Plato's own nephew Speusippus.

Speusippus, who lived from about 410 to 339, is seldom looked at by scholars today. He has been severely overshadowed by Aristotle, so much so that when scholars consider who was most likely to have debated Plato in the later years of his life, the answer is always Aristotle. But Speusippus fits the bill much better than Aristotle, for he was about forty when the *Parmenides* was written and he is known for having rejected the forms. So it is likely that Speusippus is being referred to in the *Parmenides*, and it is likely that it was Speusippus who debated with Plato in his old age more than anyone else did. And what they debated about was the existence of the forms (whose existence was necessary if there were to be moral experts). In the remainder of this article, I will try to describe the course of this debate. My conclusions will be highly speculative, of course, but the speculation will provide much light on what was formerly obscure.

I believe the debate had two phases, an earlier phase (found in *Republic* X, *Parmenides*, *Theaetetus*, and the *Timaeus* trilogy) when Plato thought he had an answer to the Third Man, and a later phase (found in the *Sophist* trilogy, *Philebus*, *Laws* and certain mysterious passages in Aristotle which speak of unwritten Platonic doctrines) when he was persuaded that his initial answer didn't work.

In the *Parmenides*, no actual answer is given to the Third Man. However, a rhetorical answer is given. Plato observed (at 135a7) that only a highly intelligent person would realize that forms exist and that only someone willing to go through a long and complicated train of argument would see this. What follows is a long and complicated train of argument. No doubt this was intended to be an intelligence test for Speusippus and his other critics.

Plato's actual answer to the Third Man is found in the last book of the *Republic*, which was probably written about the same time as the *Parmenides* and which contains a counter-argument going as follows: If instead of there being one form of largeness, there were two, then a third would emerge that would have them in common, and that would be the form and not the other two.[12] So, when there are two forms, then those no longer count as forms, and instead some third entity is the form. Thus, there can never be more than one form, and the infinite regress of the Third Man is stalled. Or so Plato thought at this time.

The *Theaetetus* perhaps contains an argument against Speusippus, but the details are too obscure to be dealt with in such a short article.[13] The *Timaeus* appeared next, and it contains the full-fledged theory of forms, with only a few hints that there is a problem. One of these hints is the question at 51d, asking whether the forms exist, after which a proof of their existence is given. That Plato was asking this question at this late date suggests that some had come to question their existence. In addition, the uniqueness argument that had appeared in *Republic* X as the answer to the Third Man makes an appearance in this dialogue, also.[14]

What is significant about the *Timaeus*, though, is that it is the first volume of a trilogy that was never completed. The second volume, *Critias*, breaks off in the middle of a sentence, while the third, *Hermocrates*, is never even begun. Why? Many hypotheses have been advanced, but as yet no consensus has been reached. However, my hypothesis about Plato's late period suggests a new one, that Plato abandoned it in connection with his debate with Speusippus. The *Critias*, after all, was supposed to be about how the Athenians, living in the ideal republic, managed to fend off an attack from the people of Atlantis. That is to say, it is a continuation of the *Republic*, but Plato may have decided to abandon this project when it became clear that his answer to the Third Man would not work.

All of this is speculation, of course, but consider the following. Suppose Plato had had a good answer to the Third Man. Then either Aristotle would have accepted this answer, or he would have rejected it after much discussion. He did neither. He simply announced that the Third Man was valid, and did this with no discussion. Sooner or later, then, Speusippus (or someone else) must have forced Plato to realize that his answer to the Third Man did not work. While there is some uncertainty as to when this happened, it is not likely to have happened before the *Timaeus*, since that dialogue uses the same uniqueness argument found in the *Republic*, nor is it likely to have happened much after, for as we shall see, the next dialogue begins a new trilogy that uses a new method and so seems to represent a fresh start for Plato. It is likely, then, that the Timaeus trilogy was not completed because Speusippus persuaded Plato that his uniqueness argument wouldn't work.

What, then, did Speusippus say to Plato? I suspect that he pointed out that the uniqueness argument has a flaw in it, and this flaw is contained in the assumption that a third thing will emerge that will be the new form. That is, the argument begins by positing two things, and it is reasonable to believe that it ought to continue positing two things. So, when Plato declares that a third thing only emerges, we can ask why a third *and* a fourth did not emerge. And once we hear this question, we see that the uniqueness proof is fatally flawed. It assumes uniqueness while trying to prove it.[15]

We now come to the later phase of the debate. Speusippus had gotten through to Plato about his answer to the Third Man, but meanwhile, Plato had gone off to Italy and had no doubt talked with Pythagorean friends. When he came back, he began writing the *Sophist* trilogy, and there is no sign in either the *Sophist* nor the second volume (*Politicus*) that there are any problems. How did Plato manage to fend off Speusippus? I believe he had a three-pronged response. Part of this response consisted of a philosophical promissory note. Plato probably told Speusippus that the Third Man was wrong, but that while he couldn't yet pinpoint the problem with it, he would be able to do so someday. Meanwhile, he would continue to assume his theory was a good one.

Admittedly, there is no textual evidence for this promissory note. No one has ever seen the slightest bit of evidence for it in any Platonic writings or in any rumors about Plato. Nevertheless, it is suggested by evidence from Aristotle, for Aristotle both claimed that the Third Man was valid *and* never indicated that Plato had revised his theory so as to avoid the Third Man. That evidence entails either that Plato never understood the force of the Third Man or that he thought he could overcome it someday. The latter is more flattering to Plato.

The second prong of his response was an *ad hominem* attack on Speusippus. Speusippus, after all, was not just a critic, but a philosopher in his own right. He had his own system, and Plato devised a ploy to both strengthen his own system while attacking Speusippus'. This ploy involved asking what the basic principles of reality were. For Plato they were unity and plurality, and he got Speusippus to agree with him. Plato then used these two principles to derive the existence of the forms. Speusippus also used these principles to derive his system, but two more or less neutral observers, Aristotle and Theophrastus, agreed that Plato had done a better job than Speusippus had. In fact, Aristotle likened Speusippus' system to a poorly constructed tragedy.[16]

The evidence that Plato did all of this is found in Aristotle and other ancient writers. It has long been questioned whether Plato believed in these two basic principles, and Plato's purpose in believing in them is not stated by Aristotle. But there is plenty of evidence that Plato did believe in them,[17] and once that is accepted, the question is why he did believe. My hypothesis provides what others do not, a plausible reason.

The third prong of Plato's attack is that he adopted a new method of dialectic at this time, the method of division. This method is similar to that used by biologists in classifying plants and animals, the difference being that Plato believed that the classifications of reality that he found were forms. No doubt he thought the method helped prove their existence. In the *Sophist*, he used this method to define the sophist, and in the *Politicus* he used it to define the politician. But the third volume of the trilogy, the *Philosopher*, in which the philosopher was going to be defined as the seeker of the forms, never appeared. Why?

Again, we can explain this if we assume that Plato's theory was under attack. Another scholar, Harold Cherniss, has already argued[18] that Speusippus had attacked Plato's theory by using an argument whose conclusion was that either the forms exist, or the method of division is valid, but not both.[19] The underlying reasoning appears to be that forms are supposed to be simple objects with no parts. If so, then there is no way they can be divided, even mentally.

In the face of this objection, Plato wrote a less definitive dialogue, the *Philebus*, rather than the *Philosopher*, and he wrote it specifically to answer Speusippus. Now in this dialogue we both see evidence that Plato was under attack and we find the answer that Plato gave to this newest attack. That the forms are under attack is shown by Plato's asking once again whether they exist (at 15b). Immediately after this comes a question that is obscure but which, based on what follows, seems to ask if the method of division is valid, so it is therefore reasonable to believe that this method was also under attack. Accordingly, it is likely that the Speusippean objection just mentioned was raised at this time. The passage that follows these questions has puzzled scholars since nothing seems to have been settled. Plato simply seems to go on to a new topic without answering his questions. In fact, though, Plato did answer them. It is true that for those who are ignorant of the debate with Speusippus and who refuse to believe that Plato accepted the two basic principles of reality, it will not look as though he gave an answer. But he did. That answer consisted of nothing other than reminding Speusippus that the two basic principles lead to the forms. Here is what he said:

> All things . . . that are ever said to be consist of a one and a many, and have in their nature a conjunction of limit and unlimitedness.

> This then being the ordering of things we ought . . . whatever it be that we are dealing with, to assume a single form and to search for it. (16c-d)

Notice that we see the two principles of unity and plurality on display here (described as one and many); it is asserted that they are the basis of everything said to be. Plato went on to say, "this then being the ordering of things." The reader might ask, "Why should I accept such a claim?" And it is true that Plato does not argue for this here. But if he were responding to Speusippus, as I have claimed, then he could say this without proof, for he knew that Speusippus had already agreed to it. Accordingly, inserting it into the discussion at this point is a reminder to Speusippus that he had no argument against Plato's claim that the forms could be inferred from the two principles. And we indeed find that after saying "this then is the ordering of things," Plato said that "we ought . . . to assume a single form." A little bit more argumentation on his part (which I won't dwell on) leads to the further assertion that the method of division is valid. So, the questions are answered.

Now this is not a solid answer on Plato's part. It doesn't really get to the heart of Speusippus' objection. It is instead an *ad hominem* remark that works against Speusippus only. (I will describe later how Aristotle answered it.) In fact, the situation that Plato was now in was somewhat more desperate than before. Before, he had only the Third Man argument to answer, but now he had this second argument as well. Introducing his two basic principles staved off total disaster, but that is about all it did. Nor did it seem likely that a promissory note would be sufficient in the face of two important objections. So, Plato capitulated, in a sense. The next dialogue he wrote was the *Laws*, in which he abandoned (temporarily, at least) the ideal form of government espoused in the *Republic*. This wasn't because he had changed his mind, for he made it clear that rule by laws was merely second-best compared with rule by philosopher-kings:

> If ever by the grace of God someone endowed with a natural character equal to the test could take over the reins of power, he would need no laws to be his masters. No law or ordinance is superior to knowledge, nor is it right that wisdom should be a slave or subject. Natural wisdom, genuine, true and free, should be ruler of all. As things are, however, it is not to be found anywhere or anyhow, to any significant extent. So we must chose the second-best, ordinance and law. . .. (875c-d)

Here we see that Plato still thought that those who had wisdom (which I have been calling expertise in morality) ought to be in charge, but he had despaired of finding such people (since they are "not to be found anywhere or anyhow, to any significant extent"). The usual reason given for this is that Plato had attempted to turn the ruler in Syracuse into a philosopher, and it hadn't worked. However, turning a king into a philosopher is only half of his formula for creating the ideal state. The other half is to turn a philosopher into a king, and he wrote the *Laws* only when this method also failed. And it failed because so many of his students had abandoned their belief in the forms as a result of the many objections that had been raised.

The *Laws* was Plato's last dialogue, and it represents the end of the debate. Plato did not exactly lose this debate, but he was far from winning it. Plato's dream of creating a paradise with true moral experts in it for the most part died with him. There have been plenty of people in later centuries who have thought of themselves as Platonists, but most confine themselves to believing that forms exist and refrain from also believing that those who could contemplate them would count as moral experts.

In addition, Plato's student Aristotle initiated a rebellion against his master that, while being less radical than Speusippus', was much more successful. To begin with, although Aristotle was willing to believe in forms, he insisted that they existed within individuals instead of some transcendent realm. Aristotle had seen the problems Plato encountered with making forms transcendent, but he had also seen the problems Speusippus encountered in denying the existence of forms altogether. Aristotle made the sensible, down-to-earth move and put forms within the things of our world. This move allowed Aristotle to avoid the Third Man, but it also meant that there could be no moral experts. If forms are in things, then as Plato had observed, their instantiation in our realm is imperfect, so contemplating them will not give one perfect knowledge of justice and beauty. Accordingly, Aristotle asserted as though it were a commonplace that we just cannot expect to have certainty in areas like ethics and politics.[20] He thus utterly rejected the idea that there could be moral experts.

What is also important is that Aristotle did what Speusippus was not able to do, namely he rejected the two basic principles of unity and plurality. For Aristotle the two basic principles of reality were form and matter. Thus, Aristotle avoided the *ad hominem* attacks on Speusippus made by Plato, for in contending that form and matter are the two basic principles, he accordingly had no reason to accept Plato's claim that transcendent forms must exist. For these and other reasons, Aristotle took his place among the world's greatest philosophers, far outdistancing Speusippus, whom the world has mostly forgotten.

For a few glorious years in the early part of the fourth century B.C., there was a thinker who believed we could produce moral experts. Had this been true, it would be like suddenly having a number of angels from heaven appear in our midst. Such creatures would have answers to many of our questions on how to live and govern ourselves, and the sensible person would accede to their greater expertise. But it was not to be.

Endnotes

[1] See W.K.C. Guthrie, *A History of Greek Philosophy* (Cambridge University Press, 1975) IV,50. I accept the further refinement of Leonard Brandwood, *A Word Index to Plato* (Leeds: W.S. Maney & Son, 1976), p. xviii, who asserts that the last book of the *Republic* was written at about the same time as the *Parmenides*.

[2] *Socrates, Ironist and Moral Philosopher* (Ithaca: Cornell University Press, 1991), p. 129.

[3] See, for example, *Republic* I 332d-e.

[4] *Phaedo* 74b-76e.

[5] *Phaedo* 63e ff; *Symposium* 210-11; *Republic* 521c-541b

[6] Gregory Vlastos, *Socrates, Ironist and Moral Philosopher*, p. 46.

[7] See my *Forgotten Debates: The Hidden Story of Ancient Greek Philosophy* (Bloomington, Ind.: AuthorHouse, 2006), ch. 12.

[8] R.E. Allen, "Participation and Predication in Plato's Middle Dialogues," *Studies in Plato's Metaphyics*, ed. R.E. Allen (London: Routledge & Kegan Paul, Ltd., 1965), p. 43.

[9] *Metaphysics* 990^{b}17, 991^{a}2-5, and 1032^{a}2-4.

[10] The most famous writings by a revisionist is G.E.L. Owen's "The Place of the *Timaeus* in Plato's Dialogues," *Studies in Plato's Metaphyics*, ed. R.E. Allen (London: Routledge & Kegan Paul, Ltd., 1965), pp. 313-338, in which it is argued that the *Timaeus* was written in the middle period and not the late period.

[11] The style of the *Parmenides* is similar to that of the *Theaetetus*, which means they were probably written about the same time. The *Theaetetus* tells of Theaetetus being wounded in a battle which probably took place in 369, and it is thought that it was written shortly afterwards.

[12] *Republic* 597b-c. The actual passage is about bedhood rather than largeness.

[13] See my *Forgotten Debates*, pp. 210-12.

[14] *Timaeus* 31a.

[15] See G.E. Moore, "Identity," *Proceedings of the Aristotelian Society*, N.S. 1 (1900-1901), 112. I thank MacNair Swanson for pointing out this passage to me.

[16] Aristotle, *Metaphysics* 1090^{b}20. See also Theophrastus, *Metaphysics* 6^{a}15-^{b}17.

[17] See my *Forgotten Debates*, pp. 221-227, for the details.

[18] *The Riddle of the Early Academy* (Berkeley, 1945), pp. 39 ff.

[19] Aristotle, *Metaphysics* 1085^{a}23-31 and also 1039^{a}24-^{b}19.

[20] *Nicomachean Ethics* I.iii.

Chapter 10

We Need Another G.E. Moore

William E. McMahon

D. C. Stove (1985) has characterized the situation in philosophy of science as being akin to the state of affairs in the Cole Porter song, "Anything Goes." In some circles what we used to call epistemological relativism is not merely in vogue; to hold otherwise is to be dogmatic, old fashioned, ignorant about the theory and practice of science, and simply anti-scientific. To regard philosophy as a pursuit of truth, or of belief justified according to some canons of rationality, is to be afflicted by adherence to an evil doctrine known as "foundationalism." To call something an "ism" is usually to treat it pejoratively, so by a clever polemic trick such old isms as historicism, psychologism, and pragmatism are relabelled by such names as "the natural ontological attitude" (Fine 1989:100-102), "an evolutionary perspective" (Giere 1989:384-386), or a "naturalistic epistemology" (Giere 1989:379-380, 386-390). This renders them philosophically respectable, while by ismizing traditional epistemology, one makes it appear that anyone who engages in it is out of touch with the world of philosophy and the scientific endeavors it comments on.

Of course, the attitudes expressed are at least as old as Protagoras, and one could attempt to combat them by appealing to Plato, but his epistemological absolutism was grounded on the theory of forms, which would surely be regarded as an unwarranted metaphysical foundation. So let me turn instead to a much more recent philosopher, G. E. Moore. Moore was mystified by many things which he heard from other philosophers, and he would have been puzzled by these recent developments. His antidote to what he found philosophically strange was a "common sense" approach, a methodology consisting essentially in arguments of the reductio type, or attempting to hoist an adversary onto his own petard.

Moore's appeal to common sense may be formulated as follows:[1]

(1) A philosophical view has certain concrete consequences q.
(2) q is incompatible with some other proposition p.
(3) p = or entails some common sense view.
(4) p is true (hence some common sense view is true).
(5) Therefore, q is false.
(6) Furthermore, the philosophical view is false.

Note that this approach does not attempt to ground epistemology on some theoretical foundation such that one can undercut it by showing that the foundation is shaky. Moore did not think he had to erect a theory of truth to make his case, but rather merely to point out a few obvious facts that everyone (except, possibly, a few philosophers) would acknowledge.

Critics (e.g., Wisdom 1942) regarded Moore's "refutations" as akin to Samuel Johnson's kicking a rock in order to refute Berkeley. But Moore's defense consisted in maintaining that common sense truths (which, incidentally, were not taken as apriori, but as contingent and empirical), if not self-evident, came as close to certitude as is humanly possible. If we couldn't believe such things, we couldn't believe anything. In contemporary parlance, both the notion of common sense truths and the methodology for evaluating claims are trans-theoretical. 'Common sense' would be at least one term that in both its descriptive and evaluative uses is not "theory-laden," or, if we maintain that all language must be theory-laden, the theory-ladenness of this concept is far more minimal than that of any theoretical notion in philosophy or science, such that a prerequisite for the employment of theoretical terms would be their capacity for being used consistently with common sense. Furthermore, if one claimed to be misinterpreted by Moore, saying that his theory and the terms therein did not mean what Moore took them to mean, Moore would have held that the burden was on his adversary to explain what he did mean. For example, a Humean would not contend that his beliefs about material objects conflicted with obvious "facts" expressed by such sentences as, "I am holding up a pencil." Moore's response, (see, e.g., Moore 1942: 667-676) to this was that prima facie there appeared to be a conflict, and if there wasn't one, the Humean ought to explain why not.

Moore addressed himself to theories fashionable in his day, such as phenomenalistic attempts to account for the physical world and idealist efforts to explain away time. I would like to bring Moore up to date and apply his method to examining the views of "radical meaning variance theorists" (see Kordig 1971: 34 ff.) in philosophy of science. For illustration I shall take up one such view, that of Ronald Giere, with the proviso that what is said here applies a fortiori to other such views. Addressing himself to theories concerning scientific propositions, Giere (1989: 383) claims that "methodological foundationalism is a hopeless program and thus. . .naturalism. . .is our only alternative." "Naturalistic" viewpoints argue from the history and practice of an enterprise such as science, so obviously the descriptive/normative distinction must be scrapped. Giere's naturalistic approach is based on "evolutionary theory, together with recent work in cognitive science and the neurosciences" (1989: 384). So the criteria (norms?) for adjudicating among theories are to be taken from what have traditionally been known as "descriptive" or "empirical" areas of inquiry. Not to do this, i.e., to follow a traditional line, is to engage in "essentialism" in epistemology (1989: 387). By failing to naturalize values traditional foundationism conflicts with evolutionary theory in espousing "emergentism," the view that there are genuinely emergent properties (such as rationality). Since these were not possessed by our evolutionary forebears, they would be "fundamentally irreducible properties that science alone cannot explain" (1989:387)[2]

The emergentist program is to be eschewed because of its gratuitous assumption that humans are a breed apart. The upshot of this is that "philosophers of science are on the same footing with historians, psychologists, sociologists, and others for whom the study of science is itself a scientific enterprise" (1989: 387). And it seems quite fair to say that, a fortiori, this would apply to philosophers in general.

It is not my intention to argue all the aspects of the issue in question. I shall especially avoid making specific contentions about the practice of science, as I have no special insights into what scientists do, and hence am willing to take what people like Giere say about that at face value. It seems to me that scientists, as human beings, behave in all sorts of ways. Sometimes they appear to display bias;[3] at others they appear to be making what we would ordinarily call "value judgments," but it might be the case in such instances that they don't really know what they are doing. Nor shall I argue as to what should be the appropriate "unit for evaluation" (or of choice among alternatives), whether it be singular sentences, specific theories within a "research tradition," or the research tradition itself. I shall further avoid attempting to explicate the relationships among these "units." There is a more fundamental issue here which I wish to address, one which Moore would have instantly spotted, and so I shall attempt to apply a Moorean analysis to it. Consider the following argument:

(a)People like Giere assert that we cannot confirm or disconfirm scientific generalizations by appealing to observational evidence. Since logic alone would not be relevant to the acceptance or rejection of such propositions, this entails that ostensibly empirical propositions are not evaluable by means of the sorts of evidence normally employed to evaluate them.

(b)That would be incompatible with the fact that both in science and in ordinary life people typically do make decisions, assess the truth of their beliefs, according to observational evidence.[4]

A few examples of this will suffice to establish the point:

(1)Giere himself holds that in geology drift models are more correct than static models, as he claims, e.g., that, "the tectonic structure of the world is more similar (in the relevant respects) to drift models than to static models" (1989: 393). So at least some scientific statements, even general statements, are corrigible in the light of "factual" evidence. If we don't hold this, how are we to make sense of what Giere says?

(2)Another domain, in which the notion of "evidence" is so commonly employed that we almost instinctively associate it with that domain, is the criminal law. A jury is even regarded as the "trier of fact." When there are a sufficient number of facts--fingerprints, possession of the murder weapon, psychological information about motive and intent, etc.--pointing to the accused, the reasonable conclusion is that that person committed the crime. Absence of such evidence constitutes grounds for acquittal. To proceed otherwise would be to have an absurd legal system.

(3)In our everyday lives factual information constantly is a basis for our decisions. Some of this information could be said to embody or entail theories. Moore (1959a: 32-35, 1953: 2-14) cites a number of such facts, which again underlie his "common sense" philosophy. Let me just note a few others. I would say we have very good reasons for believing: (a) If we sail west or east from the coasts of America, we won't eventually fall off the earth.[5] (b) If I shoot a bullet into my brain I shall die or otherwise seriously impair my health. (c) Similarly, if I put my hand into a flame for an extended period of time, or stay out in sub-zero weather without a coat, I shall incur physical damage. (d) When there are dark clouds in the sky, I should bring a raincoat or umbrella, unless I want to get wet. (e) It is very doubtful that I can lift an elephant, swim Lake Erie, or run from Akron to Columbus without stopping.

(4) Let me add just a couple of items where science and "common sense" (taken not in the Moorean sense, but as tantamount to popular belief) intersect. Certain "pseudo" or "quasi"-scientific beliefs are regarded by intellectually sophisticated people as having little credibility, and I submit this is for good reasons, not some kind of elitist snobbery. For example, the daily horoscopes, and most likely astrology in general, probably give us little information about what kind of people we are and how we should live our lives.[6] These things have been subjected to tests, and Giere himself (1984:151-172) has debunked these theories in a popular textbook. No doubt he would also agree that the "creationist" view that the earth and universe are not more than 6000-8000 years old is quite wrongheaded. To make it compatible with existing evidence we would either have to believe that God created the world with fossils in the ground, which would make God a deceiver, or that dinosaurs coexisted with humans, which is a bit hard to swallow (regrettably, Noah did not save a few with his ark).

(c) If any of the above claims about facts are correct (and I believe all are), then there are a number of routine things that we know, or have a sufficient degree of certitude so as to have little concern with the alternatives. What Moore intended by adhering to a pre-theoretical notion of "common sense" is that we have ready access to a large amount of factual information, as well as to an elementary means of checking the credibility of many beliefs. Hence:

(d) if such matters represent the truth, or a reasonable facsimile thereof, then (e) Giere's "epistemic" contentions and (f) his general theory must be incorrect.

It would seem there is something very wrong with the line of argument just used. Surely no one[7] would deny obvious facts such as those just presented, and to think that sophisticated theories based on considerable technical knowledge can be overturned by some sort of "cracker barrel" philosophizing offends one's sense of academic propriety. But this is precisely the point. Moore believed that in our sophistication we sometimes outsmart ourselves. We overlook the obvious; we ignore conflicts between our theories and information which forms the basis for our everyday behavior. Like Moore I am most hesitant to accuse philosophers of being so naive. However, if their theories appear to have bizarre consequences, what are we to make of that?

To amplify the point let us consider further the position staked out be Giere (and presumably others in the "naturalist epistemology" camp). Oddly, the philosophers in question (see also Kuhn 1989: 359-361) operate, as it were, from "the top down." Because of certain epistemological problems concerning theories and theoretical traditions they incur difficulty in formulating criteria which would enable us to make a clear choice of one theory or group of theories over its competitors. Historical information is introduced, showing there have been many cases where scientists, supported by the overwhelming preponderance[8] of available evidence, adhered rigidly to certain beliefs while rejecting others which ultimately proved be more "fruitful" (see also Laudan 1989: 370-378). Now the problem occurs when one extrapolates from these considerations to knowledge in general, i.e., suggests that the difficulties in establishing high-level theories have epistemological ramifications even for matters of everyday experience. Again, to put this into a Moorean idiom, no one cited here (except perhaps Giere) exactly says that, but their epistemological views certainly appear to have such consequences, inclining us to want to inquire into what they actually do mean.

In contrast, the traditional empiricist approach, which nowadays is the subject of much derision (see, e.g., Fine 1989: 94-100; Giere 1989: 381-383) proceeded epistemologically from the "bottom up." A simplistic version of this, taught by many of us in our logic and critical thinking classes, will suffice for present purposes: There are certain factual truths that we all know from observation. If we want to know if it is raining, all we need do is look. Generalizations concerning the observable world need not be mere inductive extrapolations from observed facts, but at least some of them can be checked against the "facts." For example if we want to know (have reasonable grounds for believing) whether a certain Indian dance produces rain, we would try to test the hypothesis, especially under conditions where there would be no other reason to expect rain. Procedures like this would ordinarily be satisfactory for testing at least low-level generalizations.[9] When we deal with higher level generalizations, such as theories and "theoretical traditions," the matter of verification (or falsification) is of course more complicated. The relationship of evidence to theory is not always very clear. There may be considerable uncertainty, so even where some theories may appear to be far more justified than others, it may be unwise to limit the possibilities prematurely, in order that views having potential not be excluded. But the gist of the position is that at relatively low levels of understanding one can appeal to empirical evidence, which is ordinarily sufficient for the purpose of inquiry. Furthermore, this epistemological account assumes the descriptive/normative distinction. No empirical statement, singular or general, would be taken as self-validating; one may always ask whether it is true, and an assertion of the form "p is true" is regarded as different in nature than one simply of the form "p" (in that, at least, the former contains a modal operator).

Now many philosophers of science would not dispute the claim that there is certain basic factual information, although some would maintain that it doesn't have much relevance to the acceptance of scientific theories (see, e.g., Cartwright 1989; Laudan 1989: 374-379). Not so with Giere, however, and here is where he seems to throw the baby out with the bath. Let me conclude, then, by making a couple of further points concerning his epistemology, showing that it surely would not have been acceptable to Moore, and suggesting that there are serious questions regarding its acceptability in general.

One may be thinking that there has been a serious distortion in this whole presentation, as Moore and Giere are really birds of a feather. That is, they could both be viewed as espousing essentially "pragmatic" theories of truth, Giere in examining scientific theories, and Moore at the level of common sense. Giere (1989: 384) rejects normative theories of rationality because he believes they mistakenly convert "ises" into "oughts." As he sees it, they are really articulating general descriptions "of situations which we instinctively regard as clear cases of rational acceptance or pursuit." Like ordinary people, scientists are "real agents facing various choices in the course of their actual scientific lives" (1989: 390). So we need a theory of theory choice, which in its "descriptive mode,. . .may be viewed as a specialized part of ordinary belief-desire psychology" (1989: 390). Giere goes on to suggest that a promising descriptive strategy would involve the notion of "satisficing," which is explained, "Agents. . .must have a good idea of their minimum satisfactory payoff--their satisfaction level" (1989: 391). So Moore's examples (and mine, for that matter) could be regarded simply as matters where the "payoff" would be the greatest for most people.[10]

However, this is not at all what Moore intended as a means of establishing the credibility of beliefs. He explicitly rejects "pragmatic" approaches to truth, noting, (1953:281-284) both that beliefs leading to satisfactory results need not be true and that "satisficing" cannot serve as a criterion of truth. Being a believer in correspondence (not necessarily as a theory, but as a prerequisite for empirical inquiry), Moore would concede that certain beliefs work, but that is not what makes them true. He would have been well aware of facts such as that knowledge of Nazi atrocities was not very convenient for Germans living under the Hitler regime. Or, to consider one of our above examples, there are many people who disbelieve in evolution, which would appear to work for them, as according far more readily with their other beliefs. If one were then to claim, "Well, it wouldn't work for our culture in general," what could that possibly mean? If, as I believe, evolution is primarily a theoretical concern, having little "cash value" for our practical behavior (hence impacting on the lives of only a small minority within the scientific community), then for most people theories without any fairly immediate technological applications need not be regarded as fulfilling any criteria of satisficing.[11]

Finally, let me note two problems in grounding epistemology on some "descriptive" discipline. First, for Moore this would be attempting to explain the less knowable by means of the more knowable. No area of psychology (e.g., cognitive science) or biology (clearly not evolutionary theory), no branch of sociology, no line of historical interpretation, could be regarded as so well established as to be taken as superseding Moore's common sense truths. If there are conflicts, he would have put the burden on the theorist to show his view was the correct one. But there should be no conflict, as "common sense" beliefs in the sense in question would all be presupposed by the various theoretical investigations. The conflict would not occur with respect to the "descriptive content" of the theories. Insofar as the theories only purport to explain the world and human behavior therein, assuming they are "good" theories, they could only augment the knowledge provided by common sense.

This brings me to my final point: Such conflicts would only occur when the theories are taken normatively, the norms in question here being epistemic ones. Thinking about this recalls to mind an experience from early in my teaching career, when I became quite agitated by hearing a psychologist colleague claim that "Freud disproved the principle of contradiction."[12] Of course, I didn't think Freud had anything to do with the principle of contradiction, and by the same token cognitive psychology has nothing to do with truth. If I were to look for some "descriptive" discipline on which to base philosophy, my choice would be linguistics. That is because I believe linguistics provides clarification of certain concepts which are central to philosophy (including "understanding," which enters into the discussion here). But linguistics does not provide us with criteria of truth (nor acceptability, nor correctness), nor is it self-validating in such a way that we could say, e.g., Chomskyan transformationalism is true because Chomskyan transformationalism says it is. Have we any reason for regarding any other science as providing norms not only for other disciplines, but even for itself?

Concerning this question, I think Giere does two things which are objectionable. First, he implicitly divides a science such as psychology into descriptive and normative aspects, then proposes that the normative aspect serve as the ground for epistemology, and then denies that there ever was a descriptive/normative distinction in the first place.[13] I have no problem with the idea that psychology provides explanations as to how human animals satisfy needs, wants, etc. There may be some problems with the specific models preferred by Giere, but let us ignore that here. Furthermore, we can grant that psychologists sometimes prescribe what the appropriate ways to achieve satisfaction, even "intellectual" satisfaction should be. When they do the latter, it has been customary to say that psychologists are "philosophizing." But let us not be nitpickers about disciplinary boundaries; let us allow that a psychologist qua psychologist may philosophize, or make evaluations. This still does not establish that he is doing the same thing (engaged in the same kind of cognitive activity), as when he is describing, explaining, etc. To say that people should achieve satisfaction in the ways that they typically do (or that some do) is still to make a normative claim, which is not per se entailed by "factual" statements (e.g., declarative utterances without deontic operators). Moore surely would not have regarded the descriptive/normative distinction as undercut by a ploy such as the one in question, for he would have noted (see, e.g., 1959b:10ff.) that it remains an "open question" as to whether what is the case ought to be the case. So even if the body of propositions within an "empirical" discipline such as psychology were taken to include epistemic (or other) value judgments (and even the correct ones), the normative propositions would not be logically reducible to the non- normative ones.[14]

The second thing that Giere does is to make a number of gratuitous remarks from the standpoint of his value system, i.e., his comments about rationality. One notes a general disregard for the "genetic fallacy" in recent philosophy of science, i.e., the conflating of motives for belief with grounds justifying a belief. Without presenting a general defense for taking that style of argumentation as fallacious, I would, however, like to comment on Giere's version, which takes the form:

y genetically follows from x

x has F (or $\overline{F}$)

Therefore, y has F (or $\overline{F}$)

That is, humans do not have rationality (as ascribed to them by some philosophers), because humans evolved from lower animals, and lower animals do not have it. Such philosophers are summarily dismissed as adhering to the distasteful doctrines of "emergentism" and "essentialism." What Moore would no doubt say to this is that we have whatever properties we have, and how we came by them is not necessarily a relevant concern. Or, if one has F, he obviously could have acquired it. It seems clear that this issue is what one would call a "conceptual" issue, concerning how best to characterize the traits that humans have. Now various theories would provide characterizations differing from one another to a greater or lesser extent. But rather than saying one theory provides a totally different picture of the human species from that within another theory, I think it makes more sense to say that they give somewhat different pictures of the same phenomenon. In other words, Moore would maintain that in a pre-analytic sense humans have certain basic traits.[15] Moore's common sense statements (and some of my examples above) contain assertions about some of the things people can or cannot do. Among these are thinking and evaluating, to which we can add such activities as the creating of art, music, and poetry. Now all these may be explainable by means of a model which does not consider the human species as unique; efforts at such explanations are to be welcomed so far as they fulfill standard criteria for scientific acceptability. But Giere is not merely trying to put forth an interesting and potentially fruitful scientific hypothesis. He is begging the question in favor of a given model and then attempting to dismiss his adversaries by name-calling.

This concludes my attempt to kick the philosophical rock. Needless to say, I have considerable misgivings about what has been said, as it seems overly simplistic. But it seemed to me appropriate to bring Moore's approach into the dialogue in contemporary philosophy science.

REFERENCES

Cartwright, Nancy. 1989. "The Truth Doesn't Explain Much." Readings in the Philosophy of Science (2nd ed.) ed. by Baruch A. Brody and Richard E. Grandy, 184-189. Englewood Cliffs, NJ: Prentice Hall. Originally appeared in American Philosophical Quarterly, 17, No. 2 (April, 1980).

Fine, Arthur. 1989. "And Not Anti-Realism Either." Readings in the Philosophy of Science. . ., 93-103. Originally appeared in Nous, 18 (1984):51-66.

Giere, Ronald N. 1984. Understanding Scientific Reasoning (2nd ed.). New York: Holt, Rinehard and Winston.

_____. 1989. "Philosophy of Science Naturalized." Readings in the Philosophy of Science. . ., 379-398. Originally appeared in Philosophy of Science, 52 (September, 1985).

Kordig, Carl R. 1971. The Justification of Scientific Change. Dordrecht: D. Reidel.

Kuhn, Thomas S. 1989. "Objectivity, Value Judgement and Theory Choice." Readings in the Philosophy of Science. . ., 356-368. Originally appeared in The Essential Tension: Selected Studies in the Scientific Tradition and Change. Chicago: U. of Chicago Press, 1977.

Lakatos, Imre. 1989. "The Role of Crucial Experiments in Science." Readings in the Philosophy of Science. . ., 344-356. Originally appeared in Studies in History and Philosophy of Science, 4, No. 4 (1974).

Laudan, Larry. 1989. "From Theories to Research Traditions." Readings in the Philosophy of Science. . ., 368-379. Excerpted from Laudan, Progress and Its Problems. Berkeley: U. of California Press, 1977.

Moore, G. E. 1942. "A Reply to My Critics." The Philosophy of G.E. Moore, ed. by Paul Arthur Schlipp, 535-677. Library of Living Philosophers, Vol. IV. Evanston: Northwestern U. Press.

_____. 1953. Some Main Problems of Philosophy. London: George Allen & Unwin.

_____. 1959a. "A Defense of Common Sense." Philosophical Papers, 32-59. London: George Allen & Unwin.

_____. 1959b. Principia Ethica. Cambridge: Cambridge U. Press.

Sobel, Dava. 1989. "Dr. Zodiac." Omni, 12, No. 3 (December, 1989):60-72.

Stove, D. C. 1985. "Karl Popper and the Jazz Age." Encounter, June, 1985:65-74.

Wisdom, John. 1942. "Moore's Technique." The Philosophy of G. E. Moore. . ., 419-450.

Endnotes

[1]   I owe this formulation to Vere Chappell, in a class taught at the University of Chicago in 1959. For the source in Moore see Moore (1959a, also 1953:19-26).

[2]   Note the resemblance of this line of reasoning to the medieval dictum that, "there can not be more reality in the effect than in the cause" (also found in Descartes' Meditations).

[3]   For example, Sobel (1989:62-63) points out that Percy Seymour's attempt to provide a scientific basis for astrology has been dismissed by some astronomers without their having read his book or examined his arguments.

[4]   Laudan (1989:376) notes that scientists often treat given theories as if they were true. This of course is obvious, for we have all heard scientists making epistemic value judgments. They could be deluded, in not realizing how their environment shapes their beliefs, but nevertheless it is indisputable that they think scientific truth or justified belief is possible.

[5]   If true, this would entail a number of facts, such as: There is a land mass called 'America'. It is on the earth, and there are oceans on either side of it. The earth is at least roughly spherical. Humans are capable of sea travel in vessels riding on the surface, etc.

[6]   The study by Seymour alluded to above (see Sobel 1989) does not support the validity of daily horoscopes or popular astrology per se. Evidently Seymour, a professional astronomer himself, believes that the magnetic activity of the sun, altered by the configuration of the planets, may have an effect on the genes of fetuses, and thereby on personality. Again, this would have to be tested by correlating planetary configurations with personality types. Sobel suggests there is such a correlation, but this is questionable. As for elementary tests of practical astrologers, let me cite one by magician-skeptic James Randi on a television program devoted to psychic phenomena. Twelve people supplied information about themselves to an astrologer, who then attempted to guess their signs. The astrologer did not get even one right. Of course one could dismiss this "experiment," using all sorts of ad hoc rescues, e.g., the individual tested could be a bad astrologer such that her ineptitude does not count against astrology in general. It should be noted, however, that in this sort of case Giere (see 1984:155-158, 163-164) is most unsympathetic to ad hoc rescues (and to astrology as well). If the move is dubious in cases like that, one could well ask why it should not be regarded as questionable in principle.

[7]   Moore (e.g., 1953:14-27) tends to think only some philosophers would deny the obvious. And as for the examples of "pseudo"-scientific beliefs, of course there are

many people who believe in paranormal theories and factual claims. The point is that such beliefs, when subjected to critical scrutiny (rational analysis), generally don't hold up.

[8] The evidence is often taken as "preponderant" because it has been accumulated within the presuppositions of the theory or tradition. See Kuhn (1989: 360).

[9] This assumes Popperian falsificationism, which has of course been attacked, especially by Lakatos (1989). A common claim is that it is useless as a criterion for high level theories; whether it is applicable on lower levels is not made clear. A few years earlier, in a more popular presentation, Giere (1984:99-110) accepted falsificationism, but he seems to have had second thoughts on the matter.

[10] His example (1953: 282) is "that my friend's belief that I had gone away for my holidays, might be true in every sense of the word, even if I had not gone away. . .it would be thus true, provided only it led up to certain kinds of satisfactory results." He adds, "And similarly, of course, for millions of other instances."

[11] Giere waffles regarding the status of evolutionary theory. At one point (1989: 394) he concedes that the fossil record does not necessarily provide "a satisfactory basis for deciding that any evolutionary theory is correct." At another (1989:385) he dismisses the argument that the problematic status of evolutionary theory undercuts his case, claiming that that argument is "equally question-begging." His own argument is:

> Three hundred years of modern science and over a hundred years of biological investigation have led us to the firm conclusion that no humans have ever faced the world guided only by their own subjectively accessible experience and intuitions. Rather, we now know that our capacities for operating in the world are highly adapted to that world. The skeptic asks us to set all this aside in favor of a project that denies our conclusion. And he does so on the basis of what we claim to be an outmoded and mistaken theory about how knowledge is, in fact, acquired.

This raises the genetic issue, which will be dealt with shortly.

[12] There is an interesting story associated with this anecdote. The psychology professor who said that to me was Father Bernard Pagano, who several years later was accused of a string of armed robberies in Wilmington, Delaware (if Moore thought philosophers were strange, what would he have thought of psychologists?). Fortunately, just when it appeared Pagano would be convicted, the real robber came forth and confessed.

[13] For example, he says (1989: 390):

Decision theory has a split personality. Sometimes it operates as an account of rational choice; other times it is more descriptive. Here we want the descriptive mode, which may be viewed as a specialized part of ordinary belief-desire psychology. Somehow these are collapsed into one another, but exactly how is not clear.

[14] As is well known, Moore devoted much attention in works such as Principia Ethica to refuting attempts to reduce ethical terms to psychological terms. Let me note that he also makes interesting comments (see 1959b:47-58) on attempts to derive value judgments from evolutionary theory.

[15] One will note Moore subscribing to the "myth of the given" here, but of course that occurs all throughout his work.

fig. 1

Chapter 11

King and Cleric: Richard II and the Iconography of St. Thomas Becket and St. Edward the Confessor in the Chapel of Our Lady of Undercroft, Canterbury Cathedral

Sarah Blick

The Pilgrim Badge[1]

The two figures flanking a stunning image of the Virgin and Child seem, at first, to be an exceedingly bizarre pairing. **(fig. 1)** Why is a royal saint, Edward the Confessor, paired with Thomas Becket, the most famous of all anti-royal saints? In a complex, but wholly understandable manner, this iconographic choice was spurred by the ruler at the time of its manufacture: Richard II, whose artistic patronage was deliberate, calculating, and partially successful.

The graceful figure of the seated Virgin holds a long, thin fleur-de-lis sceptre with a delicately-posed left hand. With her right hand, she clasps the leg of the standing Christ Child, holding him firmly in balance as he, standing on her lap, reaches out to touch the six-lobed brooch tying her mantle. All of the figures, including the nimbed child, lean back in a graceful sway. The kingly figure at left also holds a fleur-de-ly sceptre and is perched, floating, on a bald lion, while the archbishop at right clasps a cross-staff and sways atop a fluffy lamb. The elegant splay of the Virgin's fingers are repeated in the two flanking figures and even the foot of the Christ child. Below, a demi-angel, dressed in a tight diapered gown, bends its arms upward as if to lift and hold the tableaux. Some variants of this badge feature the inscription [MAT]ER CELI REGINA MONDI (Queen of heaven, mother of mankind).[2] **(fig. 2)** The magnificent image is framed by elaborate Decorated Gothic-Style architecture which closely resembles the structure of the stone screen which once displayed the sculptures behind the altar.

fig.2

fig.3

The flanking king and archbishop are cast in elegant S-curves. The presence of St. Thomas Becket (identified on some badges as Thomæ = of Thomas) **(fig. 3)** is not surprising, as the Undercroft cult lay in the crypt of Canterbury Cathedral. The curious figure in this ensemble is the king, identified as St. Edward the Confessor. Canterbury had no shrine or altar devoted to Edward's worship, so why is he shown here as the visual equal of Becket? His presence on these badges reveals broader political implications.

fig 4

fig 5

fig 6   *fig 7*

A hint as to the target of these implications can be found in the badge's date: the late fourteenth century, as demonstrated by stylistic analysis.[3] Edward's piked, low-cut shoes with fancy openwork decoration[4] and the tight sleeves covering the Virgin's hands are typical of late fourteenth- century fashions.[5] Facial features such as sharp, pointed chins and noses, high cheekbones, puffy eyes, and tubular hair curls were popular in the late 14th century as seen in the *Wilton Diptych* and in the *Liber Regalis.*[6] **(fig. 4)** Even the badge's figures' long, drippy fingers[7] and the elegant drapery patterns can be seen in manuscripts and sculpture dating to the 1390s;[8] **(fig. 5)** all of which belong to the International Style. Other works done in this style, including the Master of the Trebon Altarpiece's, *Roudnice Madonna* (*c.* 1400), the *Schöne Madonna*, and the *Madonna of the Krumau* (*c.* 1390-1400)[9] also feature iconographic details found in the badge, such as the large six-lobed brooch that secures the Virgin's cape. The lattice-work behind the Virgin is similar to the *Golden Rössel* (*c.* 1400) **(fig. 6)** and the nave windows on the west end of Canterbury (1396-1411), where it formed the background for a series of kings.[10] **(fig. 7)** More importantly, the lattice appeared earlier on funerary badges made for the Black Prince, who died in 1376 and was buried at Canterbury,[11] indicating a link to the Cathedral and the cult of the Undercroft. **(fig. 8)**

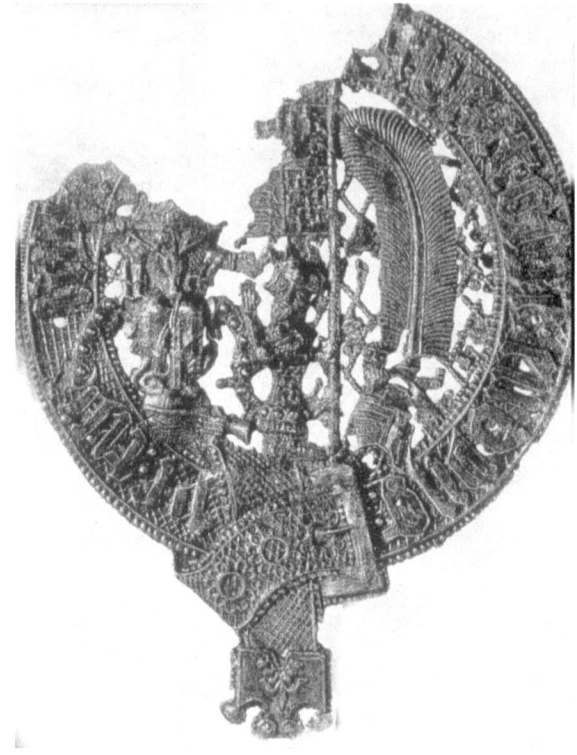

fig. 8

Iconography of the Virgin

The central iconography of these badges is the crowned, enthroned Virgin holding the Christ child, who stands on her lap, denoting the *Virgo Mediatrix.*[12] In this role, Mary turns her face towards the Christ child (as the Incarnated Word) so that she can beseech her son on the viewer's behalf.[13] This queen brings grace as well as accepts it: she mediates, reconciling conflicts. What trouble was brewing that necessitated her presence? The answer to that lies in the iconographic choice of the saints who flank her: St. Edward the Confessor and St. Thomas Becket.

Iconography of the Saints

Both saints perch on symbolic animals that reflect a wish for harmony and peace. Edward stands on a bald lion and Becket stands on a fluffy lamb-

-in effect the lion lies down with the lamb. Although the pairing of these two saints would seem to impart the same kind of symbolism-- harmony between church and state--this particular choice reflected not so much a 'canonization of opposition,'[14] but a delicate dance of mutual assurance: absolving criticism and mediating between royalty (Edward) and everyone else (Becket).[15]

Becket was the first in a rather long line of official and unofficial saintly figures whose popularity grew, in part, as they were seen as anti-monarchial. But English royalty did not stand idly by and let the popularity of these figures be used for covert protest against their rule. While they sponsored their own saints, such as Edward the Confessor and George, they also made a concerted effort to co-opt the anti-royal saints and make those potential troublemakers their allies and friends. To wit, while Becket came to be seen as the anti-monarchial saint par excellence, it was not always so. Indeed, in the late Middle Ages, royal patronage, with the aid of the Canterbury monks, made Becket their champion and source of legitimacy.[16] As Canterbury Cathedral was a locus for powerful prayers, English kings urgently and regularly requested that the Canterbury monks pray for success in military ventures, the health of the monarchy, as well as Becket's protection against bad weather and disease. They laid the fortune of their endeavors (personal and public) before Becket's purview, reminding people of Becket's favor.

English kings regularly used saints to solidify their power. Believing in the intercessory function of saints regarding state and personal affairs, sovereigns routinely granted monies to churches with important relics, witnessed important translations, made regular pilgrimages, collected relics, donated images and gems to shrines, and sponsored the production of art and architecture throughout the British Isles. Not surprisingly, the saints most keenly venerated by English Gothic kings (aside from their devotion to Christ and the Virgin Mary) were Edward the Confessor, Edmund, and George.[17] All of these saints were, in some way, connected to the monarchy, either having been a king themselves or having aligned themselves with a king, and support of royal saints was an expected part of late medieval kingship.

While general sponsorship of saints was expected, the odd pairing on the pilgrim badges indicates a deeper and more complicated situation. Henry III revived and promoted Edward's cult with the elaborate re-building of Westminster Abbey which housed it and the production of beautifully-illustrated *vitae*. These acts set Edward up as a rival and, he hoped, a superior saint to Becket.[18] Henry III wished to establish at Westminster a dynastic saint and all the holy associations found with such a figure, such as that with St. Louis at the Ste. Chapelle in Paris: while those visual connections were strong, so too were the visual and symbolic connections between the cults of Becket and Edward, interlacing their power. Both churches used unusual and expensive Cosmati pavements,[19] and both of their original tombs[20] were based on Christ's pierced sepulcher. Even their *vitae* were paired in a double manuscript by Matthew Paris' atelier which circulated among the women of the palace.[21] To encourage pilgrim crowds, in 1269 the Bishop of St. David Cathedral granted indulgences to any who prayed at Edward's shrine for 'the king' and 'the peace of the realm.'[22] Sadly for Henry III, Edward attracted only a small number of pilgrims, especially compared to the immense numbers flocking to Canterbury. So, after Henry III's death, his successors paid only perfunctory attention to Edward's cult, letting it wither. This would change dramatically under Richard II, who revived Edward and his symbolic power and would ultimately pair him with Becket.

Richard II, unexpectedly raised to the throne at age 10, experienced continual challenges to his authority, especially as his rule became more and more dictatorial. His opponents tried to protest directly, but were suppressed, so they spoke their minds through the institution of sainthood, championing the canonization of the political martyr Thomas of Lancaster[23] and drawing connections between this Thomas and Thomas Becket as an anti-royal saint.[24] Richard countered with his own manipulation of sainthood. For example, when his enemies threatened him with the same murderous fate as Edward II, he promoted the canonization of that less-than-stellar monarch. In 1387 he advanced the case for Edward II's canonization by commissioning a volume of miracles in 1390. He then sent them 'at the request of' the Archbishop of Canterbury and the Bishop of London (thereby co-opting them into his scheme), to Rome in 1395 and again in 1397, but both missions were unsuccessful.[25] More importantly, though, Richard revived the worship of Edward the Confessor because he fit Richard's view of sacral kingship where 'reverence for royal authority was part of a Christian's sacred duty.'[26]

While a number of saints personally appealed to Richard, such as St. John the Evangelist and St. John the Baptist as seen in the *Wilton Diptych*, he was particularly devoted to St. Edward. Richard wanted to be seen as a peacemaker, not a warrior, and of the royal saints, only Edward followed this model[27] Richard's intense devotion was reflected in his visits to Edward's shrine during troubled times (such as on 15 June 1381 before meeting with the rebels at Smithfield),[28] by his impaling of his arms with that of the Confessor's (1397),[29] and by his repeated invocation of Edward to curse anyone who objected to his plans.[30] He saw the Confessor as his partner: his mentor in spirituality and guide in matters of government.'[31] In 1395, Richard requested that the prior of Canterbury add Edward's martyrdom to the major feasts to be celebrated in the Cathedral.[32] He donated gems, vestments, and money to the Westminster shrine.[33] Richard left a ring at Edward's shrine when he ventured out of the country and had a portrait of himself adorned for the

Feast of St. Edward. In order to be buried himself near the Confessor's tomb, he had royal graves moved to another chapel at Westminster.[34]

To bolster Edward's importance and his own claim to sacred kingship, Richard became a major patron of Westminster, as it was the seat of royal and sacral authority. By the 1380s, the fabric had begun to decay as work had halted after the death of Henry III. Work had started fitfully on the completion of the nave, but until Richard II became involved 'out of devotion to the shrine of St. Edward the Confessor', not much was done.[35] With his money and power to obtain scarce workers and costly materials, work proceeded apace.[36] Over the course of his reign, his gifts totaled an impressive 10,000-12,000 pounds.[37]

fig. 9

His enthusiasm made sense. What was more unusual was Richard's almost equal enthusiasm for Becket and the iconographic combination of both saints. While they were sometimes paired elsewhere, such as in the north walk of the cloisters of Norwich Cathedral in a series of roof bosses from the 1430s where Thomas Becket's story dominates the fourth bay from the monks' door and Edward the Confessor's story, the fifth bay.[38] It can also be found on a 1536 painted chancel screen at Burlingham St. Andrew in Norfolk,[39] **(fig. 9)** almost all surviving examples of the pairing appear in artwork associated with Westminster.

fig. 10

fig. 11

For example, the *c.* 1307[40] painting above the sedilia on the south side of the sanctuary in Westminster also indicates a now-lost image of Becket paired with Edward. The remaining panels show two kings (one of whom might be Edward) flanking a defaced saintly figure who held either a crosier or a cross staff—and who was most likely Becket.[41] **(fig. 10)** Later, in the second litany of the *Lilington Missal* (from 1383-84), Thomas is found at the head of the five Holy Martyrs and Edward at the head of the six Confessors.[42] Much later, the early 16th-century *Obituary Scroll of Abbot Islip*, Abbot of Westminster,[43] shows the main altar of Westminster flanked by two sculpted figures: St. Thomas Becket and St. Edward the Confessor (which may have been donated earlier).[44] **(fig. 11)** These surviving instances indicate a long-standing iconographic pairing of Becket and Edward was utilized by generations of royal figures. It is in this context, that Richard II's enthusiasm for Becket should be seen, for his donations to Canterbury rivaled those to Westminster.

There was a natural tie to Canterbury with his father's burial, whose anniversary Richard kept faithfully, and prior to 1393, he regularly visited the Cathedral, giving nominal amounts to the shrines.[45] But in 1393, he became an avid supporter, donating 1000 pounds to the Undercroft Chapel and to the rebuilding of the nave as he had done at Westminster.[46] In 1394, Richard wrote to Canterbury to inquire about a new miracle that was supposed to have occurred at Becket's shrine and how that miracle might re-vitalize the spiritual life of his kingdom.[47] In the same year, he asked that the monks at Canterbury pray for his success in the campaign in Ireland.[48] When work on the nave reached the west end in 1397, Richard forgave the 160 pound tax debt owed by prior and chapter 'out of special devotion to the martyr Thomas…in aid of building of the west front.'[49] The Great West Window in Canterbury, with a line of kings, was probably sponsored by Richard II, as indicated by his armorials at the top center of the window.[50] With this, he sought 'to promote his divine right as king in major public spaces, such as the sculptural series of kings in Westminster Hall (commissioned in 1385)', becoming the main patron of Canterbury Cathedral and the Becket cult.[51] Even in 1399, when his rule was disintegrating, Richard wanted to visit Canterbury, but felt it would be unsafe until the Archbishop guaranteed his safety and took him to the shrine and back to his starting point accompanied by heavily armed men.[52]

This emotional commitment to Becket was likely spurred not only by a vague iconographic tradition, but by a deep interest in political prophecy. Political prophecies were avidly collected by all classes in late medieval England.[53] Ostensibly written by such luminaries as Merlin the magician,[54] people looked to the prophecies for guidance. The most important prophecy for Richard II was that of the Holy Oil of Becket, part of the posthumous legend of Thomas, which emphasized his visionary powers.[55] First appearing in a 1318 document,[56] it told how the Virgin visited Thomas in a vision when he was praying at the Church of St. Colombe in Sens, and gave him an eagle made of gold[57] which housed a flask filled with oil. She told him that it should be used to anoint future kings of England. The kings anointed with the oil would recover Normandy and Aquitaine without force and the first such anointed would become the 'greatest among kings'[58] recovering France without force and building churches throughout the Holy Land. As long as the king carried the eagle with him, he would prevail. Becket gave it to a monk from Poitiers, who hid it under a rock in the church of St. Grégoire until a holy man revealed it years later to Edward III, who gave it to the Black Prince, who in turn had it locked in the Tower of London, where it was found by his son, Richard II. Like the heavenly coronation oil used in France,[59] it harkened back to the Old Testament ritual, showing divine approval. In this manner, Richard, by promoting his connection with Becket, reminded people of the prophecy. Yet his real interest was not the common folk, but rather those who were a real threat to his authority: the nobility and the high-level clergy. It is this audience that he sought to influence with his patronage of Our Lady of Undercroft in Canterbury Cathedral.

The Cult of Our Lady of Undercroft

The Chapel dedicated to the Virgin Mary, called Our Lady of Undercroft is located in the crypt directly beneath the high altar. A long-standing minor chapel, it was initially revered because Becket's body rested there before his burial. However, near the end of Henry III's reign (1216-72), the popularity of the Chapel began to grow, reflected in the number of offerings made to commemorate the 'Image of our Lady.'[60] The fortunes of the cult, evidenced by records of donations, waxed and waned.[61] A good portion of these were regular donations from royalty.[62] By 1370 (the year of the Fourth Jubilee), the Treasurers accounts indicate that the Undercroft Chapel received £50, more than any other altar except the Corona and the main shrine.[63] In 1376, when the Black Prince was buried, it attracted £682, 4s.7d.[64]

The 1376 donations reflected the outpouring of grief that accompanied the death of the Black Prince at age 46. The Black Prince was devoted to the cult of Our Lady of Undercroft and asked in his will of 7 June 1376 that his body be buried in the middle of the Undercroft chapel 'so that the end of our tomb towards the feet be ten feet distant from the altar.'[65] (This wish, which was widely known, was disregarded when he was buried in the sanctuary close to the shrine of Becket).[66] His was not a choice based on modesty. Rather, as Robertson pointed out, 'This is a position neither asked by, nor granted to, any one but a founder, or a munificent restorer, of the chapel in which the altar stands.[67] Because of this, it is assumed that the Black Prince paid for the elaborate stone screens, whose Decorated Style indicates that they were probably made around 1365-80. Specific evidence of the Black Prince's connection to the Undercroft chapel can be seen in his coat of arms painted on the southeastern pier of the *sacrarium* immediately against the east wall.

fig.12

Whoever paid for the chapel's refurbishment made sure that it was done with the finest materials and workmanship. The stonework was richly painted and gilded, while the vaults were adorned with lapis lazuli forming a bright night sky which was then strewn with relief images of golden suns and silver stars. **(fig. 12)** Placed among them were painted heraldic shields of kings, nobles, archbishops, and saints.[68] Robertson dated this decoration to the period of Archbishop Arundel (r. 1396-1414), particularly before 1400, due to the prominent and multiple placement of his painted arms on the vaults.[69]

The focus was the altar which featured a sculpture of the Virgin placed in the northeast screen. In addition to the original sculpture of the Virgin Mary there is evidence for images of the Trinity and the apostles made of silver or silver gilt, given by Archbishop Courtenay (r. 1381-96).[70] Funds and gems were regularly donated to the altar and the beautiful statue by nobility and royalty. At this time, Richard II was one of the site's most generous benefactors, donating jewels and rich gifts 'at the altar in the chapel of the Blessed Virgin in the Undercroft.'[71] He gave 'to the fabric of the high altar and of the nave, beyond various jewels which he presented, and to the Blessed Virgin Mary in the crypt more than 1000 pounds sterling.'[72] This reflected not only his devotion (and remembrance of his father), it was also effective in reaching an elite audience. According to Erasmus, only the nobility and high-ranked clergy were regularly allowed access to the sumptuous chapel.[73] Everyone else had to be satisfied by gazing upon its riches through a double iron grille.[74]

The Cult of the Undercroft, Pilgrim Badges, and Artistic Reception

One could argue that it was to this select, elite group that the elegant pilgrim badge and its unusual iconography particularly spoke. The badge (and its variants) was of exceptional quality, not often seen in pilgrim souvenir production. Skilled artisan(s) that carved the moulds which made the badges might have spied a chance to profit from a more particular clientele and the high-quality design and complexity of the badges seem to indicate that they were part of the patronage (as a whole) of the Undercroft chapel and its images. The badge is unusually large 13.5 cm x 8.7 cm with two pins on the back. It was painted and apparently had a colorful backing that was once inserted between the tabs on the reverse.[75] The imagery probably depicted some of what once decorated the altar, as was typical for many pilgrim souvenirs from Canterbury such as those commemorating the Head Reliquary and Shrine of Becket. Perhaps the badge shows now-lost figures of Becket and Edward, but it is difficult to prove because even the central image, the Virgin, changes from badge to badge—sometimes sitting, sometimes standing. Nonetheless, because the visitors to the Undercroft Chapel were from the upper class, the unvarying, basic iconography (the Virgin, Edward, and Becket) of the elegant badge, rather than the specific rendition of what might have been there, conveyed a powerful message.

Although the iconography of these works indicates royal influence, it was an indirect influence, because it is unlikely that the sovereigns were patrons of the badges themselves. Rather the badges reflect royal patronage of the main works of art and their iconography which the badges sought to recall to the mind of the pilgrim. Nonetheless, their humble materials and mass production did not limit the audience to just those of wealth and status. The pewter badges with their complex iconography, reflected Richard II's wish to be perceived as specially-blessed by Thomas and as a worthy heir of Edward. Those of higher status might have understood the intricate layers of meaning, but what about the populace? I believe the average person understood quite well the meaning of the image of the gracious queen of the heavens matched with saints Edward and Thomas Becket and how Richard II's father, the Black Prince, was devoted to the Virgin. They also understood the importance of political and religious harmony and the prophecy that the king anointed with the special oil of the Virgin was destined to be one of their greatest kings.

This understanding was created by the royal point of view which was constantly put before the populace. The use of visual sacral/political symbols was widespread. These symbols were needed because the politics of the time were made up of delicate negotiations between competing interests that were often very personal and centered on the person of the king in his many roles: landlord, warlord, judge, and sacral sovereign; and these occurred in a public setting.[76] Visual symbols helped structure these negotiations both centrally and regionally, as each area of the country had competing interests. All together, they portrayed sovereignty as 'personal, familial, virtuous, sacral, and [a] purely royal affair' as well as 'dynastic self-identification.'[77] These symbols differed from literary (poems, ballads) expressions, which emphasized how the ruler and ruled were dependent upon one another.[78] The visual, in contrast, emphasized the individual rather than the communal aspects of rule.

Pageants celebrating these individual kingly virtues were organized featuring costumed performers, temporary architecture, golden altarpieces, incense, flowers, music, and more.[79] These performances were for the populace who, on the whole, understood the complex imagery, and if some nuance was missed by an individual, it would have been explained to them by a passer-by or an official. For by the late-14th century, people had grown used to a multiplicity of saints, histories, re-telling of Biblical stories and the like. Their parish churches were filled with images commissioned and paid for by patrons of all classes. Not only did individuals have certain preferences for saints (based on names, birthdates, travels, professions, particular needs), but so did groups of professions, confraternities both religious and secular, many of which made reference to royal power and virtues if it helped their agenda. This intricate symbolism was seen and understood on a daily basis.

The point of view of the monarchy was repeatedly put before the populace with not just visual imagery, but with calls for prayer throughout the cathedral and parish churches. The private and public causes were blurred as royalty asked for prayers concerning the health of the monarchy, the success of their endeavors (personal and public), and remembrance of their dead, such as for the Black

Prince's soul and King Edward III's recovery in 1376.[80] In this manner, most of England's population was informed of the initiatives of the royalty, whether military, political, or personal such as their safe travel. For instance, the Norwich crusade, led by Henry Despenser, bishop of Norwich, after being granted three bulls from Urban VI to overcome the schismatics, had copies sent to every English bishop. They were sent out with indulgences to raise funds and alms. Parish churches were used as collection points for money. In April 1383 Archbishop Courtenay ordered that prayers be said in all churches for the crusade and that Masses and processions be held.[81] So important was this announcement, that Robert Braybrooke, bishop of London, ordered that the reasons for the crusade should be spoken in English (so all could understand).[82] To encourage people to obey, indulgences were issued and suggestions were made as to how to fit the extra Masses within the liturgical week. Vivid rituals brought these requests to life, though prayers, Masses, processions, litanies, bell ringing, and more. Instructions on how these rituals were to be performed were stipulated, such as the need to go barefoot at certain times, or how psalms ought to be sung while kneeling that 'for the peace and tranquility of the king and realm special prayers, imploring divine clemency had to be said in a fervent manner.'[83] In this way, the wishes and aims of the royalty were well known not only to the elite, but to the general populace. Because of this, whether noble or not, people understood the iconography and sumptuous quality of the Undercroft badge.

Sadly, Richard's belief in these symbols paled when real life complications occurred. When Richard II discovered the oil, he asked to be anointed with it, but the Archbishop of Canterbury, Thomas Arundel, a political enemy, refused because Richard had already undergone the coronation ceremony. Nonetheless, Richard, believing in its power, took the eagle and the ampulla with him to Ireland in 1399 (remembering the prophecy of him prevailing with it by his side). When Richard was imprisoned, Arundel took possession of the oil should there be a 'future king worth anointing', which he found in Henry IV.[84] Richard was then starved to death, with no earthly or heavenly protection.

Richard had hoped to prove a worthy king, and he used saints to speak in his favor. His dual devotion to Becket and Edward were meant to guard against rebellion. The saints' purported favor did not last, but traces of their powerful pairing did, in the Undercroft badge. The figures might reflect long-lost statues given to the Undercroft Chapel by Richard (and meant to impress noble visitors), though they could also be an independent set of images. Images such as these were created not only to glorify the miraculous sculpture of the Virgin and Child and the holy presence of Edward and Becket, but also to remind the visitor (who would buy the sumptuous badge) that these saints blessed and supported their beleaguered sovereign.

Figure 1 *Our Lady of Undercroft Pilgrim Badge*, 14th century, Courtesy of the Museum of London

Figure 2 *Our Lady of Undercroft Pilgrim Badge with lower portion*, 14th century, Courtesy of the Museum of London

Figure 3 Fragment of Undercroft Pilgrim Badge featuring St. Thomas Becket, 14th century. After Michael Mitchener, *Medieval Pilgrim & Secular Badges*, p. 77

Figure 4 Detail of the face of the Virgin on the Wilton Diptych. London, National Gallery of Art. Photo: Author.

Figure 5 *Liber Regalis*, Westminster Abbey MS 38, f. 1v, f. 20, 29 (1390s). By kind permission of the Dean and Chapter of Westminster Abbey.

Figure 6 *Golden Rössel* (*c.* 1400). Photo: Author.

Figure 7 Nave windows on west end of Canterbury (1396-1411) detail of a king with a lattice background. Photo: Telemann Braun.

Figure 8 Funerary Badge of the Black Prince, 1376. Courtesy of the Museum of London.

Figure 9 1536 painted chancel screen at Burlingham St. Andrew in Norfolk. Photo: Author.

Figure 10 Painting above the sedalia on the south side of the sanctuary in Westminster (*c.* 1307). Photo: Author.

Figure 11 Early 16th century *Obituary Scroll of Abbot Islip*, Abbot of Westminster, shows the main altar of Westminster flanked by two sculpted figures: St. Thomas Becket and St. Edward the Confessor. By kind permission of the Dean and Chapter of Westminster Abbey.

Figure 12 Our Lady of Undercroft Chapel, Canterbury Cathedral. Photo: Author.

Endnotes

[1] A great variety of badges are associated with this cult. Another version of the one discussed here pictures the Virgin standing with the child in her arms as he hands her a ring (?). See Brian Spencer, *Pilgrim Souvenirs and Secular Badges: Medieval Finds from Excavations in London* (London, 1998), 128-133; Brian Spencer, *Medieval Pilgrim Badges from Norfolk* (Norwich, 1980), 28, fig. 122; Brian Spencer, 'Pilgrim Souvenirs' in Jonathan Alexander and Paul Binski (eds.), *Age of Chivalry: Art in Plantagenet England 1200-1400* (London, 1987), 222, figs. 65-67; H.J.E. vas Beuningen, A.M. Koldeweij, D. Kicken, *Heilig en Profaan 2: 1200 Laatmiddeleeuwse insigne suit openbare en particuliere collectives* (Cothen, 2001), 333; Michael Mitchiner, *Medieval Pilgrim & Secular Badges* (Sanderstead, 1986), 76-77; Geoff Egan, 'Finds Recovered on Riverside Sites in the City of London', *Popular Archaeology* 6 (1985/6), fig. 10; *London Museum Catalogues No. 7: Medieval Catalogue* (London,1940), pl. 72, no. 52.

[2] Translated by Spencer (1998), 132.

[3] Spencer (1998), 132 suggested that a badge like this was created 'for a courtly clientele preparing for or participating in' the funeral of the Black Prince. This would make sense except that the style of the badge seems to indicate a later date, one closer to the end of the 14th century. None of the badges have been found thus far in a secure, datable context because most were uncovered by metal detectors on river foreshores. That pilgrim badges were made in molds also makes precise dating difficult, because a mold carved from limestone at one point could conceivably be used for decades to produce the same badge.

[4] This shoe style was popular from the 1360s through the early fifteenth century. Spencer (1998), 131; F. Grew & De Neergaard, *Medieval Finds from Excavations in London 2: Shoes and Pattens* (London, 1988), pl. 116c, 118. See also Jesse's shoes in the Tree of Jesse in the east window of Winchester College chapel (1393-97); Dillian Gordon, Lisa Monnas, and Caroline Elam (eds.), *The Regal Image of Richard II and the Wilton Diptych* (London, 1997), 47, fig. 20. The cusping of Edward's shoes reflect patterns dating from the late 14th through the early 15th centuries. See R. Smithke's copy of the mural showing the three Magi and below the kneeling family of Edward III, now at the Society of Antiquaries, London. Paul Binski, *Westminster Abbey and the Plantagenets: Kingship and the Representation of Power 1200-1400* (New Haven, 1995), pl. 240.

[5] One variant badge features tight sleeves which cover part of the Virgin's hands, dating the work to 1380-1400. van Beuningen, *et al* (2001), 333. Pamela Tudor-Craig, 'The Wilton Diptych in the Context of Contemporary English Panel and Wall Painting', in Gordon (1997), 209 in reference to the late 14th century choir screen from the Church of All Saints at Clifton in Bedfordshire, ill. 122-23.

[6] These are all comparable to features in Bohemian painting of *c.* 1400. English use of the large, broad forehead, slender nose, and sleepy eyes with large lids above and below can be found on a *c.* 1380-90 wall painting at Park Farm, Gatehouse of St. Osyth's Priory, Essex and, of course, in the face of the Virgin in the famous *Wilton Diptych.*

[7] This style of hands (sometimes referred to as "crab claw" hands) can also be seen in the *Liber Regalis*, Westminster Abbey MS 38, f. 1v, f. 20, 29 dates to the 1390s. Bohemian influence on Ricardian painting has been much debated and mostly dismissed, but Paul Binski in 'The *Liber Regalis*: Its Date and European Context' in Gordon (1997), 242-46, suggests it as a real possibility for some images such as the *Liber Regalis*, the tester from Richard II's tomb to Bohemian wall paintings such as the Woman Clothed in the Sun found in Karlstein Lady Chapel.

[8] The drapery found on the sitting and standing Virgins also reflects the International Style of the late 14th century. The standing figure's skirt angles off to the left in long tubes with the excess pooling around her feet (but revealing the fashionable pointed shoes). The seated Virgin's drapery with one long leg causing straight folds and the other flourishes can be seen in several English contexts including the *Statutes of England* (1388-99) Cambridge, St. John's College, MS A.7, f.1.; "Coronation of the King" in the *Litlyngton Missal* (1383-84), fol. 206.

[9] There are many records of Parisian goldsmiths working in England and gifts to English royalty from French kings. Marian Campbell, '"White Harts and Coronets": The Jewellery and Plate of Richard II', in Gordon (1997), 95-114; esp.102, 105, 107, 112-13; Marian Campbell, 'Gold, Silver and Precious Stones' in John Blair and Nigel Ramsey (eds.), *English Medieval Industries* (London, 1991), 164-65. Also Public Record Office E101/411/9 (temp Henry VI) tells of great gifts from the Dukes of Burgundy and the King of France in 1396 and a New Year's gift from Philip, Duke of Burgundy in 1398 of a figure of Edward the Confessor holding a ruby. C.A. Dehaisnes, *Documents et extraits divers concernant l'histoire de l'art dans la Flandre avant le XVe si?cle* (Lille, 1886) II, 737.

[10] Richard Marks, 'English King' in Alexander, *op.cit.* (n. 1), 539-40, cat. 748; Madeline Caviness, *The Windows of Christ Church Cathedral Canterbury* (London, 1981), 231-38, cp. XVII, figs. 380-432. Lattice-work grounds can also be seen in stained glass in the first half of the 14th century in Peterborough, Stanford-on-Avon, Northamptonshire, Eaton Bishop, Hereford, and Worcester. Also note the less-complex lattice in the late 14th-century sketch of the Holy Heart surrounded by three Angels in *Hours of the Virgin and of the Cross, Boulogne-sur-Mer*, Biblioth?que Municipale MS 93 f.8; Kathleen L. Scott, *Late Gothic Manuscripts 1390-1490: A Survey of Manuscripts Illuminated in the British Isles* (v. 6) (London, 1996) I fig. 25, II, 37-39. My thanks to Laura Gelfand for suggesting the Golden Rössel.

[11] Spencer, (1998), 132; Spencer (1987), 222, fig. 69.

[12]   Aina Trotzig, 'The Iconography of the Enthroned Virgin with the Christ Child Standing in Her Lap; Søren Kaspersen (ed.), *Images of Cult and Devotion: Function and Reception of Christian Images in Medieval and Post-Medieval Europe* (Copenhagen, 2004), 245-53.

[13]   This particular iconography appeared in the end of the 12th century and became widespread in the late 13th and early 14th centuries. Trotzig, (2004), 249, 251. Jeffrey Hamburger, *The Rothschild Canticles--Art and Mysticism in Flanders and the Rhineland circa 1300* (New Haven, 1990), 101, 160, discussed images of the Mediatrix in the context of devotional and visionary images.

[14]   Binski, (1995), 3.

[15]   Sometimes the visual sources pointed out that Becket tried to protect the *vulgus* (labeled as such) or common people from the aristocracy such as on f. 2v. of the *Becket Leaves*. The figures gesture on the right hand side, asking for Becket's blessing. Janet Backhouse and Christopher de Hamel, *The Becket Leaves* (London, 1998), 6.

[16]   '. . .There was never a period between the reigns of Henry II and Henry VIII when an English monarch failed to appreciate the importance of as close and appreciative a relationship with St. Thomas's community as his other commitments allowed'. Barrie Dobson, 'The Monks of Canterbury Cathedral in the Later Middle Ages, 1220-1540' in Patrick Collinson, Nigel Ramsay, and Margaret Sparks (eds.), *A History of Canterbury Cathedral* (Oxford, 1995), 142.

[17]   Edward III not only patronized the cults of Edward the Confessor and Edmund, but that of King Arthur. W.M. Ormrod, 'The Personal Religion of Edward III', *Speculum* 64 (1989), 858, 869, n. 117.

[18]   Richard Eales, 'The Political Setting of the Becket Translation of 1220', Diana Wood (ed.), *Martyrs and Martyrologies* (Oxford, 1993), 135.

[19]   These expensive floors were almost non-existent in England outside of these two churches. As Cosmati work was mostly found on Italian tombs of high-ranking clerics and saints, it recalled the powerful symbolism of papal approval (and the dedication of Westminster to St. Peter) and the more direct linkage to Christ. The intended audience was nobility and high-level clergy who would understand the symbolism and pointed references. It was an image of 'descent, continuity, and filiation'. Paul Binski, 'Hierarchies and Orders in English Royal Images of Power', Jeffrey Denton (ed.), *Orders and Hierarchies in Late Medieval and Renaissance Europe* (Toronto, 1999), 86-87; George Duby, *A History of Private Life* (Cambridge, MA, 1987), II, 85-93. Of course, many shrine precincts were paved with colorful, exotic marbles, but there is no evidence of their being done in the elaborate *opus sectile* work. Tim Tatton-Brown, 'The Two Great Marble Pavements in the Sanctuary and Shrine Areas of Canterbury Cathedral and Westminster Abbey', Jane Fawcett (ed.), *Historic Floors: Their History and Conservation* (Oxford, 1998), 57-58.

[20] The tombs of both saints visually referenced the pierced *sepulcra Domini* in Jerusalem and the *fenestella confessionis* or "window of witness" used in many saints' tombs, including that of St. Peter and in early medieval England with St. Chad. Although neither Becket's nor Edward's tombs survive, we can surmise their appearance through multiple stained glass renditions for Becket at Canterbury and manuscript illuminations for Edward (Cambridge MS). Stephen Lamia, '*Erit Sepulcrum Ejus . . .Gloriosum*: Verisimilitude and the Tomb of Christ in the Art of Twelfth-Century Île de France', Sarah Blick and Rita Tekippe (eds.), *Art and Architecture of Late Medieval Pilgrimage in Northern Europe and the British Isles* (Leiden, 2005), chapter 14, esp. 50-51; Sarah Blick, 'St. Chad' in Phyllis Jestice (ed.), *Encyclopedia of Holy People* (San Diego, 2004) 169; B. and R.A.B. Mynors (eds.), *Bede, A History of the English People*, (Oxford, 1968), bk. IV, c. 3, 212.

[21] Paul Binski, *Crown of Becket: Art and Imagination in Gothic England 1170-1300* (New Haven, 2004), 139 also noted that their being bound in the same volume emphasized that these men were not seen not as antagonists, but rather, as complementary, even dialectical models of leadership. Paul Binski, 'Reflections of the *La Estoire de Seint Aedward le Roi*: Hagiography and Kingship in Thirteenth-Century England', *Journal of Medieval History*, 16 (1990), 334. A fly leaf on the story of the Dublin Alban and Amphibalus states that Matthew translated and drew a book on the lives of St. Thomas and St. Edward that circulated among palace ladies, including the king's sister.

[22] David Carpenter, 'Westminster Abbey and the Cosmati Pavements in Politics, 1258-1269', Lindy Grant and Richard Mortimer (eds.), *Westminster Abbey: The Cosmati Pavements* (Burlington, VT, 2002), 45; Westminster Abbey Muniments 6668 (Book 11, folio 394).

[23] His cult began to grow within a few weeks of his death leading to a *vita* and an account of his miracles written in the next twenty years. Paintings of his death and extremely elaborate pilgrim souvenirs were produced to commemorate him. In 1323, crowds assembled at St. Paul's Cathedral for a miracle-working image of Thomas of Lancaster; Henry R. Luard (ed.), *Flores Historiam* (London, 1890), III, 213-14. Amongst his followers, there was at least one person who made the pilgrimage to Canterbury as evidenced by the Becket head reliquary pilgrim badge found amongst a hoard of silver pennies found in River Dove at Tutbury, Derbyshire in 1831. Hugh Tait, 'Pilgrim-signs and Thomas, Earl of Lancaster', *British Museum Quarterly* 20 (1955), 39, pl. xvd; Brian Spencer, 'Medieval Pilgrim Badges' in J.G.N. Renaud (ed.), *Rotterdam Papers: A Contribution to Medieval Archaeology* (Rotterdam, 1968), 138, fig. Id.

[24] Enthusiasm for his cult, though, began to fade until it was suddenly revived with vigor in 1389-90. While Richard II faced troubles in 1390, Thomas of Walsingham reported that Thomas of Lancaster had been canonized, while, of course, Richard was trying to get Edward II sainted. Diana Webb, *Pilgrimage in Medieval England* (London, 2000), 173; H.T. Riley (ed.), Thomas Walsingham, *Historia Anglicana*

(London, 1864) II, 195; Christopher Given-Wilson, 'Richard II, Edward II, and the Lancastrian Inheritance', *English Historical Review* 109 (June 1994), 569. As Given-Wilson wrote, Henry Knighton in the 1390s refers to him as 'sanctus comes' and the Guild of the Blessed Thomas of Lancaster was founded at Pontefract at this time. J.R. Lumby (ed.), *Chronicon Henrici Knighton vel Cnitthon Monachi Leycestrensis* (London, 1889), I, 429.

[25] In 1383, he asked that Edward's death anniversary be celebrated at Gloucester. C. Given-Wilson (1994), 553-71; R. H. Jones, *The Royal Policy of Richard II: Absolutism in the Later Middle Ages* (Oxford, 1968), 76-87; J.W. Sherborne, 'Aspects of English Court Culture in the Later Fourteenth Century', in V.J. Scattergood and J.W. Sherborne (eds.), *English Court Culture in the Later Middle Ages* (New York, 1983), 22; Nigel Saul, *Richard II* (New Haven, 1997), 323; Christopher Given-Wilson (1994), 568; L.C. Hector and B.F. Harvey (eds.), *The Westminster Chronicle 1381-1394* (Oxford, 1982), 158, 436-438; F. Devon (ed.), *Issue Roll of the Exchequer, Henry III to Henry VI* (London, 1837), 259. Devon, 247-48, 259, 264. His support was linked with the prophecy of *Adam Davy's Dreams*. Lesley A. Coote, *Prophecy and Public Affairs in Later Medieval England* (York, 2000), 153. *Adam Davy's Five Dreams about Edward the Second*, includes a dream of Edward II standing before the high altar at Canterbury, and like Becket, was attacked, here by two knights who beat him. The king, lamb-like, did not fight back. When the knights left, four radiant bands of light emanated from Edward's head in red and white. Other dreams implied that he would be crowned Holy Roman Emperor and that Christ would accompany him on a crusade to vanquish the heathen. Rupert Taylor, *The Political Prophecy in England* (New York, 1911), 93-94. As Given-Wilson noted (569-70), Richard II wished to undo everything surrounding Edward II's deposition: roll back the strictures on royal rule, uphold the forfeiture of the Lancastrian inheritance, and overturn the treason sentences of Richard's fervent supporters.

[26] Coote (2000), 154. In order to stabilize the notion of what constituted a coronation, under Richard II the first 'definitive' illustrated *ordines* was made. Binski, 'Hierarchies', (1999), 88.

[27] Saul (1997), 312.

[28] In times of upheaval he visited Edward's shrine almost exclusively, not bothering with the other shrines in Westminster. Shelagh Mitchell, 'Richard II: Kingship and the Cult of Saints' in Gordon (1997), 116. See also Hector, (1982), lv; 8-10.

[29] Binski (1995), 87; Hector (1982), 8-9; J.H. Harvey, 'The Wilton Diptych -- A Re-examination', *Archaeologia* 98 (1961), 5-6.

[30] In 1389, he invoked a curse through the Confessor towards anyone who objected to his granting of 1000 pounds per annum to Leo of Armenia, repeating it several times throughout the years. Mitchell (1997), 117-18; PRO C 66/321, m. 21; Calendar of Patent Rolls 1385-89, 110.

[31] Saul (1997), 311.

[32] *Ibid*; Calendar of Close Rolls 1392-1396, 473.

[33] This included a gold ring with a ruby, perhaps as a reminder of the 'regale' ruby found on Becket's shrine. Westminster Abbey Muniments 9473; Hector (1982), 372; Saul (1997), 313; PRO, London, *Calendar of Charter Rolls, 1341-1417*, 311.

[34] Arthur P. Stanley, *Historical Memorials of Westminster Abbey* (London, 1869, third edition), 149-50.

[35] Saul (1997), 315; PRO, London, Calendar of Patent Rolls 1385-1389, 188.

[36] In 1393, he gave permission to two masons from Westminster Abbey to impress laborers in Dorset to mine the Purbeck marble needed for the columns and to carry it to the sea for transport. London, PRO Calendar of Patent Rolls 1391-1396, 244.

[37] The total gifts (including gems and vestments and money) was less than Henry III's 45,000 pounds, but it was still a grand donation. Nigel Saul, 'Richard II and Westminster Abbey' in John Blair and Brian Golding (eds.), *The Cloisters and the World: Essays in Medieval History in Honour of Barbara Harvey* (Oxford, 1996), 204. His relationship with the Abbey was chronicled by Richard Exeter, a prior at Westminster in *The Westminster Chronicle (1381-1394)* Hector (1982).

[38] For information on the Norwich bosses see Martial Rose, 'The Vault Bosses' in Ian Atherton, Eric Fernie, Christopher Harper-Bill, and Hassell Smitth (eds.), *Norwich Cathedral: Church, City and Diocese, 1096-1996* (London, 1996), 363-78; Martial Rose, *Norwich Cathedral Roof Bosses* CD-Rom (Norwich, 2000). Also in amongst these are bosses that depict royalty-related saints such as Edmund, Denis, and Giles. Edward and Becket feature more bosses telling their stories than any other in the cloister.

[39] It was paid for by Thomas and Margaret Benet. Eamon Duffy, 'The Parish, Piety, and Patronage in Late Medieval East Anglia: The Evidence of the Rood Screens' in Katherine L. French, Gary G. Gibbs, and Beat Kümin (eds.), *The Parish in English Life 1400-1600* (Manchester, 1997), 158-59; Eamon Duffy, *The Stripping of the Altars: Traditional Religion in England c. 1400-c. 1580* (New Haven, 1992), fig. 131.

[40] Binski (1995), 125.

[41] Pamela Tudor-Craig, 'The "Large Letters" of the Litlington Missal and Westminster Abbey in 1383-84' in Michelle P. Brown and Scot McKendrick (eds.), *Illuminating the Book: Makers and Interpreters; Essays in Honour of Janet Backhouse* (Toronto, 1998) wrote that it was probably Becket in keeping with Edward I's preferences, 103; Jocelyn Perkins, *Westminster Abbey, Its Worship and Ornaments* (Alcuin Club Collections), XXXIII (1938), XXXIV (1940), XXXVIII (1952), I,

33-4. Binski (1995), 125-26, argued that they might be founder images, suggesting that the figures might be Sebert/St. Peter/Edgar/St. Dunstan.

[42] This happened despite the erasure of the entire page of Thomas Becket under Henry VIII's orders to eradicate Becket's image. Tudor-Craig (1998), 102-19.

[43] It also shows figures of Edward and St. John the Evangelist in canopied pedestals surrounding the scene of the deathbed of Abbot Islip. Islip is surrounded by a host of saints, one of which (an archbishop, perhaps Thomas Becket?) tenders last rites.

[44] W.H. St. John Hope, *Vetusta Monumenta: The Obituary Roll of John Islip, Abbot of Westminster, 1500-1532, with Notes on Other English Obituary Rolls*, vol. VII, part IV (Westminster, 1906).

[45] For example, in 1384, he gave 6s 8d at shrine and the same at the head reliquary. Saul (1997), 317-18; Public Record Office, London, E101/401/2, f. 37r. notes that he gave 3s 4d at the martyrdom, and 6s 8d at the Undercroft Chapel.

[46] He and Prior Thomas Chillenden (r. 1391-1411) were the major supporters of the rebuilding of the nave. Richard gave 'to the fabric of the high altar and of the nave, beyond various jewels which he presented, and to the Blessed Virgin Mary in the crypt more than 1000 pounds sterling'. Saul (1997), 318; J. Wickham Legg and W. St. John Hope (eds.), *Inventories of Christ Church, Canterbury* (London, 1902), 109.

[47] Dobson (1995), 137; Reg. S. folios 142, 163; Saul (1997), 301; (ed.) J.B. Sheppard, *Literae Cantuarienses* (London, 1887-1889), III, 26-28.

[48] Dobson (1995), 137; Reg. S. folio 14v.

[49] Saul (1997), 318; PRO, London, Calendar of Patent Rolls 1396-1399, 79; E159/172, *Brevia directa*, Easter rotulus 9; Sherborne, (1983), 26-27; R. Allen Brown, H.M. Colvin, and A.J. Taylor (eds.), *History of the King's Works* (London, 1963), II, 123, 469.

[50] The armorials of his wives, Anne of Bohemia and Isabelle of France were also represented. The presence of the latter indicates that the window must have been started between his 1396 marriage to Isabelle and his death in 1399. A now-lost inscription noted that it was not finished at his death, so Chillenden paid for its completion. M.A. Michael, *Stained Glass of Canterbury Cathedral* (London, 2004), 22, 164.

[51] Michael, *op. cit.* (n. 50), 64. Richard II appointed Richard Savage as the King's Glazier in 1393, and Michael suggests (164) that he may have helped design the West Window.

[52] Saul (1997), 308; Diana Webb, *Pilgrimage in Medieval England* (London, 2000), 134; Frank S. Haydon (ed.), *Eulogium Historiarum sive Temporis Chronicon* (London,

1858-63), III, 378-80.

[53] Rupert Taylor, *The Political Prophecy in England* (New York, 1911) discussed political prophecies from Great Britain in chapter 3.

[54] T. Stapleton (ed.), *Liber de Antiquis Legibus* (Camden Society, 1846), 43; Binski (1999), 79.

[55] T.A. Sandquist, 'The Holy Oil of St. Thomas of Canterbury' in T.A. Sandquist and Michael R. Powicke (eds.), *Essays in Medieval History presented to Bertie Wilkinson* (Toronto 1969), 332-33.

[56] The oldest manuscript of the legend (BL MS. Royal 12 C XII) dates from the first half of the 14th century, but there is a reference to it in a 1318 papal letter. Sandquist, *op.cit.* (n. 55), 334; Pope John XXII in reply to inquiries made on behalf of Edward II, reprinted in Legg, *English Coronation Records*, 69-72.

[57] Christopher Wilson, 'The Medieval Monuments' in Collinson, (1995), 498 noted that 'The eagle symbolized not only kingship, but Christ, the Resurrection, and baptism. . .'

[58] Sandquist (1969), 332.

[59] The coronation of kings from the early Middle Ages was conflated with ordination and the notion that the king was anointed by God -- relating back to the Biblical anointing of David and Saul. Sergio Bertelli, *The King's Body: Sacred Rituals of Power in Medieval and Early Modern Europe* (trans. R. Burr Litchfield) (University Park, PA, 2001), 22-34. The French believed that theirs came from a dove which carrying an ampulla filled with an inexhaustible supply, gave it to St. Rémi when he wished to baptize Clovis, 25.

[60] W.A. Scott Robertson, 'The Crypt of Canterbury Cathedral', *Archaeologia Cantiana* 13 (1880), 525-26 suggested that it might reflect some unrecorded miracle. The surviving Treasurers Accounts of offerings begin in 1262, with a total of 12 d. Following that, there are records for 1268, 10s; 1270, 11s 6d; 1276 £6 16s; 1279, £8. Then its popularity declined until 1309, when that large amount would again be equaled. In 1320, the year of the third jubilee £6 13s. 4d was collected. In 1336 it earned £5.

[61] Spencer (1998), 132-33. In 1296-97, Henry III donated '£4 8s. 4d....[and] 14 minstrels, making their minstrelsy before the statue of the Blessed Mary, the Virgin, in the crypt (*vouta*) of Christchurch, Canterbury'. BL Add. MSS. 7965 f. 55v; Constance Bullock-Davies, *Register of Royal and Baronial Domestic Minstrels 1272-1327* (Woodbridge, 1986), 117. Playing music before holy images was a widespread practice; in the Church of St. Martin in Wezemaal, Belgium, three pipers played before a statue of Job. Marike de Kroon, 'Medieval Pilgrim Badges and their Iconographic Aspects', in Blick, *op. cit.* (n. 21), 390, n. 14. Queen Philippa also paid

minstrels to accompany the great cross in St. Paul's in 1331. R. Rastall, 'Minstrelsy, Church and Clergy in Medieval England', *Proceedings of the Royal Musical Association* 97 (1970-1971), 87 (83-98).

In 1297, Edward I gave a ceremonial 7s (royal donations of money were often limited to a specific size, whereby they would donate that same amount to various altars within a single church) to the 'Image of St. Mary in the Vault' on June 5 and 10. *Expense Roll*, 25 Edward I, BL add. MS 7965 fol. 7b. In 1300, he, his wife, and two sons each gave 7s and an annual gift of a golden brooch worth £5 to the image. Edward I *Liber Contrarotularis* 28; W.A. Robertson (1880), 526; Spencer (1998), 266. In 1332-33, Edward III paid 2s. for 'divers minstrels for making their minstrelies before the statue of the Blessed Virgin, in the *volta* in Christchurch, Canterbury'. PRO MS E101/386/7 f. 7r, Exchequer account, and again in 1337 for 'divers minstrels who made minstrelsy before the Image of our Lady in the Vault'. BL Cotton MS *Nero C* VIII, fol. 212.

[62] Queen Philippa gave 12d in 1352. Robertson, (1880), 527; French King John II (as a hostage) visited Canterbury, he gave offerings to Becket's shrine and the Virgin in the Undercroft. *Chronicon Joahnnis de Reading et Anonymi Cantuariensis*, pp. 208-09, 220-21; Webb (2000), 133. Edward II gave 7s. in 1311 (BL Cotton MS Nero C VIII fol. 50) and in 1316, gave 7s. to send a candle to be lit in front of the image (BL Cotton MS Nero C VIII fol. 211; BL Cotton MS Nero C VIII fol. 209), and again gave 7s. on March 6 and June 16, 1320 (BL Add. MS 17362, fol. 4a). Edward III visited Canterbury often more than once a year, giving alms at various altars including the Undercroft Chapel. He gave 7s. in 1334 (BL Cotton MS *Nero C* VIII, fol. 208, and three times in 1335 (BL Cotton MS *Nero C* VIII, fol. 211; BL Cotton MS *Nero C* VIII, fol. 212-213). In 1335, he also sent a 5 lb. candle to the image (BL Cotton MS *Nero C* VIII, fol. 211). In 1343, Edward III gave gold ships to Walsingham, St. Paul's Cathedral, Gloucester, and one to Becket's shrine and one to the Undercroft Chapel in gratitude for a surviving a difficult sea crossing. Ormrod (1989), 859.

[63] Woodruff (1932), 20.

[64] It fell to £362, 10 s. in 1381. After 1383, there is a slow decline matched by the other sacred sites in the cathedral. There are no financial records of the Undercroft until prior's rolls from 1396, 1410, and 1420 (the fifth jubilee). They show respectively: £2 5s.; £8 6s. 8d; £55. In 1436 no gifts were recorded, but the main shrine only garnered £30 that year. In 1453, it earned £1, with the shrine earning only £10. Woodruff (1932), 21, 23-24.

[65] J. Nichols, *A Collection of all the Wills. . .of the Kings and Queens of England* (London, 1780), 71; J. Harvey, *The Black Prince and His Age* (London, 1976), 160. He was to be placed on hearse between high altar and the choir before burial in the crypt. Barber, *Edward*, p. 236-37 ; PRO E 403/460 m. 23, 25, 26; V.H. Galbraith (ed.), *Anomialle Chronicle 1333-1381* (Manchester, 1927), 95; Stanley, *Canterbury*

(1906), 65-82.

[66] H.M. Colvin (ed.), *The History of the King's Works* (London, 1963), I, 487; W.H. St. John Hope, 'The Achievements of Edward Prince of Wales, the "Black Prince" in the Cathedral Church of Canterbury', *Vetusta Monumenta* VII/part 2, 1, 13-22. The flooding in the crypt may have prompted placing the Black Prince's tomb in the ambulatory. A dirt floor (now gone) was laid down in the late fourteenth century. C.E. Woodruff, 'The Chapel of Our Lady in the Crypt of Canterbury Cathedral', *Archaeologia Cantiana* 38 (1926), 153-54; W.G. Searle (ed.), *John Stone, The Chronicle of John Stone* (Cambridge Antiquarian Society) 34 (1902), 102 also complained about the flooding.

[67] Robertson (1880), 527.

[68] At center of the vault, directly over the altar, is the coat of arms of France, added after the ceiling had been painted with the stars. The others include on the north face of the southeast pier, include the Black Prince and the coat of Queen Joan of Navarre, wife of Henry IV. Saintly arms join these, including royal saints Edward the Confessor, Edmund, and George, and Thomas Becket. Cecil R. Humphrey-Smith, 'Heraldry of the Chapel of Our Lady of Undercroft', *Canterbury Cathedral Chronicle*, 81 (May 1987), 47.

[69] Robertson (1880), 535-36

[70] Robertson (1880), 529-30; Battely's *Antiq. Cant.*, 75. They might be referred to in a scratched list made by an awl at the time of the Dissolution on the east wall in the southwest corner of the Chantry of Henry IV. It sets out the weights of five images in a set of nine. It is not known whether it refers to these particular images, or another set placed elsewhere in the cathedral. The scratched inscription notes: () should be superscripted

In ye middyll Image xix(li) di(li)

It. in ye vj Image vj(li) di(li)

It. in ye vij Image xii(li) di(li)

It. in ye viij Image xj(li) di(li)

It. in ye ix Image xiij(li)

[71] N. Battely quotes from an Arundel MS which noted that Richard II gave these gems to the statue. Robertson (1880), 532; in his preface to the edition of Somner's, *The Antiquities of Canterbury (Enlarged Edition of Somner's Antiquities)* (London, 1703 reprint of 1640 edition).

[72] Saul (1997), 318; J. Wickham Legg and W. St. John Hope (eds.), *Inventories of Christ Church, Canterbury* (London, 1902), 109.

[73] Ogygius: . . . From hence we returned to the crypt, where the Virgin Mother has her abode, being hedged in by more than one iron screen.

Menedemus: What was she afraid of?

Ogygius: Nothing, I imagine, except thieves. For I've never seen anything more burdened with riches.

Menedemus: You are telling me of untold wealth.

Ogygius: When the lamps were brought, we beheld a more than royal spectacle.

Menedemus: Does it surpass Walsingham in riches?

Ogygius: It outward show it far surpasses her; what her hidden riches are she only knows herself. This is not shown except to men of high rank or great friends.

Desiderius Erasmus, *Pilgrimages to Saint Mary of Walsingham and Saint Thomas of Canterbury*, trans. John Gough Nichols (Westminster, 1849), 56-57.

[74] According to Erasmus, who visited Canterbury 1512-14, the chapel was enclosed with a double iron screen. The Treasurer's Accounts indicate that the outer grille was made 1377-80. R.C. Hussey, *Extracts from Ancient Documents Relating to the Cathedral of Canterbury* (London, 1881), 12. The innermost screen was placed between the two bays of the chapel where there is a step, while the outer screen was placed in line with the columns in the front of the chapel and continued between the columns of the ambulatory. Jane Geddes, *Medieval Decorative Ironwork in England* (London, 1999), 308.

[75] Spencer (1998), 131. A trace of vermillion was discovered when the badge was unfolded by restorers at the Museum of London. Spencer (1987), 222, figs. 66-67.

[76] John Watts, 'Looking for the State in Later Medieval England' in Peter Cross and Maurice Keen (eds.), *Heraldry, Pageantry and Social Display in Medieval England* (Woodbridge, 2002), 247.

[77] Watts, (2002), 251.

[78] They often used analogies to the body politic and the ship of state. Watts, (2002), 252.

[79] G. Kipling, *Enter the King: Theatre, Liturgy and Ritual in Medieval Civic Triumph* (Oxford, 1998), 11-19, esp. 12-13.

[80] A.K. McHardy, 'Liturgy and Propaganda in the Diocese of Lincoln during the Hundred Years War', *Studies in Church History* 18 (1982), 215-227, esp. 216, n. 8; Lincolnshire Archives Office Reg 12, fol. 133.

[81] McHardy, (1982), 218; Lincolnshire Archives Office Reg 12, fol. 259v.

[82] McHardy,(1982), 218; Lincolnshire Archives Office Reg 12, fol. 260; (ed.) J.R. Lumby, *Chronicon Henrici Knighton* (London, 1895), 198.

[83] McHardy,(1982), 220-21; Lincolnshire Archives Office Reg 15, fols. 189r/v, Reg 16 fols. 211r/v, Reg 12, fol 96v; Reg 16 fols 211r/v; Reg 12 fol. 96v. Sometimes, when people did not agree, they did not follow through. Archbishop Chichele in 1418 complained of torpor and inaction which greeted his mandates. McHardy, 224; Lincolnshire Archives Office Reg 15, fols. 189r/v, 200v.

[84] The prophecy became associated with the beginning of the Lancastrian Dynasty in 1399, with the attempt to fulfill the prophecy by Henry IV, even though they did not invent the tale. Sandquist, (1969), 335; Taylor, *The Political Prophecy in England*, 83-107 discussed it in terms of the difficulties in Edward II's reign. Thomas Walsingham used the prophecy in his *Historia Anglicana* to explain why God rejected Richard II. Coote (2000), 161; H.T. Riley (ed.),*Thomas Walsingham: Historia Anglicana* (London, 1863-64) II, 239. See also Christopher Wilson, 'The Tomb of Henry IV and the Holy Oil of St. Thomas of Canterbury' in E. Fernie and P. Crossley (eds.), *Medieval Architecture in its Intellectual Context: Essays in Honour of Peter Kidson* (London, 1980), 181-90.